From S
to Stan

CW00500540

Forty years of conflict as lived by

Derek Bumfrey

Robert Boyd
PUBLICATIONS

Published by
Robert Boyd Publications
260 Colwell Drive, Witney
Oxfordshire OX8 7LW

First published 2000

Copyright © Derek Bumfrey

ISBN: 1 899536 49 3

by the same author

A Boy's Eye View of Norfolk Village Life
All Mangolds and Muck-Cart

Printed and bound by The Alden Group, Oxford

Contents

Preface

The real object in writing "From Soigné to Standlake" is to complete the story of my life from cradle to pension book and to square a very curious and almost unique circle of events. My first book, "A Boy's Eye View of Norfolk Village Life" recorded all the wonderful boyhood experiences made possible by the freedom of living as a stockman's son on a large East Anglian estate. In reality my father was chained to his job by virtue of living in a "tied" cottage. In his case this hypothetical chain was never tightened or used as a threat by his employer, neither did it chafe my father's neck in any way. This was not universally so, for under this age-old tied cottage system friction between man and master could and often did develop into eviction cases and much distress. Being born into the system of house with the job, as a boy I hardly contemplated the disadvantage or the possible implications developing when no job meant no house or home. My open air, wander anywhere existence held no hidden terrors.

"All Mangolds and Muck-Cart" continued my early years of working as a labourer on Soigné farm, enjoying the last remnants of horse power in its original sense. As mechanisation took over, life speeded up, resulting in the loss of many pleasant aspects appertaining to rural life. We labourers were rushed from one work-site to another, with respected trades trampled under foot as a result of time and motion studies.

National Service put the final nail in the coffin containing all my dreams of an idyllic countryman's life as I failed to settle back into farm routine. Very gradually I developed a hair shirt which increasingly rubbed my back causing much irritation and blanking from my eyes all those rural pleasures so much enjoyed earlier.

"From Soigné to Standlake" commences as my real and imagined irritants become almost unbearable. The time for change was long overdue. If my reader has ever been stuck in one of lifes deep ruts, then at least the scene is set to begin this book with such a strange title. Be prepared though for a totally unexpected twist in the tail and one that neither I nor you would ever have dreamt of as we plod into chapter one of "From Soigné to Standlake".

Acknowledgements

Once more grateful thanks go out to Jean and Ian Little for undertaking the long and arduous task of deciphering my longhand scrawl for computer purposes.

Jeffrey Rye and Daisy Smith generously gave permission for me to use their "Rats Hall" poems.

All other thank you entries must be grouped under one heading. These are the readers and friends who wrote asking for the conclusion of my story to be completed and published in a third book. Coming at a time when my spirits were low after the sudden death of such a loyal friend as Irene Pitt their encouragement enabled me to work on, and I can only hope my efforts will be deemed worthwhile.

May I say thank you then to all those who helped in many ways to get my three books published. Your letters of appreciation and support made the effort so enjoyable and helped me bring a personal dream into reality.

Chapter 1

Plodding On

If you haven't already read my two previous books, "A Boy's Eye View of Norfolk Village Life" and "All Mangolds and Muck-Cart", you will be wondering what or who "Soigné" is and why a book should be written about life after it. Well, Soigné was, and still is I suppose, a large estate farm on the outskirts of the tiny Norfolk village called Westacre. The Estate, owned by the Birkbeck family, had as its headquarters the very large private house known to us as the Hall, and on the map reference as Westacre High House. I was born and bred at Westacre, living with my parents Fred and Alice Bumfrey in tied cottages, first at High House Farm and then for most of my time at No. 6, Pretoria Cottages, nearer to but still one-and-a-half miles from the village.

After attending school at Westacre, then later at Hamond's Grammar School, Swaffham, I had made the very unusual decision to drop any further education and begin work as a general labourer at the above-mentioned Soigné Farm. My first book covered school days and the second one explored fully the working practices of the 1950s, plus two years' National Service which came part way through my eight year spell on the farm. We pick up the story once more with the Estate owned and run by Captain Harry Birkbeck, who, having served in World War 2, gathered up the reins of a creaking establishment on the death of his father in 1956. At the time we all considered him to be lucky having such a lovely silver spoon in his mouth when born the son and heir to such a fortune. Hindsight of course tells me that his inheritance wasn't totally without worries, although I imagine his lifestyle, seemingly so much higher than mine, helped to take the keenest edge off most of them.

Seriously though, it was a tough task facing him for the Estate still worked on pre-war ideas and traditions in a post-war world full of new thought-lines and a much higher expectancy from working families. Men quite rightly expected better financial rewards for their labour and a reasonable level of amenities in their living accommodation. The age-old tied cottage system was still in operation, which meant loss of job led to loss of home. Actually, very little friction occurred on the Estate due to this archaic feudal system, but one always felt it to be a chain around one's neck which could be gently pulled by an employer if things were not quite going his way on the industrial relations front. Being a keen trade unionist I could see no value to the employee in the system, even if he could live at a very reduced rent.

Soigné Farm was run by bailiff Willie Thaxton, a man in his sixties and father of four grown up sons and two daughters, who lived in the farm house at Home Farm or High House Farm as we knew it. Under him came Charlie Wilson, the farm foreman, married but childless, living in a semi-detached house at Soigné. Charlie, by this time in his late fifties, was tall and well rounded, whereas Willie, although also rotund, came in several inches shorter. Both had held charge since the mid-thirties, having been promoted from head horseman and cowman respectively. Easygoing in character, and neither a slave driver, they ruled more by friendly persuasion than by fear of employment termination. Unfortunately this situation had been exploited by some to such a degree that this certain section of the workforce chose their own jobs, which left the minority always in the muck in more ways than one. Obviously both men were taking the easiest road available until their own retirement in the not too distant future.

So, as we take up the story of my career in labouring on Soigné Farm, we see a workforce apparently as a big happy family, but one with undercurrents of discontent due mainly to this insidious movement of favouritism. Life was very agreeable, there is no doubt, and many were the occasions when a laugh and a joke helped even the most strenuous labour to pass without too much pain. As mechanisation was still in its infancy regarding the replacement of gang labour there were periods when up to or even in excess of a dozen men worked together on one job. All root crop singling was still done by hand, as was the beet harvest. Threshing and harvest stacking were by now limited, but straw-bale carting, muck removal from yards and manure spreading were still labour intensive, and took up much of our time. Any moves where machines removed hard manual labour were naturally welcomed, but there was a feeling that the comradeship of numbers was in decline and a future of the lone tractor driver and his machine was progressively becoming the norm and not the exception. Lone working with a horse had been so very different as I for one never felt lonely with a wonderful cart horse for a companion. But apart from Uncle Will Bumfrey and his faithful mare, Gipsy, working around the yards, very few horses were left in the one remaining stable. Tractors constantly became stuck in small, ill-drained stock yards, which made them resemble ploughed fields even after fresh strawing had taken place. Pride in the job rapidly became a thing of the past as speed in getting over the work became paramount. Orders became more and more farcical as book-read theories replaced experience and local land knowledge. Higher geared tractors rushed we labourers from one job to the next, and one felt as if we were always chasing a machine which went faster each time we almost caught up. The days of travel between loading and unloading no longer went at the steady plod of the cart-horse. Hedges flashed past as you stood on the drawbar behind your tractor driver peeping out of a canvas cover. Admittedly one didn't have to walk, but life had lost its peace, the gentle rattle of harness chains being replaced by a constant roar associated with an internal combustion engine. On the plus side, of course a tractor didn't need grooming and feeding before seven in the morning or after four o'clock in the afternoon. A turn of the ignition switch or an energetic swing of a starting handle produced life at 7.05 a.m., whilst cutting the fuel supply rendered our noisy power servant silent until the whole process started again the next day.

I honestly do not believe these listed changes were basically to blame for my feelings of dissatisfaction. It would be very easy to find everyone else at fault and leave myself appearing to be all-knowing and blameless. Hindsight tells me that although I enjoyed most of my life at Soigné, and had the best of mates there, from the very outset I was definitely a square peg in a round hole. National Service was the watershed and I never really settled back into farm labouring after my demob. I tended to blame the "way behind the times" Estate for losing me the WRAF girlfriend I cared so much for. Looking back the bulk of the blame lay with me for not attempting to move on or to better myself. It was an impossible task I set myself to pull the Estate and Farm up to where I wanted to be, because at the end of the day neither I nor that young lady really wished to be in Westacre at that particular juncture in life. Even I didn't see then the many plus factors of that idyllic-for-some, rural life, so how could a city-bred girl be expected to see past the mud and spartan domestic facilities? That problem had been almost insurmountable for my mother in the early thirties, so what chance had the young lady twenty years on, when the world had taken huge steps forward and Westacre had stayed still. So, even after being five years parted, there was still a very raw spot deep down inside me. A few cinema trips with a lady groom from Soigné Farm House did nothing to salve that particular wound. The news of an alleged serious motor accident whilst in an American serviceman's car did nothing to annul those feelings for her, but at no time did my injured pride allow me to contemplate a renewal of contact. I felt that no one would look at me, twenty-five years of age, a shy labouring chap with little money and no prospects. Somehow I had to break out of this vicious circle between my lack of push and need to progress, but the question was how? I can see now, looking back at things from a long way down the years, that amazingly we were all estate- institutionalised, without realising it. Subconsciously we expected the little island of Westacre High House to provide for our aspirations in general life, without we going out to achieve things: we worked and then they provided. A very puzzling line of thought, but one which was present in all those of us born and bred on the Estate. It seemed as if our protective surroundings brainwashed us as we grew up. Of course, quite a few young men had been sucked into the War and had seen quite enough of the outside world, and who could argue with their need for some peace and quiet far from the madding crowd. A few decided to seek fresh pastures after demob; my uncle, Sos, always a free spirit amongst the Bumfrey family, was one of those. Why hadn't I been brave enough to make the break after National Service? What were my options then? Signing on as a regular RAF policeman, a job I could do, but I would have been even more tied than at present. My Commanding Officer gave me a good recommendation for the civilian police, but that also failed to fire my imagination. That left farming; I considered I knew no other work, so why change the devil I knew for a devil I didn't know by moving? So here I was in 1958, still basically unsettled but very unsure of how to alter the situation.

The only alteration in my life around this time was the urge to go to Church on Sunday mornings. Strangely, I cannot jog my very good and extensive memory to tell me how or why this came about. My parents certainly weren't worshippers, even allowing that my mother, whilst at school in Briston, had attended two separate chapels and the Salvation Army hall. Her motives weren't aimed at saving her soul, but to be able to enjoy three Christmas treats for good attendance. My father had even pleaded pressure of work, hand-milking cows on Sunday afternoons, in a successful effort to avoid the christening services for brothers Michael and Brian. No, I just recollect going off on my bike alone, to be greeted with warmth, although possibly with some surprise by Canon Caley who was then the incumbent rector for Westacre and East Walton. My few visits failed to help me even find the correct order of service in the age-old books seemingly designed to confuse the visiting stranger, but it was peaceful and restful as the sun shone through the side windows. It can't possibly have been that I wanted to get out of the Sunday morning wood sawing ritual. No, not that, as firewood had to be sawn at some time, so there was no escape, and anyway I've always liked the job and still do to this day. That form of exercise is very therapeutic I find. If, and I believe there is a guiding hand upon our lives, that was the first time I'd felt its influence. When something completely foreign to your nature takes place in life, then there has to be an answer somewhere. Mind you, it wasn't a flash of brilliant light experience, but wasn't it I who said of Canon Caley's predecessor, "Here comes that bl . . . y old parson", and made game of Methodist preacher Charlie Wilson singing hymn tunes as he strode along?

You will now ask if this alleged divine intervention solved my work dilemma. Well, before the end of the year there were some upheavals almost akin to the overturning of the tables in the Temple, and my life was changed sufficiently to force me out into the world well beyond Westacre.

Meanwhile I still held the post of "Lord" over the sugar-beeting gang. This meant I led a deputation setting the season's piecework price, and kept the financial book for the men. Piecework entailed agreeing a fixed price per acre to pull, top and remove the beet crop on all fields. This work usually lasted from mid-September to a week or so before Christmas. The conditions ranged from dusty, warm days, into muddy, wet and cold ones in the second half of the season, usually deteriorating as the days shortened. The weight lifted per acre generally stayed constant, although crops left to grow on a bit increased accordingly. Fields were taken in sequence, starting with lighter land where leaves turned yellow at an earlier date as growing slowed, then going on to heavier clay soils where moisture encouraged a longer growing season. As the local beet processing factory allocated loads on a daily basis, according to acreage grown under contract, supplies had to be maintained throughout the season, and work on harvesting begun as soon as the factory opened its gates.

All through one hoeing season Artie Keeley, who couldn't bear to see anyone earning more money than him, kept up a succession of gibes aimed at we sugar-beeters who, according to him, earned lots of easy money.

"Why don't you try it then, Artie?", we suggested, thinking he wouldn't relinquish his tractor seat for the mud and backache we endured.

"Right, I buddy well will", he replied, with his slight speech impediment coming to the fore.

When the suggestion was put to Charlie Wilson in September he immediately questioned Artie's sanity, but eventually agreed to let him try. To give him his due, Artie stuck it out, although at times he could barely straighten his back and had to endure much ribald comment as well as chronic backache. I doubt he earned much of that "easy money", and was quite pleased at season's end to exchange the beet hook for a seat on his International tractor. He put on a brave face to the last, but didn't turn out with us again claiming the need for his ploughing prowess was much more in demand than that of topping beet. At the age of fifty plus he ought to have known joints stiffen more readily as one grows older, and that beeting was a young man's game, unless one was well used to its rigours over years of practice. Still, you live and learn and there were times when we went as quickly as we could to put him behind the trailer with further to throw his topped beet. He was made to regret those "easy money" gibes thrown out on sunny, summer days, as he dragged his feet out of cloying mud in November.

My father had, after months of convalescence which involved lonely walks every day, returned to work on light duties which were not easy to find in the labouring field. Most of his time was spent cattle feeding with one of the young tractor drivers, and could be partially seen speeding around sheltered by one of those canvas cabs. On the occasion of one practical joke misfiring badly, Freddie had been placed with Gerry Deasley on some errand or another; it appeared that Gerry had been involved in annoying Young Laddie , and the latter planned to get his own back this particular morning. Hiding round a corner, Laddie armed himself with a bucket of water with which he hoped to douse Gerry's cab as he drove past. Unbeknown to our prankster, Gerry's assistant stood, as usual, just inside the open rear of the cab, and away they went; suddenly an apparition armed with a bucket leapt out and aimed his water at the cab side. Unfortunately the tractor was travelling a little faster than anticipated, causing the water to hit the back opening, and soaking my father in the process – hardly a helpful cure for a rheumatic fever convalescent. Shock! Horror! The expressions on the faces of both the recipient and the perpetrator must have been a sight to be witnessed.

"What the hell do you think you are up to", roared Freddie, wiping water out of his eyes.

"Sorry Fred, I didn't see you on there", apologised a very red-faced Leslie. "It was only a joke".

"Some joke, I must say", spluttered his victim, more worried about catching cold or worse. "It's about time some of you buggers grew up".

All's well that ends well, they say, and a fast dash down to Pretoria for a change of clothes, amid profuse apologies from Laddie, saved the day, as no adverse health problems arose from the incident. Without doubt, my mother had a few choice words to say about the infantile mentality of some members of the Soigné staff after having nursed her husband back to health during the previous twelve months or so. I never witnessed the incident, but it was re-told so many times that I've had no difficulty in piecing the details together, complete with the rapidly changing facial expressions of the main participants.

A couple more jokes which failed to raise a laugh spring to mind and these both included poor old Alfie Dann. In neither case was any vindictive thought involved, although I suppose thoughtlessness was more to the point. Alfie Dann had been employed at Soigné on the insistence of the late Major Birkbeck, who admired the former's fortitude in being prepared to walk the four or more miles each way from Castleacre to find work. Not that Alfie was in the forefront of physical power or mental capacity, being the product of closed village inter-breeding over several generations, I would presume. He was a spindly-legged, hump-backed figure, possessed of a shrewd brain mostly concentrated upon how to avoid too much work after having walked those long miles. Eventually the Major had purchased a tricycle for him and it was on this machine that Alfie slowly wended his way past Pretoria on a dark, winter's morning. At the top of the hill leading from our houses to Soigné, Leslie Lloyd, my brother Michael and myself came up behind the three-wheeled cyclist, and Leslie called out, "Come on, Alfie, get a move on". As we passed him Alfie suddenly sprang into more active life as he ground out, "Get out of my way, Lloyd, before I run over your wheel". Of course, a mock race then ensued, with Leslie just keeping a few feet in front as our three-wheeled hero trod on his pedals to gain speed. No one gave a thought to the sharp White Gate corner which we trio of two-wheeled cyclists took with ease, but not so the Castleacre pursuit champion on his more cumbersome machine. A fearful crash echoed out behind us, which sounded so ominous that a quick about turn was executed. There lay Alfie, trilby hat alongside, and a tricycle with one wheel in the air. With great trepidation I gently lifted the groaning figure, fearing the worst, but having got him to his feet, no apparent injury seemed to present itself, and the victim seemed more concerned about his bike than his person – that was until he touched his head and felt a little blood on his fingers. This discovery sent him into a succession of moans and muted cries, and me into wild panic. By the light of a cycle lamp we examined the wound, and found it only to be a superficial graze. Calming our man down, we right-sided the three-wheeled machine, and tried to lighten the situation by joking about the race. This ruse worked a treat, and soon Alfie had re- mounted, all the time swearing profusely about "that bloody Lloyd", whose fault, as usual, it was. We piled on the agony in order to keep his mind off the injury, and by the time we reached the cart-shed Leslie had become, in Alfie's mind at least, the perpetrator of crime most foul. Increasing daylight revealed only a slight graze upon the injured party's cranium, and very little paint scrape on his tricycle. Alfie never missed an opportunity over the next couple of days of telling all and sundry of how that "bugger Lloyd" caused him to crash on the White Gate corner.

The second prank to misfire happened at Elbreck Barn where a large gang of us engaged in various jobs around the area, gathered to shelter one very wet morning. It was Springtime, and all the bullocks had gone to Lynn Fat Stock Market, leaving muck-filled yards awaiting our attention prior to the onset of the hand-hoeing season. As we lounged around on straw bales waiting for the rain to ease, mischief began to itch in bored brains The hunched figure of Alfie Dann nodding off under the hovel quickly nurtured the idea of launching a missile at his battered trilby, and a hunt for a suitable weapon ensued. A wizened mangold left over from bullock feeding was rejected as too heavy and dangerous. Just as the project was about to be abandoned due to lack of missile material, Brum Chase discovered a piece of tractor inner tube which, tied in a ball with string, presented an ideal solution. Taking careful aim, and unfortunately with too much arm power, the rubber ball was propelled towards the slumbering figure, catching the poor old chap on the side of his face with a resounding crack. Howling more in fright than agony, the recipient fell in a heap clutching his head. His trilby hat, the intended target, rolled on to the soiled straw, and a shocked silence fell upon the company looking on to enjoy the joke. Once more we rushed forward to help pacify the injured party, doing our best to play down a prank gone horribly wrong. Doubtless Leslie Lloyd would have been blamed had he been there, but this time Alfie's curses could only be aimed at an unknown assailant.

It would seem on the surface that our sick jokes were always targeted at one of the weakest in society, but I can assure you that Alfie Dann Boldero, with a fork in his hand, was very far from weak, and could have possibly wreaked a horrific revenge on anyone caught in the firing line. I think it fair to say everyone was a likely target for the many pranksters in our midst. Fork handles became mysteriously covered in tractor grease, doors were often tied from the other side causing stock-men a long walk round in order to gain entry to a stable or cow-house. Many have been recorded in previous books, but one I believe has escaped, and that occurred whilst my father was still cow-man at High House. When he returned from dinner, Freddie always propped his bike at the end of Willie Thaxton's house whilst he collected milking pails from the dairy. Other minor tasks needed his attention, which usually meant about a ten minute stay. One afternoon, on his re-emergence, he found his rear bike wheel flat, and felt quite miffed as a new inner tube had just been fitted. A closer examination revealed a loose valve, and after tightening prior to pumping up he had no more trouble. The following afternoon the same thing happened, which raised father's temper a few degrees, and made him vow to catch the "silly bugger" messing around with his bike. On the third afternoon a trap was duly set for the prankster as Freddie hid to keep watch. No sooner had he settled in position, poised to catch his annoyer at work, than round the corner came a flock of geese led by their notorious gander. This gentleman stopped beside the propped machine, and then proceeded to peck at the shiny new metal valve in the rear wheel. A hiss of escaping air sent the flock into a loud cackle as their triumphant leader sped off before them en route for the pond. Hardly able to believe his eyes, the irate cycle owner retrieved his flat-tyred bike and pumped up once more. It seemed the shiny valve metal had attracted his lordship, and then ceased to be of interest when air came out. By pushing the machine down to the dairy doorway further sabotage was averted until natural metal discoloration meant that all "goosey" interest ceased. Before witnessing the true culprit, all members of the Thaxton family were under suspicion as they carried a strong reputation as practical jokers. No one would have given a thought to this trend extending to their flock of innocent-looking geese.

Most of my days during the last winter at Soigné were spent working with Leslie Lloyd who, like me, was beginning to chafe at the collar of permanent labouring tasks. Unlike me though, Leslie craved to return to tractor driving, a job he had previously held at Southacre before his violent verbal confrontation with "Flicker" Bensley, the foreman, causing a quick move into labouring at Soigné. I must admit there did seem a concerted move on the management's part to block any opportunity for my mate to resume his natural career, except in an emergency when he became the man of the moment. So it was that my unsettled spirit, coupled with his feeling of unfair treatment, combined to produce a couple of hair shirts for us to wear during 1958. We were fast becoming anti- everything, and anti-management most of all.

I recall being sent to replace a broken gate post on Little Strawberries, the one in fact I had tried to dislodge with my wagon in the first days of holgy boy. On that occasion, the oak post had withstood my gentle pressure with horse-drawn transport. Unfortunately, a much more powerful tractor implement had succeeded where I failed, and a replacement post was needed. An eight-inch square oak post, nearer in length to a telegraph pole than a gate post – in my opinion at any rate – had been delivered from Westacre sawmill. Leslie and I hauled the massive timber on board a tumbril, collected tools, one digging spade, and a short crowbar, and then set off for the Little Strawberries gateway. After tying our faithful mare to a hedge stump, we surveyed our task for the day. One drunken, gnarled post, possibly round in its heyday, to be removed and then replaced by our huge piece of English oak. After an hour of digging, wriggling, sweating and swearing, the near one hundred year old post remained stubbornly in its appointed place. We both agreed that the devil himself must be hanging on its bottom end. At long last the twisted old devil did come out, and we breathed a sigh of relief, stupidly believing the worst of our problems must be over. As we sat taking a later than usual breakfast I thought back to the days almost ten years ago when Jimmy Lane and myself toiled with rusty shovels and forks moulding up seemingly miles of potato hales. Nothing had changed, for hadn't we been given today a set of tools just as old and useless for the job in hand?

For most of the next couple of hours we scrabbled around, trying to get soil out of a narrow hole with a straight spade, after loosening the chalky subsoil with a much too short iron bar. Knuckles were grazed, and knees muddy as we worked almost upside-down at our task. Eventually we decided enough was enough, and shot the new post into our excavations. Wedging it up straight, we stood back to admire our handiwork. It looked alright until we compared it with its partner holding the gate on the other side. Without a word of a lie, it was at least two feet higher and stood out for all to see like a heavily bandaged sore thumb. Our already sagging spirits sank lower than the post hole bottom, I can tell you. Urgent action was required, and fired with the fear that Leslie Richardson, or some like mickey-taker, would pass and see our disaster, we struggled the oak tree out of the hole. Sweating profusely in the strengthening Spring sunshine, we scrabbled away once more with our puny efforts to deepen our post receptacle. Viewed from outer space, I suppose an alien could have mistaken us for members of a backward native tribe, well-digging with primitive tools which had, by this time, become mainly our hands, as a straight spade will not, by design, lift loose chalk from a narrow, deep hole.

Having our noses so near the ground prevented us from enjoying the bright sunshine and fresh, green growth around us. The growing warmth and worry combined to make our metaphorical hair shirts prickly and uncomfortable, and we both wished ourselves miles away from that prehistoric and outdated farm, as we saw it that day. A sudden stroke of inspiration flashed upon us, which sent me back to the farmyard to fetch a shaped spade or a longer iron bar you might suppose. No, a hand saw from Barney Hooks the carpenter in order to reduce the length of our offending post, thus saving us from more digging. My bright idea was douched when Barney learned the reason for my request. With shock and horror registering large in his eyes, he explained that gate posts had to be almost as far in the ground as out of it. No saw was forthcoming from his workshop, so a crestfallen, doom – laden labourer trudged slowly back along the road where my spring-like steps had brought me a few moments earlier.

"Silly old bugger", said Leslie. "Who the devil would have known?"

Eventually we rammed in the post, maybe not quite level with its partner, but passable, and rode back to learn of the next mission impossible Charlie would dream up for us. I doubt whether our oaken monument would stand as long as its predecessor, possibly no more than a decade, as it would soon bar the passage of wider and larger farm machinery, and be unceremoniously uprooted in the name of progress, and no one would have cared if we took eighteen inches of it home for firewood at the outset.

Change was coming, albeit slowly, but it was destined that I would not be working at Soigné long enough to see it, let alone enjoy its fruits.

Chapter 2
The Last Straw

It was on one of those occasions during the winter when Leslie and I worked on separate jobs that the final straw of unrest and unfair treatment caused me to think at last of using my brain instead of my limited brawn. Muck was being spread from trailers on to Lightning Breck, and I had, for my sins, the redoubtable Alfie Dann as my unloading partner. The idea was to spread the farmyard manure evenly by fork as the tractor slowly drew its load across the field. By this time a front fork loader, mounted on a tractor, filled the two-wheeled trailers at the muck heap, thus saving much manual labour. This initial labour-saving conversely made our job harder because the manure came out in large, undisturbed lumps, whereas previously the hand forks had partially broken it up. When the loaded trailer pulled up, we let down its sides and scraped a foothold, one at the front corner and one at the rear on the opposite side. Once up in our positions the tractor driver drew forward slowly to allow us time to spread the load over fresh ground. I began working towards the trailer rear, distributing my half of the muck fairly thickly, and leaving my partner's half for him to work towards the front. When Alfie and I met to pass halfway along, I found I was left with three-quarters of a full trailer to get rid of. This situation continued without comment until it became obvious that Alfie's natural aversion to work prompted him to clear barely enough room for his rather large feet to find purchase on the trailer bottom.

"Damn me, Alfie", I finally exploded, "if you carry on like this you'll fall off the side. You've hardly moved enough muck to make standing room."

As we looked around, the half-mile long field shewed dark and light strips where our manure coverage varied to such a degree. It became very clear to me then that Charlie Wilson didn't care who carried the rapidly increasing number of lame and lazy ducks, as long as somebody did. I vowed then and there it wasn't going to be me for much longer. I just had to get out, but still the question was how?

I had taken the Farmer's Weekly for some time, on the pretext, I was really kidding myself, of seeking another working position. Eventually an article caught my eye regarding possible entry to farming colleges. This, in turn, triggered my long-slumbering brain cells into thoughts of further education, a thing that had been resisted for ten years after over-pressurising myself in gaining the Cambridge University School Certificate at Hamond's Grammar School. Nothing was said outside my immediate family as I took one day's holiday to attend an interview in Norwich, after filing an application for a grant to the Norfolk Education Committee. For the first and probably only time, my academic achievements stood me in good stead, although my age caused a few problems, but these were overcome. A one-year general agricultural course became the best bet, and a number of letters were sent out to farm institutes in an effort to find a vacancy on 1959/60 courses suitable for mature students. This went on at the slow pace associated with any form of officialdom, taking up the last nine months at Soigné. Strangely, at no stage did anyone require a reference from my employers, and consequently no one knew anything of my plans. There was no real need for secrecy, but as nothing surfaced sleeping dogs were left to lie. Deep inside I was glad no one knew about it as my residual thoughts of self doubt and failure surfaced quite frequently, leaving me all for it on bad working days and against the idea when things went well and the sun shone.

These "stop, go" visions regarding my future did little to help me enjoy working at Soigné. I began to see reasons for complaint where none existed. The grass grew lush and green on the other side of the fence, especially after Union gatherings which I really enjoyed. Books on the hard lives of early trade unionists became my avid bedtime reading, rendering Willie Thaxton and Charlie Wilson into the fat, overbearing characters depicting farmers in Land Worker cartoons. Of course they weren't, for in reality their station was very little above ours, both living in tied houses, and drawing their pay from the same purse as us. I've never known a worker who couldn't do a better job than their immediate superiors, and I was no exception.

My last harvest was spent working in the barn alongside Gerald Andrews and Uncle Will Bumfrey. This again was hard work, but enjoyable, in good company. Unfortunately I became unwell, with a flu-like complaint, nearing the end of proceedings, and was confined to bed. John Thaxton took my place, being both strong and unafraid of work. It appeared that an influx of extra combines from the Abbey produced more grain than could be handled by the dresser on a 7 a.m. to 9 p.m. shift, so a night shift was instigated. Charlie Andrews, Hans, the German cow-man from High House, and Captain Birkbeck himself arrived to man the fort. As the following poem indicates, the idea didn't last too long; in fact, when Captain Birkbeck dropped out and Brum Chase took his place the latter came up with a bright idea to mark the passing hours by striking them on the corrugated pit shelter side, with a heavy-headed yard broom. This new innovation failed to win the approval of Charlie Wilson who lived in the nearest habitation, and the night shift ceased to be, on the pretext that harvest was almost at an end. As a convalescent pastime, I penned a poem which I found my mother had kept, along with other personal papers. A few lines of explanation as to the characters first of all: Captain Harry Birkbeck was known to we barn-men as "Our Father" or "Har, the Paymaster"; Charlie Andrews, the cow and pig man, carried the nickname of "Lop"; his son, Gerald, had been "Dilberry" from early school days; Leslie Richardson, "Young Laddie", also came up as "The Borr" behind his back. He had continuously taunted us with the tremendous feats of corn clearance achieved by pensioner Billy Briston, single-handed at the Abbey Farm. Udale worked at the Hall in the dual post of butler and personal servant to the Birkbeck family. With that background outline, let us creep into the dust-filled barn, with the hum of machinery and rattle of whirring sack barrow wheels drowning our footfalls.

The Night Shift

The sun goes down, the darkness falls, outside the world is still,
But in the barn the work goes on, by Dilberry, John, and Will,
Their backs are bowed, so great their load, Their eyes are near to weeping,
With pit still full and more to come, they dare not think of sleeping.
But "Our Father's" on his way, the barn-men need not fear,
For Har the pay, Hans the cow, and Lop the pig are here.
They mount the stair with measured tread, three men of might are they,
To do their duty they have come, or perhaps they need the pay.
"Now, off to bed", they order Will, "to bed both Dil and John",
No need to tell them more than once, for they are off and gone.
Now Lop's the sacker and head-man, he fills the boots of Will,
The other two have sack barrows, for they have got no skill.
So off they go, the corn comes in, their zest is plain to see,
But poor old Har has lost his way; says Hans, "You come wid me".
For hours and hours they struggle on, 'tis near the break of day
Before they can shut down the barn to softly creep away.
They tiptoe out, no noise to make, for fear they wake "the Borr",
'Cause if he knew the work had stopped, he'd rush out and cut some more.
The job goes on, night after night, no rest for man or piston;
Still Laddie roars, "Not fast enough, let's send for Billy Briston".
Once more night comes, the pit is full, but Harold doesn't come,
Instead he phones, his feet are sore, can Willie send for Brum?
Up in the Hall the master sits, just listen to his moans,
He holds his back and loudly yells, "Hey, Udale, bring the Sloans".
Now Har's laid low, who'll take his place, will Chas or Willie go?
Please write and tell me which it is, I'd dearly like to know.

So my last harvest at Soigné ended with me confined to bed suffering a severe flu-like throat infection, which left me feeling weak and very tired, hardly a good preparation for a heavy beeting season. I am certain my poor health considerably shortened my temper, which, in turn, eventually led to a final confrontation with poor old Charlie Wilson who was nearly always the man chosen to fire the bullets made by those above him in the hierarchy. These confrontations had occurred between us at regular intervals since my National Service. One, I remember, clearly concerned the unfair treatment of my brother, Michael, when he had a school holiday harvest job. A very hot harvest period followed a wet June, which had caused high growth of straw on the grain. Michael had the task of riding on the sledge behind a straw baler. He stacked the heavy, for a boy that is, bales of straw in eights before releasing them on to the ground. The high temperatures, dust and heavy crop proved too much for a boy, so he bravely asked the foreman for a change of job.

"Certainly not, my fellah, it's this work or none."

To say my mother was upset when her work-weary son came home was an understatement. "I'll give that fat-gutted old "bee" a piece of my mind when I see him", were her exact words.

After a council of war, we decided that Michael would go to the cart-shed the next morning and wait for fresh orders. This he did, only to be completely ignored by Charlie. Keeping a watching brief from my barn vantage point, I controlled myself until the foreman came out from breakfast, and then the storm broke. The language I used cannot be printed, but all my pent-up rage at the preferential treatment given to those who wouldn't work came out. Charlie's blustering words about obeying "his" (Willie Thaxton's) orders were blown sky high as my temper reached boiling point. Meanwhile Michael, in his own unique and deadly determined way, stood his ground even under Charlie's insinuations that almost branded him as lazy. Unbeknown to us, an almost identical scene was being re-enacted at High House, and when Willie was imprudent enough to almost say the same thing to my father, he was told in no uncertain terms to go and try the bloody job himself. I don't think my father went as far as threatening to down milking pails, but I threw in my final card when I went off to fetch my bag and leave on the spot.

"If there is no other job for Michael, then there's no job for me either. Come on, let's go home."

Suddenly the storm abated as a partial olive branch was offered in the form of, "I'll go and ring "him" and see what he says". I can't remember what alternative job came up, but one of the Thaxton clan went on the sledge. What a sacrifice, you may think, but as he was old enough to change with Bill Johnson on the tractor, the job was shared by two full men, and

Michael's stand was vindicated. Charles and I never spoke for some time after that for I found it hard to forget his bully-boy tactics towards a junior, whether my brother or not. I can only think that this insidious need to protect almost three-quarters of his staff from heavy, manual work had warped his sense of fair play. As for me, an active trade union man, recently inspired by reading the stories of early Agricultural Union stalwarts such as Joseph Arch and Will Edwards, any unfair treatment was like a red rag to a bull. The more I read, the more I aspired to lead the labouring men out of their shackles. What I didn't realise was the basic fact that very few of those labouring men wished to have those shackles removed. They were happy to keep in step with Estate thinking by making the best of things as they were, and letting sleeping dogs lie. The tiny minority of us who thought otherwise would have to go elsewhere to make our mark, as I was to find out only a short time later when I finally burned my boats and bridges in a self-manipulated head-on clash with the Soigné management, backed up by the autocratic ruler of the entire Estate, Captain Harry Birkbeck – he who was born to be obeyed.

So it was in a state of poor health and low morale that I began the beeting season once more. Three months' hard graft lay ahead, but at least we all knew where we would be working and with whom. As "lord" over the gang, I went through the farce of setting a price for the season. This usually meant adding about half-a-crown per acre to last year's price, irrespective of the likely weight of crop to be moved. An unusually wet spell during the main growing period meant a much heavier crop, although, in fairness to the farmer, a lower sugar percentage would be recorded. Eventually, the price paid by the contracting sugar-beet factory was based on this percentage which was taken from a sample removed from each load delivered. Damp, mild growing conditions continued well into the Autumn, and we found ourselves lifting as much as eight tons more per acre than the usual average of twelve or so tons. Having strategically placed the oldest members of our gang at the rear of each trailer, we were able to lift a few beet from their rows when they dropped behind. Horrie Everard occupied this "rear gunner's" position in my gang, and I took up to a quarter of his beet, thus helping to speed up our progress. Owing to the increased size of beet our tractor men found it difficult to keep us supplied with empty trailers, so often we found ourselves resting but earning no money.

As discreet growls of discontent reached my ears, I felt obliged to do something positive in order to balance our financial books. Overtures to the foreman brought an extra trailer, but no more money. At the end of the day, I felt drained both mentally and physically, often falling asleep on the settee after my tea and not much more refreshed the next morning. Life for me, and I suspect my family, was becoming intolerable. At work I was being squeezed between disgruntled workmates and management who were mortally afraid of setting a wage precedent above the level of Captain Birkbeck's other farm in Westacre. There, lighter, sandy land was yielding much less weight per acre, but this practical point just couldn't be taken into account by them for this one-off abnormal season. At home I had no hobby, girlfriend, social life – apart from supporting Norwich City which on most occasions lined up in the minus column – or future prospects either. I imagined the vultures, who ten years before had strongly advised me against agricultural work, circling above shouting, "I told you so!". After my initial years of enjoyment things had turned sour for I had outstayed my welcome through my own weakness of being afraid to move on at the appropriate time. The cloying mud held me fast in more ways than one.

They say it's always darkest before the dawn, and so it turned out for me, although the first thin shaft of light hardly merited a dawn chorus. A letter arrived from the Principal of Kesteven Farm Instutute in Lincolnshire inviting me to an interview for a possible place on their one-year General Agricultural Course for 1959/60. I quickly wrote back affirming my acceptance of the interview which was timed for early on a Saturday afternoon, thus allowing me time to get there by a cross-country train and bus route. At last things seemed to be set fair for me to start a new career, a light at the end of the tunnel, a ship's sail sighted by a marooned man. What better time could I have found to attempt to shoot myself in the foot? If anyone has doubts about my sanity, then what followed can only convince them of my need for the men in white coats.

Let us forget for a moment my scholarly aspirations, and go back to the beet fields where bumper crops were being pulled from the mud, and trailers, grossly over-loaded, were sinking axle-deep and holding back what little earning power we had. As previously stated, all overtures to Charlie Wilson for an increased price per acre had fallen on deaf ears. On Thursday, when the foreman came to collect my book for him to work out our wages, I made what I considered to be a last-ditch request as a matter of personal principle.

"Charlie, if you can't pay us a half-a-crown more an acre out of this extra eight tons of beet, then I for one shall down tools and go on day rate."

"Don't talk silly, Derek. You can't do that", was his snotty reply.

My hackles were up and so were his because we didn't just have differences of opinion, we often fell out completely, we had that kind of temperament. On the other hand, one just couldn't row with Willie Thaxton as he always turned anger aside, and one ended up half joking at any rate. The back view of Charlie swinging away from me with his exaggerated rolling gait so infuriated me that I swore to myself I would stand by my word, whatever happened. Not only did I swear it to myself, but I also issued my resolve loud and clear to those of my fellow workers in earshot.

Temper ruled me for the rest of the day, and my fire was stoked up by a few so-called mates who thought it worthwhile to keep the row going if only to help break the monotony of work. I don't think anyone really cared if we achieved the extra 2s.6d., for it would only mean about three old pennies extra to each man, and that before tax. The dull November afternoon closed in on the Soigné Wood end of Fifty Acres. Distant hedgerows slowly disappeared into the fog as the monotonous swish of beet hooks severing tops was drowned by revving tractor engines dragging half-bogged trailers along the rows. At ten to four backs straightened, hooks, muddy leggings and sack aprons were stored in our old shepherd's hut, and away we all went, a straggle of motorcycles, autocycles and bikes, with all riders intent on reaching a warm fire and cooked tea as soon as possible. After a wash, brush-up, and good meal, my temper cooled, leaving me to reflect on my actions and likely consequences. Without doubt, my paranoia over principles and the strict adherence to them had forced me to paint myself into a corner. If Charlie threw the half-a-crown per acre extra into the pot, then at least I would gain a moral victory, even if it was financially a hollow one. On the other hand, if, like me, he was hell-bent on sticking to his word, I would be literally up the creek without a paddle. I couldn't lose face before my workmates, I never had, and life would be intolerable if I did. Their sly references to it on appropriate occasions, one or two were just waiting for it, and my conscience would give me hell. Mulling over my dilemma, I fell asleep on the settee, worn out both mentally and physically.

I still felt tired the next morning as I biked to work. A day of destiny lay ahead, tomorrow an even bigger day as it was the date of my Kesteven interview. As I tied my still wet leggings over my trousers I asked myself why I put this kind of pressure on myself, and for what good reason. Did I have to go round picking fights with management? Did I have to go for interviews when I could have remained quiet and gone to a football match? As the afternoon progressed, and pay-packet time approached zero hour, the atmosphere on the beet field became electric. Furtive glances towards the farm sought out the first sight of Charlie's car. It was well past "High Noon", but "The Fight at the O.K. Corral" was about to be re-enacted. Slightly later than usual the little black car came slowly to a halt by the gate. The huge figure of our foreman rolled out and then strode across to Blackie's trailer and stopped for a few words. Then to the second gang, and again a few words as pay-packets were handed out. Then the moment everyone, with the exception of myself and Charles, had been waiting for.

"Afternoon, not very nice again today", ventured Charlie.

Silence!

With a quick look at the brown packets in his hand, and then with a snatch and a jerk, Gerry was given his packet through the back of the tractor cab, and then Leslie Lloyd received his. Round behind the trailer went Charlie to deliver Horrie's, and then to me. Eyeball to eyeball I received mine, and then the fateful words had to be spoken, the answer to which could well end my life at Soigné.

"Are you increasing the price per acre then, Charlie?"

"No, Derek, we are not, so that's an end to it."

Well, he couldn't have spoken a truer word, for so it turned out to be. With a dramatic flourish I flung my hook at his size twelve boots, luckily it landed just short.

"Right then, Charlie, that's me done. I won't be in tomorrow, and I shall be on day work next Monday. I will not do piece-work at this price".

Charlie never tired of repeating in the next few days, "He just chucked his hook down and left". Not quite true because I did return on the Monday, but that was after my trip to Kesteven, and then it wasn't to back down from my late Friday afternoon stand.

It wasn't until I sat quietly contemplating my future on the train that it suddenly came to me that the College might well ask my employer for a reference. My God, what had I done? Probably shot myself in both feet. Imagine the kind of reference I would get in the circumstances. Recalling all the worst scenarios recorded in my trade union books where frustrated employers turned all their spite on upstart workers, my journey was not a happy one. Could a principle be worth the risk of losing job, college place, and ultimately a new life? Was it for an extra sixpence per week at the most I had flung it all away? No, it wasn't just for that, but for the honour of my word which was always to be my bond. Let the devil take the hindmost, and to hell with all employers. If sticking to my guns meant starving, well I wouldn't be the first. With these thoughts of being a workers' martyr, I entered the gates of Kesteven Farm Institute, and prepared to meet the interviewing committee who, to my mind, would be a motley collection of rich farmers and retired Army Officers.

When the secretary ushered me into the Principal's office, I met only two men, Mr. Rowland, whose office it was, and his deputy, a Mr. Treble. Neither looked over- academic, and as was soon apparent especially in the case of Mr. Treble, were more interested in practical things than book work. Both men put me at my ease, well as easy as it was possible to put a bag of nerves like me. My nine years on the farm more than covered the one year practical experience required, and also helped me to answer their varied questions from a practical angle. The one dreaded question, "Who is your present employer?", never came. After briefly examining my school and RAF reports and references, they concluded, with a firm handshake, and made it clear that my place would be reserved and details forwarded in due course. Walking on air back to the bus stop, I gave no thought to how I would earn my living during the nine months up to the following September, a time when a saving period would be sorely needed in order to bolster my limited grant finances whilst at College. Anyway, this wasn't the day to think depressive thoughts, my star was in the ascendancy, and if going back to school at 26 meant a little hardship, then it was worth it. If anyone at home had reservations, then no one dampened my temporary high spirits. They must have been pleased to see me out of the doldrums for once. Black Monday morning seemed a long way off that Saturday night. I wonder now what my father really thought as things I had got myself into were way outside the quiet country lifestyle he always craved for and was uncomfortable without. A man of peace, he hated upsets, and it took quite a lot of adverse treatment or criticism to rouse him, but then he would become as stubborn as anyone, and nothing, not even my mother, could shift his chosen point of view. "You Bumfreys are as stubborn as mules", would be her final shot as she conceded defeat or, as was the usual case, defeat for the time being.

Sunday passed almost uneventfully as our Sabbath days tended to do. Traditionally firewood was sawn, after Dad returned from his milking duties, but since his return to a five-and-a-half day week, this ritual had been allowed to slide. In summer a game of darts with our very worn board hung on the shed door helped pass the time. On bright, crisp winter mornings a walk round the fields bordering Field Barn might appeal as we searched for that elusive rabbit dinner. Since my recent forays to Church, most of these pastimes had been put on the back burner, although Michael, Colly and Gerry Deasley, or maybe John Thaxton, surfaced from their only "lay-in" morning to indulge in these time-fillers. Without much doubt, we all went off to Lynn in the late afternoon. Biking to Westacre in order to catch Jack Eagle's bus, we could then take our pick from three picture houses, having time to see the complete programme round before quaffing a quick pint at a pub adjacent to the Saturday Market. Jack's bus parked on the open market space, which was overlooked by the familiar outline of St. Margaret's Church. Another familiar outline would be the hunched figure of Alfie Dann, our aforementioned tricyclist from Castleacre. He usually spent his time mooching around the Lynn streets, no matter how inclement the weather, and I can assure you the windswept streets of King's Lynn can be very anti-social when the north-east wind whips up from the river. Occasionally one of us would weaken our resolve and buy him a pint, but then he haunted us for weeks, so the move wasn't all that popular. It was a shame, for Alfie was a rather pathetic figure, but his crafty outlook on life often proved his undoing. One night, as we returned home, Alfie sat eating a large bar of chocolate. Edgar Coe, sitting a few seats behind, began to pull his leg, pretending to urge him to share it round the bus passengers. Edgar, who had been indulging in a few pints of beer, kept on ribbing our hero until Alfie turned and flung the half-eaten bar at his tormentor with enough force to have decapitated Edgar.

"Have the bugger if you want it, Edgar Coe of Westacre", ground out Alfie.

We heard him swearing away to himself all the rest of the way home.

Just before seven o'clock the next morning I set off to bike the short distance to Soigné. Instead of accompanying Leslie & Co through the farmyard and on to Fifty Acres, I drew into the cart-shed. Charlie spent half-an-hour circumnavigating my position before he finally approached.

"Well master, why aren't you on the beet field?" was his opening gambit.

"I told you on Friday I wasn't prepared to work at that price, and therefore you are obliged to offer me alternative day work, and that you know very well."

"I can't do that. He" (again Willie Thaxton had to do the ordering in his absence) "says it's either piecework or nothing".

It was at this juncture both of us, deep down, wanted to back off, but each of us had a point to prove and so the opportunity for sensible negotiation was lost. Instead our arguments remained in deadlock as the final shots were fired.

"So you are telling me there is no work for me at Soigné Farm then, Charlie? You are therefore sacking me."

"I didn't say that, my fellah, you can go back beeting."

"Day work rate or piecework?"

"Piecework, or nothing, as I said before."

"At the same price per acre?"

"At the same price as everyone else is working for, and will be for the rest of the season."

"Not for me then, Charlie; I shall take it I am sacked."

The foreman, sick of hitting his head against a brick wall, barked out, "Have it your way then, and go home".

Away swung Charlie, taking huge strides across the yard, whilst I, still seething with anger, remounted my green Sunbeam and cycled down past the cow house and out of Soigné Farm life for good.

Charlie Wilson and I never spoke another word to each other for around twenty years. It wasn't until I visited my mother in her council bungalow at Westacre where she lived next door to Miss Eva Wilson, Charlie's sister, that contact was made. Charlie, with his wife, had retired long since to a bungalow at Toftwood near East Dereham, and said he wished to see me, having heard that I was an active member of the Salvation Army in Oxford. Presumably, unable to believe the age of miracles still existed, he needed to see me for himself. I enjoyed an hour or so with him as we discussed things past and present over tea and biscuits. Looking back I feel our meeting illustrated the strange but unique ties that united we people who were born and bred on the Westacre Estate. Almost like a family tie in that however much we fell out, there was still a bond of concern and interest maintained. It is this bond, which, after almost forty years away from Norfolk, has almost forced me, in the most enjoyable way, to record my days spent living on the Westacre High House Estate. As for the other two people involved in the argument, Willie Thaxton and Captain Birkbeck, they being well behind the firing line, we shall hear more of them in the next chapter as my story unfolds.

Chapter 3

Life on the Dole

As I cycled slowly back home in the half-light of that late November morning, I was consumed by two very conflicting emotions. First and foremost was the feeling of defeat in that I had taken on the might of authority and lost – a feeling that had always sat uncomfortably on my shoulders and one I wasn't very accustomed to experiencing. The second emotion was one of freedom, that at last I was my own man, answerable to no one, and free to cast my nets wherever I wished. This second line of thought quickly gained the ascendancy as I came to terms with the fact that I had, almost subconsciously, talked my own self into getting the sack, and in the process destroyed all chances of reinstatement under the existing circumstances. The disagreement had been so loud and consequently well publicised that there was no way in which the ruling parties could be seen to back down, even if they wished to do so, a thought very far from their minds at that point in time, I am sure. It wasn't until tempers cooled and both sides became influenced by the genuine feeling of Estate family unity that the extent of this chasm was realised. That situation only came to the fore after weeks of attrition, for remember, whatever the rights or wrongs of the argument, we were really friends who had fallen out over a principle, and very little else if one discounts losing face.

The next few days and weeks seemed to have an outside influence which turned the usual "peace at all costs" management of Soigné Farm into hardened "never give an inch" employers with, in my eyes, even a vindictive streak rearing its ugly head. As is often the case when potentially weak leaders eventually decide to act tough, they tend to go over the top and whip one of the very people who had encouraged a much less lenient view on the disregard of orders. At that juncture I felt I had become that whipping boy. In the end, of course, this "we'll teach the workers not to get stroppy with us" attitude served only to strengthen my resolve not to weaken towards any olive branch that might be offered, not that it seemed likely, and remain free from my shackles whatever the cost.

Propping my bike by the house wall, I entered the back door to be met by my mother, and the question, "Well, what's happened now?". Slipping my haversack off my shoulders, I carefully placed it on the floor, before sitting down beside the living room table and giving her the latest on my fiery exchange with Charlie Wilson. I feel fairly certain her summing-up would have been in the words, "Trust old Blunderskull to take that attitude", which was slightly unfair as he was at the sharp end, following instructions from his superiors. With a contest between "Blunderskull" on the one hand and "Bullskull" on the other, there could have been little hope of a negotiated settlement, especially with feelings running high on both sides.

After making a cup of tea we resumed our seats and began to analyse the whole situation. I had put myself well and truly out of work with the possibility of another job being at least five miles away, due to the huge area of the Estate. No tenant farmer within that area would even consider it a wise move to take me on. Being "on the dole" held a certain unpleasant stigma, implying that anyone who was unfortunate enough to find himself jobless was very likely lazy or, even worse, unemployable. This tunnel vision stemmed entirely from the Estate-institutionalised ideas that work was always there for the taking, and no one should need State support, unless too lazy to take it up.

Older family members could well remember the 1920s and 30s when the dole queues were long, and being "in work" meant the difference between living and starving. Grandfather Bumfrey had once reputedly squeezed a farmer in a gate in order to extract his owed wages. I believe he spent many months knapping flint stones at the roadside for very meagre wages as a result of seeking justice. To them, nothing had changed, so consequently they were much more worried about the situation than me. So my first move was to seek the dole office telephone number in the 'phone box at the bottom of our row. My enquiry gave me information to the effect that a mobile office called at Swaffham market town on a day later in the week.

With no clear idea of what course to take next, I dredged through my latest edition of "Farmer's Weekly". The jobs vacant column was extensive, listing various posts for stock-men, tractor drivers and labourers, all over the country. Nothing interesting caught my eye, and deep down I considered if the touting farmers had exhausted their local labour and been forced to spend money on national advertising, there had to be a catch in the job somewhere. No! I would report to Swaffham and stay on the dole for a while and wait for an opening.

Another doubt about the future entered the equation as I waited for confirmation of a place at Kesteven Farm Institute the next September. If accepted, and I was pretty sure I would be, only a temporary job was needed, and that should be far easier to obtain. What an unworldly country lad I was at that time. I was to learn quite quickly the outside world didn't owe me a living, especially in December when winter economies left the labour market over-subscribed.

Riding my bike into Swaffham on the appointed day gave me a feeling of complete freedom as I passed carrot-pullers and sprout-pickers working on light-soiled fields between Southacre and Narford. These were the far-flung acres on which my mate, Leslie Lloyd, plied his tractor-driving skills before falling foul of Flicker Bensley, the farm manager. From the vantage point of my bicycle seat I felt lord of all I surveyed. I could sign on with a ganger, bagging carrots at the drop of a hat, and the money would be good. Perhaps I would try it later, if nothing better turned up. What I didn't realise was the fact that those workers came by lorry from the Fenlands, where gang labour was intensive and gang bosses ruled the roost. Compiled mainly of women, my hopes of a job there were practically nil.

Crossing the Lynn to Norwich railway line via the hump-backed bridge previously crossed daily when attending the Grammar School, I thought of the firework factory just beyond the station. Being newly established, perhaps they had vacancies. Again it would have been a non-starter as female labour held sway there as well. I only gave it a passing thought as I had with the carrot gang.

The mobile office I sought was parked directly opposite Hamond's School where I had spent five years and left with high hopes for an idyllic life on Soigné Farm. Life had been very pleasant until National Service had given me a taste of the outside world, and itching feet, both of which had become badly out of step with the Estate on which I lived and worked. Still, I didn't need them any more. At last I was a free man and would undoubtedly go far. Eventually I had to go far to find that job I felt then would be mine, even before I left the unemployment office. How wrong I was, poor fool.

Going through the usual official channels, I submitted all details required. Yes, I had been sacked as myself and employer could not agree a piecework price, and day work had been refused. What experience in other jobs? None, except for RAF Police. Had I any preference for types of work? Farm labouring only, as I had no practical experience in machines or stock. All these questions were asked of me, and answers noted. My first question back became my last. What jobs are on offer? None, and at this time of year, little hope of anything either. Call again in a fortnight. Any money due to you will come by post. Interview at an end.

Thanks for nothing, I thought, as I pushed my bike round to our grocer's to collect shopping for my mother. The lace-curtained front windows of my old school frowned down upon me. The Pedlar of Swaffham stood on his pedestal, wearing the same expression as he did on the day Harry Carter, my old woodwork master, carved him. A few desultory shoppers hardly gave me a glance, and my feelings of freedom and wellbeing left me to be replaced with the chill of a cold Autumn wind, so familiar to those who know Swaffham in the short daylight season.

Cycling back home, under increasingly thickening cloud, I passed the carrot-pullers now huddled under a very sparse hedge to eat their dinners. The thin winter sunshine, which had made the job look inviting on my outward journey, had disappeared, taking with it the mirage of a pleasurable job. Now muddy boots and pinched faces told me the true story of frozen fingers and aching backs. My late career on a sugar-beet field, left with such high dudgeon, looked vastly preferable to this, for at least we had a hut for shelter and a fire for warmth.

It looked as if I was on the verge of learning a very important lesson in life, a lesson I tried very hard to learn through future years, but never really mastered. It was to make sure one had a job to go to before letting principles and temper throw in one's notice on present employment. They say you live and learn, but I'm afraid I never did, certainly not in that particular area of life.

As I had never been a spendthrift, I had a nest-egg of money saved which meant I was nowhere near destitute. By cutting my suit according to the cloth, I calculated that, with these savings and my small amount of dole money, life could go on normally for a time. My bread and cheese dinners (we ate a hot meal in the evening) worried my father who thought, as I was at home, I should have something hot as he usually did on cold days when he came in to dinner. But I was adamant, and stuck to my guns in proving I wasn't sponging off my family who were at work.

My financial calculations took a slight knock when I returned to Swaffham in the fortnight specified, complaining that no dole money had been paid. Sorry, explained the gentleman in charge, it appears you will not be entitled to anything for six weeks. Your employers state that you sacked yourself by refusing to work. Gulping down my fast- rising temper, I again explained the Union and Employer's agreement appertaining to the acceptance of piecework. Both sides must be in agreement as to the price and conditions of the job, or day work rates apply. These facts were carefully noted once more, but no change of their policy was forthcoming. Boiling anger trod my pedals round as I sped home, vowing to bring all the fires of hell down on my late employers' heads.

At this point, I think one should use the aid of hindsight to defuse any thoughts of Charlie Wilson, Willie Thaxton and Captain Birkbeck all having grown horns and sprouted forked tails. I would like to think that, to protect their good names as employers which the Estate always enjoyed, they slightly adjusted the true facts in order to achieve this, whilst not realising my frail income would be seriously affected by their actions. On the other hand, perhaps they failed to grasp the subtle difference between dismissal and handing in one's notice. At any rate, as Willie said to my father when he gave him my final pay packet, "It should never have happened, Fred", but it had, and I for one didn't regret it, for hadn't I subconsciously engineered it?

As soon as tea was over I set off to cycle the four miles to Castleacre in order to put my case to Don Clarke, our N.U.A.W. Branch Secretary. Again outlining the facts, I was very gratified to hear him agree that my case appeared to be watertight and the dole entitlement was mine by right. Promising to contact the District Organiser, Mr. Jack Boddy, he told me not to worry and they would be in touch. From standing alone I suddenly felt I had the full support of all my Union colleagues for whom I had worked hard during my short adult life. Unfortunately, my glowing picture of those linked, muscular arms of the working man, was soon to be shattered by the person I naïvely imagined would emerge as my knight in shining armour.

I had never met our Local Organiser before, and unfortunately took an instant dislike to him the moment he opened his door in answer to my tentative knock. Whether it was his short, black cheroot, or the foul cigar smell that hung round him like a cloud of incense, I don't know. Probably both, coupled with his barely disguised contempt for this young fool who had put himself out of work over a paltry principle, to him that is, but not to me. By almost dismissing my case out of hand and then telling me he would discuss it with Captain Birkbeck at a shared function the following evening, he made me so mad that I would have torn my union card up in front of his face had I carried it with me. As it was, I left him with a curt goodnight, to cycle back to Westacre. As I pedalled, my mind went back to those union stalwarts I had read about, those hardy souls, many of them Methodist local preachers, who had risked jobs and homes to further that cause to get justice for the agricultural labourer. If my experience of that evening was anything to go by, it was no wonder people in like situations as mine fought a lone hand. To be fair, I suppose nothing short of seeing blood spilled would have satisfied me, and I was in no mood to consider methods of conciliation over a glass of wine in civilised surroundings. To give my cheroot-toting mediator the due I think he was entitled to, my dole money was reinstated from day one, so perhaps his overall methods worked, but I never forgave him for that first "not another thick-skulled, labouring oaf, causing problems" resigned attitude with which he "welcomed" me.

After getting that fight over, my feathers lay down for a peaceful spell over Christmas. I knew it was no use seeking gainful employment before the New Year, so I settled to taking stock of my overall situation. But, first of all, I went to football. A drawn F.A. Cup game at Swindon gave Norwich a mid-week afternoon replay at Carrow Road, so, after biking to Swaffham station, I took the local train to Norwich, and was rewarded with a 2 – 1 win for the Canaries. This set up another home game, this time with Manchester United at the beginning of January. It seemed very strange going down to the ground from Thorpe Station, without the usual crowd from Westacre, but there, wasn't this part of my newly-won freedom? The only negative thought came from the fact that I was spending my nest-egg money with nothing coming in to replace it.

Mulling this over on the way home, a sudden idea struck me which seemed sweeter the more I considered it. The Swaffham Coursing Club always held a day's sport pursuing hares with greyhounds by special invitation on the Birkbeck Estate. Why not book up for a day's beating and walk those broad acres from which I had technically been banished? Another cycle ride into Swaffham the following Saturday saw me entering the Greyhound public house, and nervously enquiring about the day's employment. Yes, that would be O.K. – meet up at Westacre – no problem. The practical side of the event was organised by head keeper Hinxman who had very recently taken over from Fred Welham. If the latter had been in charge, I'm certain his Estate etiquette-soaked old heart would have given out at the sight of yours truly presenting himself for work. As it was, apart from a few individuals looking askance at me, and Captain Birkbeck's eyes almost leaving their sockets, the day was very enjoyable, for my part at any rate, although perhaps most of the poor hares wouldn't have agreed with me. So a small sum of money went into my pocket, and although it was only a token amount, it helped my self-esteem enormously.

To help fill my time, I decided to take a day trip to Briston in order to deliver a few items for Granny Eke, my maternal grandmother. Taking a leisurely ride the four-and-a-half miles to Massingham Station, my intention was to catch the Melton Constable train at around 9 o'clock. Imagine my mortification as I cleared the trees at the top of the steep station hill only to see the train snaking off towards Melton. The winter timetable meant a fifteen minute earlier departure. What now? How to fill three hours' wait on a cold country platform. As there was a train due going in the opposite direction, I decided to spend a little more of my fast-depleting cash reserves, and go to King's Lynn. It was much more comfortable there in the warm waiting room with a cup of tea. As I sat there, with two hours until the next train to Melton Constable, which would of course pass through Massingham, I once more set up thought processes regarding my future. It suddenly dawned on me that if I could drive then a whole new vista would open up on the job front. Why not strike whilst the iron was hot, and seek out a driving school in the town? Still encumbered with those parcels for my grandmother, I found the British School of Motoring office, and made enquiries. They were very helpful, and explained first of all a provisional driving licence was required and gave me details of how to obtain this almost unheard of document. Still on a high of firm decision, I booked my first lesson to take place a few days before Christmas. Not until my now much shorter wait at the station did the size and scale of my actions come home to me. Self doubt assailed me as I felt sure I would never have the nerve to sit behind a steering wheel, let alone drive a vehicle in traffic. Why take on this extra expense when finances were at a low ebb? That was the trouble with having time on my hands as it cost money to fill it. What I didn't really take account of was the fact that, for the first time, I had made a very positive move to claw my way out of the rut in which I had buried myself, a rut of self doubt well- cemented with lack of ambition and fear of failure in the sight of others who, in my biased opinion, were far cleverer than I. Still, there was no turning back, the die was cast, and for once my nerve didn't fail me, although I must admit my stomach played a few tricks on me the morning of that first lesson.

Continuing my journey to Melton Constable, I picked up my bike at Massingham as pre- arranged, in order to cycle from Melton Constable to Tythe Barn, Briston, where Granny lived. She was, as always, pleased to see me, although slightly surprised at my lateness. A quick shuffle round provided me with a dinner as the provision of meals was her forté, even at her advanced age. Telling her of my morning and the driving lesson plan brought encouragement from her, for she had always been a forward-looking lady. The people of Briston were very independent, with many working for themselves, and I had always been envious of them. Our many enjoyable holidays there had often roused the spirit of independence in me, but this had soon subsided in the Estate environment of Westacre where every field and property belonged to one man. As I sat in the old armchair by the fire I thought back to the day when, as a boy, I idly swung my hand under it, only to be rudely brought back to life by the mouse-trap set thereunder to catch a rodent coming in from next door. I can confirm that the spring leaves a nasty bruise across one's fingers, so can do a great deal more damage to the neck of a mouse.

Christmas 1958 came and went without much fuss and bother, as far as we were concerned. The cockerel, which had been fattening since the previous summer, made an excellent Christmas dinner. Dad, as was his habit, again remarked his preference would have been a nice piece of cheese instead. Mum gave him a withering look which, in itself, questioned his sanity, and withheld a reply. We others took no notice as this was an old chestnut trotted out annually. Anyway, this was just about as near a compliment as he ever uttered, as romantic gestures weren't in his line.

Our parents' marriage was built on a rock of practical living, and would never have foundered in a hundred years of adversity.

After my flare up with Charlie Wilson, and the dramatic flinging down of the sugar-beet hook, I had very little contact with my late fellow workers. It seemed as if everyone was sitting very firmly on the fence, waiting to see the final outcome before throwing their caps into the ring. One or two voiced an opinion that I was a damned fool, but made the mistake of expressing it within earshot of my brother Michael. Blood being thicker than water meant that he immediately took up cudgels on my behalf, and threatened to ram those said opinions back down the throats of the men expressing them, along with a few front teeth for good measure. I've no idea who the transgressors were, but I suppose we didn't nickname one of our number "snake" for nothing, but I could be wrong.

In the week following my dramatic gesture, and before the dole-withdrawal battle, I was summoned to Captain Birkbeck's office in the Hall. Propping my bike along the side wall, I entered the room through a low sash window thrown up for this purpose. We discussed the matter amicably, and to give him his due, my late employer seemed quite concerned about it. He explained that he was unable to offer me my job back as it would undermine the authority of Wilson and Thaxton. I put it rather bluntly that I wouldn't work under them again if I never obtained another job. I added that anyway I would be going to college in September, and only needed temporary employment. This latest fact came as a complete surprise to him, the authorities having never asked for references, employer's observations, or character assessment. Eventually he wished me luck, we shook hands, and I left the way I had come before cycling away down the Hall drive, thankful that no offer of reinstatement had been on the table, thus weakening my resolve to leave the Estate for good. I had a great fear that there was a chink in my armour still, which could have made me go back to the status quo, based on the age-old saying of, "better the devil you know than the one you don't know". The trouble was that the "devil" I knew wasn't so bad really, and many would even say he was very good, and that just had to be said for those two men under him as well. Needless to say though, at the time, my opinions were much less complimentary.

The search for a part-time agricultural job, that is for a span of eight months, failed to make much progress. Most of the column inches in the Farmer's Weekly sought stock- men for what appeared to be small farms in Devon and Cornwall. The requests for short- term labourers were conspicuous by their absence. Nothing seemed worth exploring, although I did send out one or two tentative letters to which I never had one reply. The nearest I got to a job was when Captain Birkbeck leapt from his Land Rover on the road one day to express his worry at my lack of employment.

"I must ask around my friends, Bumfrey. We can't have you without work any longer".

I politely thanked him and silently hoped nothing would be offered. In answer to my silent prayer, nothing was all I heard, thank goodness.

A trip to Joplin's barber's shop meant also a look into the boot repair emporium where Reggie Eggleton still held court. A few – no, rather a lot – of communistic propaganda words were forthcoming on the subject of worker control and the overthrow of the landed gentry. In his opinion I had struck a blow for the working man, a hero for the cause and all that, but at the end I still had to pay for my shoe repairs despite giving my all for the party. Mind you, I was a Labour man, which wasn't really red enough for Commissar Eggleton – what a fiery little character he was. It was a wonder he didn't swallow his mouthful of tacks when in full verbal flow.

A big uplift to my spirits came in the field of football. In the third round cup-tie at Carrow Road, Norwich defeated Manchester United to trigger off their greatest F.A. Cup run ever. We couldn't believe our eyes even when the much sought after "Pink-un" blazed the headline for all to read. We returned to Westacre in Jack Eagle's coach, riding on cloud nine, but was it to be that I was destined to leave Norfolk in this, the Canaries' greatest season? Could a mere Division 3 South team reach even greater heights? I never saw the following games, it's true, but could only follow it all through the newspaper. Their great run finally finished with a narrow semi-final defeat by Luton Town, and then only after a replay. To fall just short of Wembley was sad, but it was great to have lived through it all.

My first driving lesson was very traumatic, although I don't think I actually moved the car. Just sitting behind the wheel whilst learning the function and use of controls reduced my nervous system to pulp. Mirror, gear, handbrake, mirror again, how could I get my eyes, hands, and feet to work in conjunction with one another, and then, remember hand signals – no indicators allowed then – accelerator and steering all at the same time? I lost more sweat during that short lesson than a whole day's threshing would have produced. Why on earth did I volunteer to pay good money for such mental and physical torture, I asked myself, as a pair of very shaky legs carried me away from my instructor. Not only that, but another session was booked for a week's time. In all I managed three hourly lessons, and by that time found myself driving through the narrow streets of King's Lynn, struggling to avoid jay-walking pedestrians who stepped off pavements with no apparent thought for learner drivers or their own safety. The experience changed me from a lifelong irresponsible pedestrian to a traffic-wise individual overnight.

It was in the midst of these last two recorded events that I spotted an advert in the Farmer's Weekly which caught my imagination: "Wanted – for a limited period only – an energetic young man to assist with construction work on a mink farm. No previous experience necessary. Apply in writing to E.W. Spilman, The Manor, Standlake, Nr. Witney, Oxon." That advertisement was destined to change my life and transplant me from East Anglia into the heart of Middle England.

In composing my application letter I explained that I had experience with stock (I had no idea what mink farming consisted of), wire fencing, and general agricultural work. I was single, only required work until September, but would need lodgings. A letter came back by return offering to pay my train fare enabling me to travel, stay overnight, and then after the interview, return home. I needed no second bidding, and immediately wrote back giving the day, and time of expected train arrival (I had checked the tortuous route with British Railways). It was arranged that Mr. Spilman would meet me at Oxford Station in the afternoon of a late January day. I felt that whatever lay at the other end of the correspondence was my key to leaving Westacre. I might just as well have taken the job blind, as my Grandfather Alfred Bumfrey had the job for Alfred Lewis which brought him and his family to Rats Hall on the Westacre Estate in 1927. My days here were over, and I couldn't wait to be on my way. The only real regret was having no further part in the village cricket team set-up, for which I had been Secretary and Treasurer alongside Gerald Andrews, the Captain, for a number of years. The summer Saturday afternoons as scorer I would surely miss. Still, there could be no looking back now for this was the real beginning of life after Soigné.

Chapter 4

Pastures New

When the invitation arrived back from Mr. Spilman suggesting I visit Standlake for an interview my mother was away, leaving we three men to fend for ourselves. As mentioned previously, my maternal grandmother was well into her eighties, and Mum liked to help her as much as possible. This was one of her periodic visits, which could last up to a week.

When searching for a small overnight case I realised that the only one we owned was in use at Briston. No bother, I just wrapped my few necessities in some thick brown paper, tied it with even thicker string, and was ready to go forth and seek my fortune. It never crossed my mind to attempt to make a good impression on my prospective employers by going to King's Lynn and buying a new case in order to look at least semi-civilised. Steeped in farming's "make do and mend" policies, the first practical and least expensive solution was taken without further thought.

Leaving my bike at Narborough Station I took off into the unknown, putting myself in the hands of British Railways. I believe the route took me from Narborough to King's Lynn, then round to South Lynn, and from there we steamed across the fen land, flat grey and uninviting, arriving eventually at Cambridge where the express hurtled me towards London. After flashing through town and country, the scenery became more and more urbanised, and as the metropolis gained the ascendancy, we eventually drew into a very grimy Liverpool Street Station. Country boy had come to town, and now the maze of underground tunnels beckoned me. Actually, the London Underground system has always been my easy way to cross the Capital, and I had no problem getting myself and bucolic-looking parcel to Paddington in order to proceed westwards. A quick cup of tea and a cake prepared me for the last leg of my journey. Train travel itself I enjoyed, but making certain one was on the correct train could be traumatic as often a double check with a second porter gave conflicting information, thus causing steam to rise from inside my thick East Anglian coat. This blanket-like outer garment, designed to withstand the rigours of January at the North Pole, had become a burden as the more balmy temperatures of the softer west became apparent. In fact, when I did eventually work in Oxfordshire, my greatcoat was never worn again, and a much lighter outer covering came into use.

As the train passed Reading, with its famous Huntley and Palmer's biscuit factory, my stomach muscles began to tighten in anticipation of the imminent arrival at Oxford. Green fields with grazing cattle and sheep did little to calm my nerves as we rattled on towards the dreaming spires of the famous university city where it seemed my destiny lay. Now the stomach-churning went into overdrive as the crowd spilling from the London train dispersed, leaving me perspiring from both overcoat and nervous tension. Where was my prospective employer? As my anxious eyes scanned the area outside the Station I could see no one searching for me. Eventually I was the only person left on the forecourt, and with a sinking feeling in the pit of my stomach, I considered my next move. Should I give up the job and return home, or try to get out to Standlake under my own steam? At least I had an address to guide me, although in which direction the village lay, or how far out it was remained a mystery. Just as I turned to re-enter the Station in order to make preliminary enquiries, a light-blue Ford Consul roared into the parking area. A rather thickset man of medium height leapt out, and made haste towards me. Extending his hand he greeted me warmly, taking for granted I was the man he had come to meet, and proceeded to apologise profusely for being late. Whether it was the traffic, the car, or his watch which was responsible, I can't remember, but with hindsight it could have been all three. On the other hand, I learned that whereas I was usually ready ten minutes early for an appointment, the Spilman family was at least fifteen minutes late, that is if they remembered it at all. Be that as it may, I warmed immediately to the man who drove me out of Oxford into the countryside, so perhaps it is true that opposites attract.

Along the road known to me now as Botley Road, up the steep Cumnor Hill, and away right through Cumnor we went. It was all strange land to me, but I liked what little I could see as we flashed along. A narrow road through Eaton led down to the River Thames, on whose edge we stopped as, to my amazement, there was no bridge. This was no brook, I thought, as I peered out over the bonnet of the car. A sharp peep on the horn brought a shambling figure to the opposite bank, and what to me was almost like a figment of my imagination. The hunched form scrambled on board a large raft-like contraption, and by means of some form of arm movement, propelled it across the river. Grounding on the incline in front of us, he beckoned my driver forward, and the car slowly inched on to the wooden deck. Good Lord, I thought, they haven't even invented bridges in Oxfordshire, and remembering the fact of not being able to swim, I kept everything crossed until we reached the far bank. After parting with sixpence my companion explained that the ferry, as it was known, had existed at this crossing point for hundreds of years, and he had brought me this way as a matter of interest. I was of the opinion that the poor old man still operating it had been there almost as long as the ferry. Later I learned that he was a displaced person from Eastern Europe, who could speak very little English, but on occasions could swear well in his native tongue should a vehicle need his services at an inconvenient moment – inconvenient to him, that is.

Darkness had by this time closed in, so I saw little or nothing of Northmoor or Standlake as we wove our way along narrow roads. Arriving at the rather imposing Manor House, we were greeted noisily by two dogs, Cheena, a long-legged "spotted Dog", a Dalmatian, and Snippet, a short-legged Corgi, the former quite safe to pat, the latter needing caution as her temperament was suspect, to say the least. When her lip turned up, showing a set of off-white teeth, I decided to keep my distance. A tall girl, dressed in trousers and an old baggy jersey, appeared from a lighted shed at the drive end, and was introduced as Gillian, who ran the mink farm, being part owner with her father who did the introductions. Taking his case from the back seat and handing me my parcel, Mr. Spilman led the way into the house via a back door. Following behind I thought how well it was all going. The bosses seemed, on the surface, to be very civilised and easy to get on with, putting me at ease, which wasn't the easiest of jobs. I walked through into the roomy kitchen dominated by a large cream-coloured Aga cooker with two chromium lids, and two dog baskets, one either side of it. The lady of the house came through from the front, and again introductions were made. Quite how well my then fairly broad Norfolk accent acquainted itself with her ears, I don't know. I did notice she spoke with very rounded vowels, which would turn "foxes" into "forkses", and "off" into "orff". She also cast rather disbelieving glances at my personal luggage still well intact inside its thick string binding. She probably thought I was only one step up from that poor old Polish displaced person on the ferry at Bablock Hythe.

The last member of the family came bouncing in from school, dressed in grey uniform, with round felt hat. Auburn-haired and very outgoing, she didn't just glance at my parcel, but asked outright what I had brought. My embarrassed explanation about not having a small case sent her into gales of laughter, but not with any malice. In fact, she helped break the ice that had descended when Mrs. Spilman found the situation of meeting a prospective labourer rather difficult. Bounding up the stairs to show me my room for the night and the bathroom, the young lady chattered away nineteen to the dozen, leaving my three bosses to discuss me in peace. Judy was to turn out a bit hot tempered, as her red hair warned, but we got on very well, especially in later days when I helped to fence in her very wayward horse which she adored.

What do I remember most about my first night's stay in Standlake? The highly-scented toilet soap! Ever since Uncle Billy Eke came home from lodgings in Doncaster pre-war, and sported scented soap, Granny Eke had declared a ban on the "stinking" stuff. This ban had extended to Westacre, and the only soap allowed in the Bumfrey household was carbolic or Sunlight washing (linen, that is) soap. This "modern" scent permeated the whole upstairs, and the smell remains imprinted on my mind to this day. Was this a new civilisation I was about to enter? Could this be the brave new world I craved for? Yes! I knew before we discussed wages and conditions that this was the temporary job for me. Like many a temporary move, this one was to be more permanent than anyone imagined.

When I returned downstairs, it was suggested we take a quick look at the mink sheds by torchlight, and with Gillian leading the way, we set off down the drive. Really, all I could see was an open-sided shed with wire cages on either side of a central walkway. Our presence activated some small, furry animals, which looked to me like a larger version of a stoat. Their feet, on bare wire-netting cage bottoms, set up a whirring, drumming sound, which seemed to be taken up by an indefinite number away in the darkness. Each cage had a wooden box hanging on the end of it, lining up along the central alley, a small water cup on the outside, and an empty wooden fish box upside down on the top. The mysterious purpose of this latter item I was to learn later. The only other thing I noticed, this time without the need for a torch, was the very strong smell permeating the whole area, and the sea of mud on all tracks outside the actual shed. If I hadn't been wearing rose-coloured glasses, there is no doubt I would have seen the whole set-up as a "Heath Robinson" backyard affair, and turned my back on it at the outset. The business, if one could call it that, smacked of an over-indulgent father using his money to pander to the whims of a favourite daughter, unwilling to find a niche in the outside working world. But this wouldn't have been strictly true, although perhaps it did start like that. As I came to discover, Gillian spent almost every waking hour working in some way with her animals, and was deadly determined to make a profitable success of fur farming, leaving no stone unturned in her efforts to achieve this. I was soon to be swept along by the enthusiasm expressed during that evening, which completely blotted out the foul smell and poor wages offered with business promises of higher dividends when mink coats on the hoof increased next year. Both sides conveniently forgot, on purpose, my temporary form of engagement. If my plans materialised, I wouldn't be there to share in those enticing high dividends. Dick Spilman was a great talker, as well as a great dreamer. The thing was that he really did believe there was a profitable future in mink farming, and so it seemed at that time as more small farms sprang up around the country.

After agreeing to pay me the basic agricultural rate, and let me live in their house as no lodging had been forthcoming, we shook hands and I was due to return to Standlake the next week. It turned out that Gillian and her father were going up to the Hudson Bay Fur Company next morning, and would drop me off in London. The very mention of Hudson Bay conjured up visions of fur-clad trappers amidst the snow-covered woods. This was adventure, and gave colour to my description of the new job when I returned home. I don't think I stressed the muddy tracks or the stomach-churning smell. No, I was off into a new life, full of challenge and opportunity. I believe I even boasted of returning with a huge car the length of Pretoria Cottages. Dick Whittington had nothing on me as I set out to make my fortune.

Such were my dreams as I shook my pyjamas out of that brown paper parcel and went to bed in that freezing bedroom, without my home comforts of a hot water bottle and warm chimney-breast running up inside the wall. The old manor house creaked and groaned, as did my stomach minus its usual big cooked meal at tea time. When you are out seeking your fortune, these things cannot be considered, although they did creep into account a bit later on. Also, was this bed damp, or was it just very cold? I curled up and hoped I wouldn't contract rheumatic fever, which Mother always warned us against should we sleep in damp beds. Best not to mention it in her hearing.

All too soon it was time to get up into a freezing January morning. A 6.30 a.m. start had been planned, and after porridge and toast, I climbed into the canvas-covered back of an ex- RAF truck, and set off for London. Clutching my parcel, and huddled in my heavy coat which yesterday was a hindrance but this morning a life saver, we swung away over the eight hundred year old "New Bridge" spanning "Young" Father Thames. Peeping through gaps in the canvas that let in a steady flow of arctic air, I might well have been in Canada. A very heavy frost covered the landscape, and everything sparkled with rime in the candle-powered headlights. As we entered Marcham, a lean-to window set in the wall at an angle of 60° looked very strange, and stuck firmly in my memory. It is still there to remind me of my early morning ride every time I travel along that particular road. On through the historic town of Abingdon we sped, and away to London. By the time we pulled up outside a convenient tube station, I was nothing more than a block of ice, almost too stiff to get out, and vowing never to complain about the lack of comfort on British Railways as they were known then. Shaking hands (I kept still, allowing the cold to shake for me) with my future employer, and promising to return to Standlake the next week, I staggered off underground. Eventually, a hot cup of tea at Liverpool Street Station helped to thaw my bone marrow, and I returned home without further incident, being able to enjoy the passing landscape without suffering a churning stomach caused by fear of the unknown.

My feeling of euphoria, generated by the thoughts of a new life well away from the claustrophobic restrictions of the Estate, soon evaporated as I began to feel very unwell. My mother, who had just returned from caring for Granny Eke at Briston, now turned her nursing skills to me. There was no chance of me getting back to Standlake as planned, for I had full-blown flu which confined me to bed for a week, and left me in a fairly weakened state. After enjoying good health generally, I considered this latest setback a strong case of "sod's law", but thanked my lucky stars the virus had appeared before I set off for pastures new. Whether my imagined damp bed, or the marrow-freezing ride to London had anything to do with the affliction, I don't know, but at any rate they didn't help. Contact was made with the Spilmans, who agreed to wait the extra month for me to take up my post. Presumably they had liked what they saw at our initial meeting, and being unable to find local labour, they hadn't much choice.

So at last the scene was set for me to depart, leaving the world I had known since my arrival as a tiny baby some twenty-six years before. A large case, along with an ex-RAF kitbag with army coat and wellington boots tied on the outside, carried my worldly goods away from the bosom of the family. Frank Clarke provided the taxi to Narborough Station, as he had done on the last occasion when I left home for RAF National Service. Fortunately he didn't find me so tearful this time, for I was looking forward to a new life filled with opportunity. This departure was of my own freewill, whereas before conscription had forced me to leave home for the first time. Settling into my carriage seat, I could really enjoy the train journey, for I knew where I was going, and even better knew how to get there. A man of the world, you might say? Well, not quite. Even if my case and kitbag were one step up on the brown paper parcel tied with thick string, I would cut a peculiar figure in the metropolis with khaki coat and worn wellingtons tied alongside an RAF-issue kit conveyor. Still, it wasn't for my cut of fashion that my employer needed me, but for my ability to work, and of that capacity there was no doubt.

The final ride through the Berkshire countryside, on the last leg of my journey, produced a slight tightening of the stomach muscles. The late winter sunshine lit my way, and soon the dreaming spires of Oxford welcomed their new son into the County. I should have realised things were going too well, as was proved to be the case. After an agonising half-hour wait outside the Station failed to produce my motor transport to Standlake, I knew the spires' smiling welcome had been a sham. Having come this far, I wasn't going to turn back, so after consulting my map, I discovered that the town of Witney was closer to Standlake, so decided to take a single ticket to that Station, on the Oxford to Fairford branch line. After a short rumble through such places as Eynsham and Barnard Gate, the little tank-engine steamed into Witney. Enquiries here told me that I was still about four miles from Standlake, and not being too keen to walk that distance with case and kitbag, I at last resorted to the telephone, a thing I should have done in Oxford, and contacted the Spilman household. After a muddled explanation of how we had missed one another in Oxford, I was instructed to stay put until Gillian arrived at Witney Station. This simple exercise was soon accomplished, and I rode into Standlake in Ford Consul style, to begin my new life, without knowing a single soul or them knowing me.

The room allocated me was the same as I had spent the night in before. It faced west, and the last rays of the setting sun made it look very welcoming. Gazing out over the house lawn, I saw a huge walnut tree to my left, and a wall-enclosed garden with thatched farm buildings beyond where a herd of cows were picking their way through thick mud and into a milking shed. Mr. Hill, later I discovered this was the farmer's name, slammed the gate shut behind them, and prepared to tackle his twice daily chore. This scene was to become very familiar to me through the coming months, and was very scenic, especially on a slightly misty summer morning when I woke to the cows' muted lowing as they plodded in to have their bulging udders relieved of milk once more. Memories of High House Farm and my father ushering his faithful few charges into the old milk house – yes, I missed my family very much in those early days, and proved to myself the truth in the saying that one never appreciates a thing until it's gone. Well, at least my family was still there, even if at a distance of approximately 150 miles.

My first task that evening, before taking to my bed after quite an exhausting day, was to pen a few lines home telling of my safe arrival. Being always well equipped with writing materials, this was soon accomplished. With my clothes neatly stacked away in wardrobe and drawers, and a book on the bedside table, I felt quite at home as I settled down for the night. My alarm clock had been set for 6.30 a.m., just in case I overslept, which would be unusual, but chances must not be taken as there was no ever-wakeful mother to rely on now. The new starting time of 8 a.m., however, did allow some leeway in the mornings, as opposed to the Soigné Farm 7 a.m. kick-off, but of course one hour had to be added at the end of my shift.

Living and working with my employers, in this totally strange environment, proved to be very exhausting. The only place in which I could totally relax was my bedroom, and I tended to sink down there in relief at the end of the day. Being unheated meant that I couldn't very well spend much time there, except for sleeping, but of course when the weather got warmer I could spend more time in peaceful isolation. It wasn't that the Spilman family harassed me in any way, but it's a fact that your soul isn't your own in someone else's house. Going down to breakfast always seemed a mountain to climb. My nerves were on edge, especially on that first morning, as I hovered at my bedroom door trying to ascertain the amount of progress being made by others towards the kitchen. Was that a rattle of plates I could hear? Were those footfalls going downstairs? Was it better to risk being first, or wait until last? Why couldn't I have been satisfied with my home life, where everything was familiar? I felt worn out before the day had hardly begun. An effusive welcome from Cheena, the big spotted dog, helped to break the ice for both myself and Mrs. Spilman who, I am sure, felt uncomfortable with this strange, half-civilised, Norfolk peasant, who, through force of circumstances, had been dumped in her household. A low growl from Snippet half rebuffed me, and told the younger dog not to make quite such a fool of herself with strangers.

So, with breakfast over, I prepared to go out to work for the first time. When passing the kitchen sink I couldn't but notice the enormous pile of washing up, and was soon to learn that the lady who came to work there on certain mornings had to face that unwelcome sight on each occasion. I was also to learn that, on these mornings, we had a proper cup of coffee made with real milk, but on the odd days it was a poisonous concoction, brewed by the lady of the house, with dried milk powder.

All these idiosyncracies slowly came to light as strangers became people who would play a big part in my new lifestyle. I would also mark down the fact that Mr. Spilman came out with Gillian and myself to begin work, but very rarely repeated the action after that. I think the post held him up on most mornings, or so he said, and he joined us when the sun had risen just a little higher in the sky. On the other hand, he was the boss, so this lack of appearance remained a private joke between his daughter and myself when we were more acquainted. At any rate, both people who came out with me that morning were very easy to work with, and weren't afraid to get their hands dirty.

The growing daylight gave me my first real sight of the mink farm. It consisted of a short, open-sided shed, as I said before, with wire cages suspended on each side of a wide walkway. The roof was of stretched, black plastic, held down by battens. The floor of the walkway was covered with wood shavings and sawdust, which I found out later had been thrown out by the over-energetic mink as soon as it had been placed in their boxes as a form of bedding. Some cages stood outside, with an assortment of covers over as protection. The whole conglomeration was contained within a four feet wire fence, with a twelve inch flat tin baffle along the top. The wire, I learned, was also dug into the ground. A metal gate of similar construction had to be kept closed at all times to prevent any loose animals from escaping into the wild. Mink, being natural killers, can wreak havoc in poultry houses should they get free. They can climb, dig, swim, and squeeze through any hole larger than one inch in diameter. They are vicious beyond belief, lithe, wonderful athletes, and smell worse than the proverbial polecat to which they are closely related. A native of North America, they had been imported for breeding, their winter coat being used extensively in the fur trade. Savage with tooth and claw, they were always handled with thick hedging gloves through which they could still pierce your finger quite painfully. Even with all these antisocial traits, I loved them from the start, and found them to be the most interesting and entertaining animals to work with. From the outset they were determined to outwit us, their captors, and escape by any means they could, always gnawing, pulling and pushing lids and gates with little wet noses, their shiny, intelligent eyes flashing the message of defiance at all times. Moving faster than light, an unsuspecting hand inadvertently rested on a cage top would receive a slash before its owner could move. That kind of reception moved one's reactions up a gear or two, I can assure you.

Opening the slip bar of the gate, and carefully closing it behind us, Gillian explained things to me. Prevention of escape was emphasised, for not only were the animals dangerous to ducks and poultry, they were also valuable stock which could be ill-affordably lost. Empty nest boxes had been placed in the run corners, with the hope that any escapees would tire of their new-found freedom, and curl up therein for a sleep. As I found, this very often happened, and a metal slide whipped across the entry hole kept the animal trapped until the box was hung on the miscreant's repaired cage. This saved maybe hours of ducking and weaving whilst trying to catch one of nature's most slippery customers with an indiarubber body wrapped up in an expensive fur coat. After a few months' practice, I found myself diving around with reflexes akin to any cricket wicket-keeper, and having great fun pitting my wits against one of the keenest little brains ever made.

The first objective, for me at any rate, was to construct a second shed before the mink mating and breeding season, which always begins around 10th March, when females start to come into season. Having lost almost a month of planned time, due to my flu infection, this was to prove a very tough order, but we could only do our best and this we proceeded to do. Even this rough carpentry looked daunting, for remember, I only produced one tiny scissors rack after five years in the school carpenter's shop. But I was keen to learn, and was very thankful that my boss had donned his coat to show me what to do. As the sun slowly appeared above the bare branches of the old orchard apple trees, the unlikely trio of teenage girl, ex-Flight Lieutenant of the RAF and farm labourer, set about making a fortune as mink farmers. Hope springs eternal, they say! Maybe no one made a fortune, but we did enjoy the pioneering spirit that this trying engendered.

Chapter 5

"Mink Mad"

Before starting work that first morning I nervously asked how far away the post box was. Under instruction to turn right at the gate, I walked the short distance past Florey's Stores, two cottages, the butcher's shop, over the Bell forecourt, and found the letter box in the Post Office wall. Well, I thought, how handy all the services are. Food, drink, and Post Office, with even a bus stop over the road just outside the tiny doctor's surgery. Without spending any more time sightseeing, I posted my letter and returned to base.

The second mink shed planned was to run parallel to the existing one, that is straight down the orchard. It was explained that two rows of ancient apple trees had been pulled out to make way for the mink run. This had been done by hand, with assistance from a winch worked by a handle. The rear of the winch was connected to the base of the second tree in the row, whilst its pulling chain went back to the first one. By working the handle and ratchet, slowly but surely the poor old tree keeled over, and progressively lost its root hold. This work I observed at first hand later when the need to extend the sheds beyond their existing perimeter fence became a necessity.

My first job was to dig four holes in a line across the shed end. These were marked on a measured length of wood, so I was sure of each position. As the posts were only 4" x 2" there was no need to have a large diameter hole, but one only big enough to work the spade in – nothing like the width and depth of that gate post hole Leslie and I excavated on Little Strawberries. The soil compaction wasn't too bad either, and I made very impressive speed at the job. A large pile of second-hand timber lay beside a saw-bench situated at the rear of an ex-Army-type half round, galvanised shed. A hole in the back wall facilitated a belt from saw-bench wheel to electric motor inside. I had cast a wary eye on this machine, hoping that I would not be asked to use it, for a fast-whirring circular saw blade always sent shivers down my spine. As luck would have it, my boss much preferred sawing timber to digging holes, so the problem never arose. Every so often a gut-rending shriek would come from the saw blade as a hidden nail was struck. This metal to metal confrontation called for a break in operations, as Mr. Spilman applied a file to one or two blunted teeth – the machine's, not his own! We two labourers, Gillian and myself, selected four posts, two longer than their mates. Across the top of these we fixed an apex truss, ready made up at the correct angle, and constructed of 3" x 1" rough cut timber. A thin, temporary timber nailed across the posts half way up held them steady enough to allow us to upend the whole structure in our holes. After much adjustment with an instrument called a spirit level wielded by my teenage supervisor, we could tamp in the posts firmly, leaving the first structure of many standing alone, straight as a die. I had no idea what a "die" was, but my Grandad Eke, who was an engineer, always used the expression for the ultimate in straightness. Another tool new to me was that spirit level. We hadn't really needed one of those in the beet fields, and certainly wouldn't have qualified to have one for our Little Strawberries gate post. After all, remember, Barney Hooks wouldn't even let us loose with one of his carpenter's saws. But I was open to learning, and I must say neither of my new bosses made any mention of my glaring lack of tradesmen's skills. I, on my part, was determined to make up with brawn any deficiency on the technical side. Under their quiet tuition, I soon learned what was, in reality, just basic, rough carpentry, and enjoyed myself whilst doing it. The sun had risen above the mist and bathed the orchard in late winter sunshine, the chickens scratched around outside the mink run, and ducks paddled their webbed feet in the mud, making a bigger mess than was already there. That was my first meeting with a big Muscovy drake, whose face was beginning to take on a boozy colonel's red colouring, as the mating season approached.

Judy's horse rubbed itself on the tin baffle which topped the mink yard fence, bending it and causing Gillian to threaten all sorts of dire punishments if it didn't desist. A call from Mrs. Spilman, indicating "corfee" was ready in the kitchen, straightened everyone's back, and muddy boots were shaken off by the back door before proceeding into the warm kitchen. The dogs gave only a token acknowledgement from their respective baskets; Cheena especially had only a thin coat and would sit as close as possible to the Aga, even on relatively warm days. A short break, a visit to the toilet, and off we go again, eager to get on with the job in hand.

All the time we were at work we had an interested audience watching every move from the confines of their cages opposite. Each shriek of the tortured saw blade sent small brown bodies hurtling back into the shelter of their boxes. Then, tiny minky noses would appear, followed by a sharp face dominated by shiny, black, button eyes. Those small ears were finely tuned to pick up any sounds of danger. Slowly, as the suspected risk of danger subsided, the sinuous body would almost flow out of the bolt hole, and a mink would creep over the netting floor of its cage to finally climb up the end wire to get the best vantage point for observation. Another sudden move would send them all scampering back into their boxes like rabbits into a warren. It intrigued me to such an extent that I had to take myself in hand and concentrate harder on my work. The only blot on this otherwise blissful environment was the constant whiff of foul odour coming from deposits under the cage ends. It took me several weeks to condition my nose to this, although it was vastly reduced when I undertook the job of "mucking out" with shovel and wheelbarrow, and then strewing fresh-smelling wood shavings over the floor. But all the time I was fascinated with the antics of those highly intelligent, ultra-mobile animals, and did not realise at the time that their lives would end prematurely in order to donate their fur coats to the fashion industry.

After dinner, or lunch as my new-found employers called it, we returned to our task of shed building. A second batch of holes was now required, and I set about marking them out, under strict supervision. The distance from the first set of posts was crucial, as the intervening space had to contain six cages on each side. These wire cages were 18" wide, with a 2" minimum gap in between to prevent the occupants fighting, for if there is one thing a mink hates more than its human captor, it's another mink. Again, the excavations were done in record time, for this was one job I could manage without too much worry.

At about 3 o'clock Gillian disappeared into the larger shed, and I could hear the hum of machinery for a time. Then she reappeared armed with a bucket filled with what looked like anaemic mince. I had noticed the mink becoming more active, but this was nothing to the frantic acceleration which occurred as soon as she entered the mink run gate. Every animal proceeded to climb the wire sides, rush up and down, and some even walked sloth-like upside down along the cage roof. To each animal a scoop of this strange mixture was allocated, it being placed carefully on the cage top and then covered over with those inverted empty fish boxes. The climbing mink delicately pulled a mouthful of food through the wire and ate greedily. The cloud of starlings, which had miraculously appeared in the apple trees, squabbled noisily, their hopes of an easy meal being thwarted by the boxes. One or two braver birds flew on to the cage tops furthest from where we were working, and continued their noisy protests there until a lightning thrust by one of the mink sent them squawking skywards. On occasions their evasive action failed to save them as the vicious and unrelenting jaws of nature's lightning killer closed on a leg. The victim either died as a result of being partially pulled through an inch square wire mesh, or escaped leaving one leg behind as a trophy of war to be stored for later in a wooden nest box. After witnessing this exhibition of nature in the raw, I was doubly careful not to leave any part of my anatomy resting on an occupied mink cage.

After the feeding had been completed, it just left the task of refilling the metal water cups situated inside the outer end of each cage. Gill, who must have been heartily sick of watering twice every day, suggested I take this job over. Equipped with a metal watering can, which was filled from a standpipe tap, I slowly worked my way along each side of the shed. The small female animals were standing up beside their cups in the hope that some water would overshoot and give them a bath. This they enjoyed, being animals of streams and rivers in their wild environment. Some would stick their heads into the cup, thus emptying half the ration straight away. A few cages at the end contained much larger animals, the breeding males. These chaps lumbered along, a vast contrast to their smaller and more active mates – or hopefully to be during the last three weeks of March. Their apparent slow movements were no more than a blind, because I soon found that when one escaped they could travel like the wind, and give me a run for my money.

As the light began to fade and 5 o'clock approached, it was time to pack up for the day. The two Spilmans seemed very pleased with the day's progress, and it looked as if we would soon erect this vital second shed. In fact, I wondered how this temporary job was going to last me out until September. I needn't have worried because the lady of the house also had an eye on this new labour, and earmarked me for quite a few jobs in the garden and around the house, jobs which her husband had very cleverly side-stepped, pleading the acute necessity for him to work on the mink farm. Now he would either have to do them himself, or give his blessing for me to work at them instead – hoist by his own petard, one might say.

Being in lodgings meant a change of clothes before tea was taken, whereas at home one could lounge around in working gear as long as the day's jobs hadn't been connected with pigs in any shape or form, although the new form of cattle fodder, known as silage, carried a pretty persistent odour, so much so that my mother once threw my boots into the shed when I worked at Soigné. The evening dragged as, after reading the Telegraph, no Daily Herald here, and half listening to the Archers, I had nothing to occupy myself. The much-enjoyed simple games of Ludo, in which Dad always held everyone up with his yellow barriers, had been forfeited without a thought in my quest for a wider and more fulfilling life. Mrs. Spilman had enquired whether I rode, whilst offering me a copy of Horse and Hound. I refrained from the obvious answer of, "Yes, but only a bike", and instead expressed my love of horses, but rather the working, heavy horse with which I had quite a lot of experience. That piece of conversation exhausted, we lapsed into an uneasy silence. After an early supper drink I excused myself, and retired to my room to read a book on mink rearing lent to me by Gillian who, from that point on, gave me all the literature available on these small, furry animals. Quite quickly we became "mink mad", to coin a favourite phrase of Judy's. She, on the other hand, was "horse mad", and went riding whenever possible, usually with Susan Walker who lived a few yards down the road opposite the Post Office. I'm sure Judy's friends looked with some amusement at this strange, labouring fellow with an even stranger accent, but the two Spilman daughters did their best to make me feel at home by involving me in their interests as much as possible.

The Manor, in which I now lodged, was a rather imposing, half-timbered building, with an extensive Cotswold slate roof. It appears there had rarely been a Lord of the Manor in Standlake, and much of the surrounding land was at some time or other owned by various Oxford colleges. The house itself had been allowed to slip into a poor state of repair by a succession of owners; the last of these, Doctor Slee, sold to the Spilmans and moved to Ducklington, quite a bit nearer his Witney-based practice, although he still covered Standlake and was my first doctor in Oxfordshire. Being a very old house, it repeatedly creaked and groaned at temperature changes, and Judy lost no time in telling me of the ghostly figure that frequented the Rose Room, a bedroom overlooking the High Street. I was to have a much closer encounter with this apparition before too long as will be recounted a bit further on in my story.

On Friday morning I made the acquaintance of the lady who gallantly tackled the mountain of dirty pans and dishes. Mrs. Pitt came in for three mornings a week, and after spending an hour wading through this enormous task, cooked lunch and cleaned the house. Mondays, Wednesdays, and Fridays were highlighted, not only by coffee made with real milk, but also by some wonderfully delicious meals for she was a cook second to none. Thankfully the Aga provided unlimited hot water for dishwashing, and two large hot plates, and an oven for her to cook with. Occasionally the cry would go up, "The water's nearly cold", and a second cry from Mrs. Spilman, "Dick, did you remember to do the Aga this morning?" Yet another lapse of memory, similar to that when I was marooned at Oxford Station, had occurred, and no fuel had been poured into the fire. Under the withering gaze of two women he would riddle away, tip anthracite into the belly of the stove, and hastily withdraw to take refuge down in the orchard until water warmed up and ladies cooled down. Such was life for the master of the house who had been totally outnumbered by females until I arrived to bear him company. Even the domestic pets lined up against his gender with two bitches and an elderly female cat.

Saturday was to be a half working day for me as, in fact, it was then for all agricultural workers. Having occasion to come up to the workshop situated opposite the back door, I found two men there preparing to do some house maintenance. The younger of the two quickly introduced himself as Bert Coombs who, with his father, also called Bert, came along on Saturdays to carry out work on the house. As was clearly indicated by brown water stains on ceilings inside, the Cotswold slate roof was causing problems, and it was on these the two men intended to concentrate their labours. Whilst drinking my mid- morning refreshment with them I learned some more about these friendly work-mates. Bert, the younger, or Albert as I later found his mother always called him, had completed his apprenticeship as a bricklayer, and now worked with his father for a building firm in Witney. He, like myself, had served two years' National Service in the RAF, which gave us some common ground to build a friendship which lasted from that day until cancer claimed his life at the age of 54. Also, like me, he had attended the grammar school, and left to take up a manual trade, although of course bricklaying came much higher on the blue collar scale than muck-cart, and was a skilled job. The one big difference between us emerged as our friendship increased. Bert possessed a stack of self-confidence, and was prepared to try his hand at anything and everything, whilst I saw disaster in even the smallest deviation from work I had done before. Eventually some of his enthusiasm for tackling whatever problem arose rubbed off on to me, but it was many years later before I became semi-self-sufficient, as the financial cramp of being a property owner forced my over-cautious hand. My new-found soul mate also disclosed that he was engaged to Mrs. Pitt's second daughter, Gillian, so a pattern of local life slowly began to unfold. My village knowledge now extended outside the Manor gates, and I felt a tiny sense of belonging to this new community.

Another fact I learned from Bert was that, if I needed to go into Oxford, a bus passed through about 1.15 p.m., and I could catch it at the stop opposite the shop. As it was a nice day, I decided to go forth and explore the city for myself. The only part of it I had seen was back gardens from a train window, and of course the Station itself. So, after a wash and quick lunch I stood in the late February sunshine, awaiting the red double- decker Oxford City bus which was to carry me to this world-famous city of learning.

Chugging along the country roads at a much reduced speed to that of a Ford Consul, I could take a more leisurely look at the fields. These were much smaller than those I had been accustomed to working, and there was a much higher percentage of pasture land, with many tiny pocket handkerchief-sized meadows holding a couple of cows or a horse used for riding. Being on the top deck did little to settle my quickly eaten midday meal, but the view was first class. I was very pleased the bus didn't turn down to the Bablock Hythe ferry, but ploughed on through Stanton Harcourt where I noted, with some surprise, a set of stocks next to the bus stop. As there was no one sitting in them, I assumed their very presence kept the local population law abiding. Notwithstanding, I was fully prepared to see a gibbet round the next corner with the remains of a sheep stealer swinging in chains thereon. After leaving the narrow streets of Eynsham, we met up with another blast from the past in the form of a toll bridge. Well, at least that was a good step up on the ferry propelled by manpower. After these eye openers I began to wonder if I had progressed at all from my native Norfolk where I had considered things were very out of date. The old adage of grass being greener on the other side of the fence was beginning to take on a real meaning for me.

After negotiating the quite considerable traffic entering Oxford, the bus pulled into the depot which was part of the market place. We had skirted the railway station on our left as we came in, after passing under a very low bridge. This particular bridge was a constant hazard to double decker buses as only certain vehicles were low enough in design to pass under. Many Oxford Mail headlines carried the news that yet another bus had been opened up sardine tin fashion by this obstruction. As I was disgorged with my fellow passengers, I asked the conductor for information regarding the return journey. It transpired that the timetable gave me a good four hours to explore, before the next bus back so, taking my bearings, I set off into mainstream Oxford. The fire station and a cinema on the corner gave me a return point should I become lost. My first objective must be to buy a street map of the city, and this I proceeded to do. W.H. Smith provided this vital necessity, and with its help I began to take stock of my surroundings. The first thoroughfare I had entered was George Street with, to my delight, a theatre advertising a mouth-watering selection of shows with stars known only to me on radio. The New Theatre was to be well patronised by me as matinée performances took place every Saturday. In addition to this building, another theatre, The Playhouse, was situated on the far side of this block, rubbing shoulders with the famous Randolph Hotel and almost opposite the Ashmolean Museum, yet another attraction for my leisure time enjoyment. Two nearby picture houses gave me a wealth of entertainment without going more than a stone's throw from the bus depot on Gloucester Green. At least I needn't run the risk of getting lost, or spend too much valuable time getting back to the bus should a show overrun.

A strong smell of fresh coffee assailed my nose in Carfax encouraging me to enjoy a cup in the Cadena whilst studying my newly acquired map. Taking a seat by the window, I gazed out at the milling, cosmopolitan crowd outside. King's Lynn and Norwich had always been busy on a

Saturday afternoon, so that was nothing new. The thing that struck me most forcibly was the great variation in skin colour and dress of the people. To see a coloured person in the streets of Lynn or Norwich was very rare indeed – Americans in uniform perhaps, but not otherwise. Here there were all shades of black, yellow and white, dressed in bright colours, weird fashions, to me that is, and talking in many foreign tongues. There were even undergraduates wearing mortar boards, with black gowns hanging from their shoulders, clutching huge quantities of books and discussing deep educational theories with one another as they shoved through the crowd. This certainly was another world, very much like the seething metropolis of London which my mother described so graphically from her domestic service days of pre-marriage. But, to tell the truth, I felt rather lonely as I sat there watching all those people hurrying to and fro. They seemed to be part of some big family, whilst I didn't even have a home of my own to hurry back to when my afternoon jaunt was over. Still, at least I could send a postcard back to Norfolk to give my family an insight of my impressive historical surroundings.

I spent the rest of my afternoon peering through gates of various colleges, admiring their neatly trimmed grass quadrangles, and vowing to visit them all in turn, but of course this never came to fruition. The theatre billboard proclaimed the coming next week of the Crazy Gang, featuring Flanagan and Allen, Nervo and Knox, Naughton and Gold, along with "Monsewer" Eddie Gray. This show was pencilled in as a must to mark my first ever visit to a live theatre. This promise to myself I certainly did fulfil, with many other performances to follow in the next few months. Well before my bus was due to depart, I returned to Gloucester Green, and filled the waiting time with a cup of tea in the depot café, which would have won no prizes for presentation but served a very nice cuppa. Reading the back page – I always read papers in reverse – I caught up on the news of the local football team. Headington United was then a part-time professional team, playing in the Southern League and experiencing a pretty poor season at that. Reading on, I discovered they were in grave danger of finishing below a cut-off point at the end of the season, thus condemning them to an inferior league next year. What a come-down for me as a supporter! I had left a Norwich City team carrying all before them in the F.A. Cup, and occupying a reasonable position in the dizzy heights of the Football League Division 3 South. Outlook as a lifelong soccer supporter was certainly grim, to say the least. Still, perhaps later I might find the whereabouts of this Headington United ground and give them a try for, after all, they had once visited Norwich for an F.A. Cup tie, and had performed pretty well. At that time I hadn't any idea where Headington was, but now I realised it was part of Oxford, rubbing shoulders with

Cowley, the industrial area of "Town and Gown". William Morris, the motor car mogul, had built his factories on the edge of Cowley village, and expanded to such an extent that thousands of men and women were employed there, many living locally, but the majority commuting in from surrounding villages. It was from this source that most of the football support came as professional soccer failed to make much impact on the academic mainstream of this university city. The true blue amateur team, playing at the White House ground under the name of Oxford City, drew some support, as had the combined Oxford and Cambridge University team of Pegasus who won the Amateur Cup a few years previously, but had by now passed into the history books.

All this information I gleaned over the next few weeks by trawling back pages of the local Oxford Mail and Oxford Times newspapers. These sources of information were greatly enhanced when I discovered the Saturday evening sports paper, which was a "Green-un" as opposed to the "Pink-un" so avidly read at home in Norfolk. Swindon Town and Reading, being the two nearest Football League teams at that time, held pride of place in headlines, but Headington United were poised to begin a long climb to join their two more illustrious neighbours when they became Oxford United a short time later.

As the bus rattled along narrow roads back to Standlake, my stomach muscles began to contract in their by now well-known manner. Peering through misted windows into the darkening countryside, I worried in case the conductor would forget to warn me of my requested destination. At last he called, "Standlake High Street", and with a word of thanks, I tumbled off the wide step and found myself outside the village shop, only a few yards from my temporary home at the Manor.

The rest of my weekend seemed to stretch ahead with nothing beyond letter writing to fill it. At the moment my time seemed to be all stop, or all go. Saturday had been full of work in the morning, and exploration in the afternoon, but now I had an evening and all day Sunday to face without everyday, homely tasks to complete. I longed for Monday morning to come round so that I could get involved in work once more.

As is often the case, my worst fears were unfounded, and my first Sunday in Standlake passed quite easily. You may remember that I had started attending church at Westacre, and on the strength of this interest, I tentatively enquired about local services. It turned out that Gillian and Judy were both bell ringers and choir members, so immediately they invited me along. Ten-thirty was the starting time for them at the bell tower, and so, true to their tradition, they tore out of the house at twenty-eight minutes past ten, and with me in tow, flew up to the church, allowing me little or no time to view my surroundings as we went. I was introduced to Mr. Dan Costar, local farmer and tower captain, who invited me to watch, after enquiring as to whether I was a bell ringer myself. Again, as was the case with horse riding, I had to reply in the negative. It seemed as if I had a great lack of experience in any pastime, except that of spectator. At any rate, the welcome was warm and an invitation was extended to attend practice during the coming week. My natural reserve and fear of anything unknown held me back, and I silently resolved to give this job a miss. Of course, I had reckoned without the persuasive powers of my two companions, especially Judy, and I was destined to be amongst the company for practice on Wednesday. One thing I did stand firm on was the church choir. When, a few weeks later, Mrs. Gibbon, the rector's wife, invited me to join their practice on Friday evenings, my polite decline held firm against all persuasion. Not being able to read music (could I do anything, you may well ask!) was my excuse, and I stuck to that. In no way could I imagine myself dressed in frilly choir collar and flowing gown.

The weather being fine in the afternoon enabled me to walk through the village, on this occasion with time to look around and admire the Cotswold stone cottages with stone slate roofs. Almost all the properties were of this material, and well weathered, although a few were thatched, and even the odd one bore blue Welsh slates. I expect that, in the days before planning authorities, a property owner used whatever materials came most easily to hand.

Another trip to church in the evening filled my day far better than I had envisaged. Returning to the Manor through a darkened village, I considered I liked what I had seen of it, and had been warmly welcomed by the people I'd encountered along the way. Yes, the new environment met with my approval; how, I wondered, did I match up to the local expectations. If they respected hard work and willingness to adapt, then I was in with a chance, only time alone would tell on that score.

Chapter 6

Finding my Feet

Monday morning found me once more down in the orchard with more holes to dig and new shed sections to erect. As each set of posts went up, the tops were secured to the previous ones by narrow timbers. Again, the spirit level came into its own both for keeping the roof struts at a constant height, and for ensuring each post was exactly upright. Slowly the framework took shape, giving us a skeletal pitched roof structure, almost on the pattern taken by modern steel and concrete buildings for industrial use. As the roof was to be stretched black plastic, there was no need for heavy timbers, and the wooden supports designed to hold the wire cages gave additional strength. Before actual roofing took place all timber had to receive a coating of creosote, and this was my job for most of the afternoon. Gillian disappeared into her mysterious shed, from which issued the hum of machinery, and the boss had been absent all day, leaving in his car just after 9 a.m. This left me happily brushing away on my set of steps from whence I was able to view my surroundings.

As previously stated, the mink run was situated just inside an old apple orchard at the bottom of the Manor vegetable garden. I suppose at one time this had been kept in first class order by an employed gardener, but now, like the house itself, it had fallen into half-wild state with acidic land weeds gaining an upper hand season by season. Wild horse-radish, and mare's tails grew in profusion, almost hiding an antiquated mechanical rotovator, which looked very forlorn after standing outside for the winter. Compared with my Dad's neatly-tended garden, it looked a mess, and had I realised Mrs. Spilman nursed ideas that I could turn it into a mini-market garden for her, then my afternoon could have been sadly blighted. Blissfully unaware of some of the impossible tasks I would be set later, my creosote brush splashed over the wood with gay abandon, watched by a host of little eyes set in sharp faces whose owners were climbing their cage ends to get a better view of the interesting operations. Nothing moved in or around the mink run without Mrs. Mink fixing her beady eyes on it, although the males tended to live a much less active life, or were less nosy, as the case may be. Mr. Hill's cows lay chewing the cud away on the western side, beyond the overgrown orchard hedge. To the east, the orchard ran along the rear gardens of Florey's shop and house, two cottages, one of which housed Mrs. Pitt and her three daughters, meeting up with another pasture owned by Mr. Back of Eagle Farm. At the bottom end it adjoined arable fields, also part of Eagle Farm. From my vantage point, coupled with the absence of foliage, I could see for quite a distance. A green Fowler tractor moved ponderously over the ploughed land, stirring the surface in preparation for spring sowing, its single piston "thump" carrying plainly across to me. Judy's horse grazing in the corner completed a very peaceful scene which, coupled with my easy-to-accomplish afternoon job, set me up in buoyant mood. My drastic change of scene seemed to be working out very well, so I felt like whistling while I worked. This was certainly a big improvement on the back-breaking monotony of a sugar beet field.

Gillian came in with her bucket of mink food, and suggested I broke off creosoting for a few minutes whilst she demonstrated the amount of food to be given to each animal. It seemed such a small amount, and I remarked on this fact, which brought an explanation. Mink, being natural inhabitants of the cold North Canadian forests, would be subjected to a diminishing diet as winter progressed, using their body fat to keep going. This meant that by mid-March , their mating season, they would be almost skin and bone, and this slim-line state stimulated their reproductive organs, which produced more female eggs, and consequently larger numbers of young. Later on their rations would be increased to provide sustenance for milk production, and then eventually a thick winter coat, which was the end product or, in other words, the mink farmer's harvest. The males, being much larger animals, had a double ration, although again it was essential to keep them thin and active. A sluggish male would prefer to sleep rather than chase a fiery, spitting female playing hard to get in the mating cage. With me replacing those empty fish boxes over the food we soon completed the job. An ever-present afternoon audience of starlings chattered and squabbled in the trees, thwarted once more in their search for an easy meal. If they had been brave enough to come under the cages they could have enjoyed quite a feast as the very hungry animals dropped quite a bit in their frantic efforts to pull down their food. Again I went round with the watering can, noting that one or two animals had loosened their metal cup, thus enabling them to tip the water out as fast as I filled it up. Fearing the silly creatures would die of dehydration, I reported back to my superior.

"We had better tighten the wires again", she said, and I had visions of putting my bare hand into the cage and ending up with a finger or two augmenting the animals' tea.

Gillian appeared with her wire cutters, and a flat metal slide with about an inch turned at right angles on one end. Walking up the centre aisle, she stopped at one loose-cupped cage, and by gently scratching the back of the wooden box, quickly enticed the curious mink inside. A deft slip of metal down from above trapped the animal inside where a furious scratching of claw against metal ensued.

"There you are, Derek, you can secure the cup safely now, but just keep an eye out in case she manages to get a claw round the side of the metal in order to pull it aside."

You can bet I kept a weather eye open, but everything went according to plan. Most metal slides were wide enough to prevent escape, but I found later there was one slide a bit narrower which did occasionally let the prisoner escape from her box, and this in turn encouraged a quick exit of any body extremities from her cage.

Mr. Spilman arrived back at about 4.30 p.m., with some large, metal, butchers' trays in his car boot. One contained large, brown objects, covered with cows' muck and resembling old hooded overcoats. These, I learned, were tripe, or cows' stomachs turned inside-out. Another bin held a large liver and some lights or lungs. A third tray held a conglomeration of fish bones, mainly plaice from which fillets had been taken. This was basic mink food to be used during the next few days. Whilst unloading these, I saw for the first time the inside of Gillian's secret shed. This mincing shed, as it was called, contained a large walk-in fridge into which the fresh food went, a small mincer, large sink, and one or two bags of meal and bran. The overall smell was of manure coming from the tripe which needed much washing, and the residue from this operation just ran out through a hole under the shed side, hardly a satisfactory sewerage system, even in cold, winter weather. I could well imagine what the smell would be like in the height of summer..

After enquiring as to our progress during his absence, the boss explained the pattern of his working week. It transpired that he owned two automatic, coin-operated laundrettes in Swindon, which meant regular trips there to oversee their working, although he employed a manageress at each establishment. On the way back he called at a slaughterhouse to buy offal on which the mink depended for food. Fish offal came from a wet fish shop, also en route, so in actual fact, at that time he had no additional transport expenses. The only snag was that his wife complained about the residual smell in the car boot, and entreated him to use the old ex-RAF truck, which I suppose did little for the status of a laundrette owner when parked outside, with bluebottles surrounding its open back in high summer. Well, another day was done as far as work was concerned, and I had learned quite a lot about the small animals I had come to build sheds for.

As we sat in the lounge after tea, Mrs. Spilman enquired if I was able to kill a chicken. Not wishing to appear ignorant of everything asked of me, I admitted I had disposed of poultry in the past. What I didn't say was that I had seen my father break an old hen's neck when her laying days were over, and it looked quite simple.

"I will leave the poultry shut in tomorrow morning, then perhaps you can pick out one with a pale comb, a non-layer, and kill it for me."

This I agreed to do first thing, surmising that this small act of kindness would not hold up my shed building project by more than a few minutes. Poor, simple soul, I had a lot to learn, I'm afraid.

Approaching the dilapidated hen house next morning with trepidation, I wondered why on earth I had admitted to knowledge and experience I didn't have. Cautiously opening the door, I peeped inside. A strange head in the confined space of their house is not conducive to quiet, ladylike behaviour by hens. They cackled and flew around, raising dust and poultry mites into the air, thus preventing me from seeing at all, let alone able to select a pale-combed matron. Coughing and spluttering, I grabbed the nearest feathered fiend, and withdrew, trying valiantly to hold on to the legs of my victim who, in turn, tried to raise her head in order to attack my hand. Gripping her head, I pulled on it with more force than was necessary, and succeeded in almost decapitating her completely, rather than just breaking her slender neck. After a few minutes' frantic flapping, during which time my hair and clothes had been even more liberally covered with feathers and fleas, my chicken ceased to twitch, so I could assume success with the execution. After proudly presenting the body to the lady of the house, I was instructed to hang it in an outhouse.

At coffee time the next question was fed to me: had I experience in plucking poultry?

"Yes", I replied, gullible to the extreme.

"Gillian", rang out the voice of authority, "it will be alright if Derek plucks that chicken for me? The mink shed won't miss a few minutes' lost time".

Gillian didn't seem best pleased, which made me feel like "piggy in the middle", not wishing to fall foul of either side. After pulling at the by now cold feathers, I knew the job was going to take more than a few minutes. If I had been given the task straight away, the warm body would have released its feathers easily, but now the stumps from a part-moulting chicken would take some finger-tearing effort to remove. I sweated away, torn between doing a clean job without ripping the skin, and getting back to shed building. Later I was to learn that, in the past, Mrs. Spilman had paid Barb. Nichol to pluck her poultry, the fee having to come from housekeeping money, and now of course a cheaper method had been devised. This was the beginning of a running battle of wits to monopolise my labour between mink farm and domestic tasks, which I didn't care for at all, especially as I found Gillian quite moody when I eventually got back to my carpentry duties. Her father was in an even more unenviable position, for either way, he lost out. By keeping marital bliss by agreeing with wife, he fell foul of his daughter, and by taking a reverse stand, he suffered the age-old punishment of being sent to Coventry for a day or so. Eventually the tug of war usually took place on his Swindon days, so at least he escaped unscathed. As for me, I soon learned to say to myself that the pay was the same wherever I worked, and just left them to sort themselves out, although I would have preferred to have been left to do the job for which I had been hired, namely shed building.

The nearer we came to March, the more I heard talk of this mating season and its crucial importance to the economics of mink farming. The furry animal upon which the whole financial venture depended only came into season once a year, and at a specific time. Only between 11th March and that month's final days would a female accept advances from a male, and then often only after a terrific fight. If a female failed to mate within that time she would remain barren for the whole year, and have been fed for nothing except the value of her rather small coat. As every minute of every day had to be concentrated on that one job for three weeks, the Spilman family wanted to take a few days' holiday beforehand. This meant I would be left in charge of the animals, and therefore needed to learn how to make the feed under supervision, distribute it and make sure everything was kept as fresh as possible, for mink are very susceptible to botulism, a very serious form of food poisoning. When I heard of these plans I was mortified, to say the least. To be left in charge after a few days' shed building was taking a big risk I must admit. They were either very desperate to have a holiday, or had great faith in my ability to learn quickly. Perhaps it was a little of each, or that Gillian turned out to be a very good instructor. I think she warmed to the fact that I was eager to learn every aspect of mink keeping, so our lessons went well.

Cleanliness seemed to be the key to food preparation as everything had to be washed well before being cut into strips for easy feeding into the fast turning, electrically driven mincer. All trailing pieces were pushed on to the worm with a stick, keeping fingers, hands and any loose clothing away from machinery. By wearing a rubber apron for protection, one could slosh around with hose-pipes, although the pressure wasn't very high as no mains water existed in Standlake at that time. An automatic pump from a bore supplied our needs, it being situated near the house. Hot water for washing off grease came from the Aga, and collected in a bucket from the kitchen sink taps.

Tripe, fish, liver and lights were mixed in various amounts with bran, milk powder and minerals being added. The percentages of the first four constituents varied according to their availability for, at that time, we were subject to slaughterhouse vagaries of supply and demand. Sometimes we had small, softer tripe from sheep instead of the heavier cattle variety. These tended to make a wetter mix, so more bran had to be used to get a correct consistency. I soon got the hang of it, but always sweated as to the freshness of perishable ingredients, spending much time in smelling every item. My ultra-caution paid off, for there was never even the mildest outbreak of botulism in all my seasons in mink farming. Nerve-jangling reports came out in the Fur Farmer giving graphic details of whole farms being wiped out after one feed of tainted food. What a catastrophe, to get up in the morning and find all your breeding stock dead in their cages. Every morning of those first few days in charge found me shaking the box of any animal not showing itself in the run. I received some very indignant looks from rudely awakened tenants as their bedroom suddenly became an earthquake zone.

The two dogs and one cat were to be fed on tripe cooked on the Aga top. The smell of cooking unblanched tripe, has put me off that supposed delicacy for life. The kitchen reeked of it for hours afterwards, but the animals enjoyed it. Chickens were fed on grain and any old mink food left over from the previous day. The ducks also joined this feast as soon as it was thrown down. They also enjoyed dabbling in the effluent that ran out of our mincing shed, which did little to assist it to soak away. The Aga had to be riddled, cleaned out, and refuelled each morning, with a top up of anthracite before bed. Mrs. Pitt saw to my food supply, and I lived like a lord in his manor for those few days. I also had an invitation to go to her house and watch T.V., where I met Bert again, and also Gill, along with John who was the boyfriend of Jean, her eldest daughter. The last of the three sisters was Jackie, who had just passed her seventh birthday, being a long way behind Jean and Gill who both worked in Oxford. After the initial fear of being left in charge, the short time passed very pleasantly, and I was sorry when my virtual freedom was finished. But all good things have to come to an end for I would have run out of fresh mink food, and as I couldn't drive, it was impossible for me to renew the stocks, even if I had known where to go.

On 10th March it was decreed that all work in and around the mink pen must cease, for mink need peace and quiet for their mating operations. So, as I was not needed in this field, my work became centred on the workshop, a prefabricated building opposite the back door.

The main occupation was to make up cages in batches of six, which would fit exactly between each set of posts in our new shed. The necessary wood and wire netting had been purchased, and with the help of a scaled plan, I commenced this new task with a great deal of trepidation for, apart from that now famous scissors rack, I had never completed a usable item in a carpenter's shop, and that was after five years of close supervision. First of all I had to cut down a long roll of 1" mesh wire netting. By rolling it out across the lawn I could measure my depth, and then laboriously cut along its length by means of an ancient pair of hand-operated wire snips. As each wire separated, the pliers closed with a severe jarring sensation to my wrist. The first half mile, or so it seemed to me, produced the first blister, and by the time I had reached the far end of a fifty yard roll, my whole hand was a strong contender for the Radcliffe Hospital casualty department. Through my pain from raw flesh I despaired in case my measurements had been wrong. What if I had done all that painful work for nothing? What if the whole roll had been ruined? My nerves played havoc with my tummy and forced me to take a quick toilet break so soon after breakfast. Of course, all the sweat and worry were needless because, having measured correctly in the first place, and checked it half a dozen times after that, the job was a good one. As well as the plan, Mr. Spilman had left me a ready- made partition as a guide, and as there were no joints required, only nailing, the second part of the job went well. My slightly angled sawing and often off centred nails didn't matter as stiff wire on either side held the whole thing together quite firmly. Five of these partitions took me most of that first day to make, but the boss seemed quite pleased with my progress when he inspected the work. Considering my close proximity to the rear of the house, the lady therein hadn't come out with any odd jobs to break my concentration. This was too good to be true, and succeeding days brought various "five minute" jobs, which tended to need an hour to complete, and which began to make considerable inroads into my cage construction output. Feeling that my two mink bosses, hidden away in the orchard, had no idea of these interruptions, it began to worry me as they could well imagine I was swinging the lead behind their backs. After I tentatively mentioned my second line of jobs, the frequency of calls became less for a while, and this enabled me to produce a steady flow of cages. On completing the first one, we wheeled it down the drive on a trolley. Mink-mating being finished for the day meant we could try it in situ. Imagine the knots in my stomach as we raised the structure between its holding posts. To Gillian's joy, and my immense relief, it was a perfect fit, so without further ado we set the spirit level along the top and nailed the batch of six cages firmly in position. That made our shed look really something, and as each section was completed, our pride in the work grew stronger. My cage building contract went on until the last few days of March registered an end to the mating season, with only a few of the most ferocious females left barren.

During this time my leisure activities were widened. I was introduced to Mrs. Mooney who worked a couple of mornings a week doing secretarial work. Her parents had hailed from Peterborough, and as I later learned, Mr. Tee, her father, had driven the Flying Scotsman for a period of time. After retirement he had moved next door to his daughter and son-in-law in the High Street of Standlake. Mrs. Mooney was very friendly, and invited me to join her husband, Horace, and father in a trip to a pub in Eynsham. I was not sure this would appeal to me, but felt it churlish to refuse point blank. I went along for the trip on a few occasions, playing darts and dominoes quite badly, and losing them a few pints in the process. Being a poor pub conversationalist, I found it hard going, and as the evening light lengthened, found repeated excuses why I was not able to go, and eventually it all fell through, with obvious relief on both sides. I'm very glad to say that Mrs. Mooney remained a very good friend for many years until after Horace's retirement, and then they migrated eastwards to live in Suffolk, near Bury St. Edmunds.

As the weeks passed, I spent pleasant evenings at Mrs. Pitt's cottage, being plied with a selection of home-made cakes whilst watching television. Often Gill and Bert, Jean and John were there, but on other occasions only Jackie and her mum were at home. At first I was afraid I might outstay my welcome, but if Jackie could have had her way, I would have been a permanent fixture. If she hadn't fallen asleep before I tried to leave, another game or book would be produced. For a young lady of seven, she was very persuasive with determination second to none. I like to think my new-found attraction left John and Bert in relative peace to watch T.V. In truth, poor Jackie missed her dad, and perhaps the family as a whole, so recently bereaved, found a stranger helped to channel their thoughts away from the vacant chair. I never had the pleasure of meeting Jack Pitt, but I only ever heard him spoken of as an honest, likeable, family man, who was a sad loss to everyone, not least of all his own family who I was to get to know very well through the coming years.

Bell ringing practice became a regular Wednesday night time-filler. I never became very proficient, but neither did I forget to let go the bell rope when required. I'm sure you have seen cartoons depicting the beginner being carried upwards by the weight of a bell, to bang his head on a false ceiling. I made very sure to follow Mr. Costar's instructions in that field, even if my non-musical ear failed to pick out the deep tone of my tenor bell. I fear that even years of practice wouldn't have qualified me for my campanologist's badge, but I did try, and it was good fun in excellent company. Mr. Dan Costar was of stocky build, sporting a fine moustache, and the very epitome of a farmer, which of course he was, along with his two sons, Gordon and Bernard.

Repeated calls to join the choir continued to fall on deaf ears, my only reply being, "Have you a death wish and would like to empty the church?".

They must have taken me at my word for the invitations dried up, to my intense relief. I could imagine my Westacre mates rolling in the aisles with laughter had they learned of my choir member's official dress. No, that was not part of my "gone off to make my fortune" propaganda which I envisaged sending home for publication.

The Saturday after my trip to see the Crazy Gang gave me a chance to visit "The Manor", where Headington United played their home games. Taking a bus from Oxford centre, I was again able to get a seat on the top deck in order to see the sights. Down "The High", over Magdalen Bridge, round The Plain, and up the steep Headington Hill we lumbered. Bright sunshine blessed my afternoon once more, and I marvelled at its warmth so early in spring. Several other football supporters, wearing their colours, were on the bus, so, as soon as they made for the stairs, I followed them. A slow drift of obvious spectators led me to the ground which, even as kick-off approached, seemed only sparsely filled. Having bought a programme, I sat down on wooden sleeper steps to acquaint myself with the home players and the local news. Reading on I discovered that a well-known name in football management had just arrived at the club. Arthur Turner had been quite successful at Birmingham City until his face failed to fit for some reason, and he had moved on. He had come to work in Oxford, promising to revitalise the club and build up the support by his success, until Football League status was a possibility. Firstly, though, points had to be obtained in order to stay in the premier section of the Southern League. To further this aim, two new players had been signed, and who, as it turned out, would develop into the most loyal club servants ever. They were Ron "Tank" Atkinson and fullback, Cyril Beavan. Ron became the new captain and driving force from midfield. Released then by Aston Villa, he was to become a famous manager who eventually returned to Villa Park as their manager. So, on that first Saturday, I was inadvertently part of the build-up of Headington's rise to fame as Oxford United, who did gain league status and went on to win the Milk Cup at Wembley. Arthur Turner had by then long since ceased to be their manager, but it was his hard work and football knowledge that set the club on its road to success.

To return to that first Saturday, the standard of football wasn't great as I stood on those wooden steps in the sunshine. My open air view point was from the end which now houses the London Road stand, home to all fanatical United supporters of modern times. The play might not have been of the highest standard, but an exciting game, won narrowly by the home team, encouraged me to go again, thereby commencing a support which has continued on and off for almost forty years. This support has not been regular, I must admit, but Oxford's result still comes a close second in importance to that of Norwich City at 5 p.m. each Saturday during the football season. I must record here that Headington United did finish in the top half of the league at the end of that season, qualifying for Southern League senior status, and that limited success signalled a steady climb to greater things.

Whilst on the subject of spectator sports, I also watched some cricket in the Parks when our summer game took over. Oxford University played home games there against county sides, and in those days had quite a good team. Captained by the bespectacled Mike Smith, future leader of both Warwickshire and England, they produced some exciting games. The flamboyant Alan Smith kept wicket and wore, I remember, a pair of huge, floppy, keeper's pads, a stark contrast to those narrow, short protectors worn by modern wicket-keepers. These matches took place in May and early June as warm-ups before their annual Varsity match at Lords. This early start was needed as the University "went down" in early summer, with their leading players turning out for county sides, often to the exclusion of young professionals. This long-established tradition caused quite a lot of bad feeling in the game, but remember, it was still an amateur and professional set-up. All the former were recorded in score books with initials before their surnames, but the latter were surname first, denoting their lower status. All county captains were amateur, again by tradition, and although many were very good, others were hardly worth their places in the side. Unfortunately, but predictably, warm summer weather didn't accompany summer activities, and I often shivered in the Parks, whereas I had basked in sunshine watching football. Still, I was determined to sample all forms of entertainment available whilst the opportunity was there, for remember, I was only a temporary resident of Oxfordshire and would be off to Lincolnshire in September. At least if rain stopped play I was able to go to the Ashmolean Museum for an hour or so, and as both venues were free, my Saturday outings cost little more than a bus fare and a cup of tea. This principle was essential, as I was trying to put away a small sum of money each week as a nest-egg in readiness for my wageless year at college.

Chapter 7

Mink Mysteries Unfold

As soon as the mysterious mink mating season was officially over, work on the second shed began again in earnest. The first task was to roof the finished sections in order to keep the new cages dry. As mentioned previously, the material used was black plastic bought in a roll about six feet in width. First of all the end was fastened to one side of the roof timber by means of staples delivered by a large gun, an adult edition of the machine used for paper clipping in an office. Carefully unrolling the heavy bulk up over our roof, we repeated the operation on the other side. By pulling the material as tight as possible, we achieved a drum-tight result, which looked very professional. Thin, wooden battens were then nailed along all edges to make it secure. Of course, a windless day was required, and on that very still morning we made good progress. In fact, the lack of air movement finally produced a very warm day, and looking back along our roof, we noticed how the original drum-tight sheets had become much looser. Not being able to reach a conclusion as to the reason, we continued to pull our sheets as tight as possible, if anything even more so in an effort to counteract the sagging. It wasn't until the next morning that we realised the error of our ways. Close inspection showed numerous slits in the plastic where the nails and staples had entered, although every section was now well stretched. Then the penny dropped. In the hot sun black plastic sheeting expands, and then contracts when temperatures drop at night. On our over-stretched sections, the pressure of contraction caused the plastic to rip from its holding nails, thus weakening the sheet. We decided not to replace our worst mistakes, but to be more careful in future. Eventually autumn gales whipped those faulty sheets away, leaving mink cages and their furry occupants open to the elements until a calm day enabled repairs to be done. That was one of the many trial and error experiments we tried, only to fall foul of some problem along the way. Luckily they were relatively cheap materials we were using for, in business, one cannot afford to make too many mistakes. Obviously corrugated iron sheets would have made a much more permanent job of it, but the extra expense in thicker timber and the sheeting would have been prohibitive at that early stage. So we worked on until mid-April when the in-kit mink mothers-to-be regained our attention and labour.

If you think I had been allowed all my time on the mink shed, you would be wrong. After Mr. Spilman had struggled to start his garden rotovator, and waded through the sprouting jungle of horse-radish and mare's tails, I had the unenviable task of trying to clean the land. It's amazing how many pieces weeds can be cut into by whirring rota blades, and how well they can spread thereafter. My first job was to attempt to fork them out. Being well used to manual work, I suffered very little from muscle fatigue, and as there was no cold East Anglian wind, my jacket could be removed without fear of lumbago. I was soon convinced that however hard I worked, the result would be the same – a garden choked with rubbish before any seedlings could take hold. A weed- infested stack bottom in Norfolk would have been a Garden of Eden in comparison. This infestation was by two weeds, which were then almost impossible to get rid of. I struggled on, but my heart wasn't in the job, and sure enough, before the month was out, all garden seedlings had disappeared under a sea of indigenous weed cover. Poor Mrs. Spilman did try hard to establish a kitchen garden, and saw me as her knight in shining armour riding to her rescue, but before long that armour had rusted, and she had to give up the unequal fight, with the exception of a small section for potatoes. My first lesson in weed infestation had begun before reaching farming college. Twitch grass may have been public enemy number one in Norfolk, but here two much worse opponents had stolen the thunder.

Mink always have their young, or "kits" as they are called, during the very last days of April and first two weeks in May. The kits are born naked and blind, and run a serious risk of being eaten if mother is disturbed or frightened in any way. Thus, every precaution must be taken to prevent this catastrophe from taking place. Add to this the risk of dying from exposure or dampness , the first few days of a mink's life are very precarious, and without the survival of these tiny, pink creatures, no mink coats would be there to market around Christmas time.

The first operation was to exchange the 9" square boxes for much roomier nesting boxes. These had ample room at one end away from the entry hole for nest making. They also had solid floors to prevent up-draught, and loss of heat and bedding. As soon as the exchange was made, the lady of this new house set about rearranging the contents. A bunch of wood wool had been placed inside each box, and its hinged, sloping lid secured with a hook and eye fastening This new bedding was furiously tugged out into the cage, and then carried back in again, presumably to the satisfaction of its new owner. This whole operation was carried out at a frantic pace, which should have caused the house- proud matron to abort forthwith, but this must have been part of her hormonal change. Eventually peace returned to the mink run as each nest was completed to its owner's satisfaction, although some bedding had to go out and in several times before perfection was achieved. It all turned out to be very amusing to us onlookers, if not to the mink whose facial expressions indicated that a very serious operation was taking place.

Next we set about constructing light wooden frames which were then covered with clear plastic sheet. Again this was secured with the staple gun and battens, but experience taught us not to tighten it in direct, warm sunlight. These panels were designed to fit across the outside ends of the cages, keeping out draughts from our nesting mink, but were not put in place until a few days before kitting was due to commence. The blocking off of cages from outside meant moving all water cups inside the shed. This fiddly, time consuming work was carried out with Mrs. Mink shut inside her box by means of that metal slide. A furious scratching came continuously from inside, causing more than a slight concern for one's exposed fingers should the slide move enough to allow the enraged bundle of tooth and claw access to her cage.

At last everything was in place for a warm, secure and peaceful atmosphere in which the mink could have their kits. Only Gillian entered this hallowed sanctum from now on, for any strange persons or sounds could cause panic enough for those temperamental females to eat their young. All male mink were moved to the far end of the run and caged securely for fear an escapee might enter the kitting shed and cause mayhem therein. Husbands are definitely banned from the maternity ward in mink circles, to the extent that males are classed as public enemy number one immediately after mating takes place. As I was surplus to requirement in the mink run, my work reverted to cage construction in and around the workshop.

A pile of empty, army ammunition boxes had raised my curiosity, and now came the day of explanation. This military surplus had been bought in the hope that the wood could be re-used for mink boxes. The stout, well-seasoned timber looked very suitable for the job, but one slight drawback, of how, in the first place, the well-constructed and heavily- nailed box could be dismantled, hadn't been fully investigated. Many of them split beyond practical use whilst prising off their reinforced sides, and so the work turned out to be time consuming and was a financial loss when compared with using new wood cut specifically for size. At any rate, our mink box pile grew steadily in readiness for all the young mink we hoped would emerge from the carefully guarded maternity wing.

During the Easter holidays Mrs. Pitt brought daughter Jackie along with her to the house. Being a very inquisitive seven-year-old, she soon tired of watching housework, and moved her attention to the much more interesting workshop. We soon became workmates as she busied herself with offcuts from the boxes, trying to make patterns by nailing them at various angles. More by luck than judgement she managed to miss her fingers, and the time passed in friendly chatter as we worked at our separate tasks. The little girl was so taken up with her new pastime that she made impassioned pleas to be allowed back after dinner, but eventually she was persuaded to leave some work until her mother came next time.

Every alternate morning saw Jackie beavering away at her appointed task of turning all available offcuts into works of art. Sometimes the finished article failed to come up to expectation, and I was prevailed upon to draw the nails holding it together. This didn't detract from my box output, and we had plenty of old nails taken from our dismembered ammunition crates. The dual output from our workshop went swimmingly well until one morning when Jackie's domestic traits took over from her carpentry leanings. She suddenly took it into her head that the workshop was filthy and needed sweeping out. Admittedly months of sawdust had accumulated on the concrete floor and did cause some nuisance when struggling to prise the ammunition boxes apart. But this small inconvenience was nothing compared with the dust storm raised by a seven year old bundle of energy, swathed in one of her mother's aprons, and armed with a broom almost as big as herself. Immediately working conditions became impossible, as did the stopping of the jet-propelled broomstick. The self-appointed cleaner was determined to rid the floor of every dust particle if she died in the attempt, and no amount of pleading on my part could deter her from this goal. Gasping for air, I took the coward's way out and withdrew to the relatively clean atmosphere outside where I continued to work. Considering the pall of dust pouring through the door, it was a wonder the cause of it didn't die of clogged lungs, but the will to succeed must have seen her through. Eventually a dust-covered apparition appeared in order to gulp some fresh air. Thinking the spring-cleaning madness would have evaporated, I congratulated her on a good job well done, and thought that, with any luck, the dust would have settled by the time my afternoon session began. No such luck, for my words of praise only served to send her back in again to do an even better job. Fearing that her mother would chastise me for letting a little girl get into such a filthy state, I implored her to stop, but to no avail. I learned that morning the fact that nothing short of a brick wall would turn Jackie away from any chosen objective once her mind was set upon it. When eventually I returned to my workbench, I discovered most of the floor dust had been transferred to every other surface in the shop, causing a mini-fog each time something was disturbed. It was with great trepidation I greeted her on the next visit, but thankfully the cleaning bug had died a death, although it was only by good luck we hadn't all died with it. By the time the next holiday came round new jobs were being tackled out in the sunshine, and the workshop was left alone in its dusty state, much as Barney Hooks had left his carpenter's shop during summer at Soigné. Strangely, my recently abandoned life on the farm seemed worlds away from Standlake and only fleetingly brought back by frequent letters from my mother.

Every fortnight Mother and I exchanged large parcels of washing. Wrapping my dirty clothes in thick, brown paper, I sent them home from the very handily placed post office. Mrs. Dobbs received my securely-tied parcels over the counter, and Marg. Couling left the returns inside the front porch of my lodgings. Marg., of course, delivered using a bicycle in those days, and must have been pleased to be able to relieve her front carrier of such a large parcel only a few yards from her starting point. They also must have wondered why laundry was sent almost 150 miles to Norfolk when my boss owned two laundrettes. The cost wasn't very high, although of course my mother had to cycle to Westacre in order to post the clean clothes back. Anyway, if the laundrette had been used, the question of ironing would still have been a problem, as I had no experience in domestic matters at that time. Every Monday Percy Tuckey brought a tiny parcel to the door, which went to Swindon, where the manageress put the few items through a machine. Percy was a retired postman, and lived with his wife, Dolly, in a small cottage overlooking the Green. Percy regularly attended at church on Sunday evenings, where he took the collection, his best boots creaking over the quarry tiles as he tried to tread softly in the sparsely-filled building. He also partook of a boiled sweet to help digest the sermon, and we could hear the paper crackling as again he tried to operate in silence. The effect was almost akin to fire crackers echoing round the high vaults of the roof. I imagine poor old Percy was partially deaf, so never realised he could be heard. At any rate, the Reverend Andrew Gibbon, or "Gabby", as we irreverently called him behind his back, never gave any indication that he heard or was distracted.

The Reverend Gibbon was a tall man in his late fifties, a rôle model for all village fiction writers who needed to paint a picture of the rector, even down to the dewdrop on the end of his parson's nose. He rode a high bicycle at a moderate speed, and never fast enough to unseat his trilby hat. A Christian man down to his boots, he went about doing good works in a quiet and unobtrusive way. One might have imagined him to be too heavenly to be any earthly good, but this was far from the truth. The forthcoming years proved him to be a deep thinking man, and a very good mate in times of trouble and stress. Mrs. Pitt worked for him also, and perhaps he too experienced a taste of Jackie's spring- cleaning efforts during school holidays. The huge rectory, in which he and his wife, Margaret, rattled around, had already been divided into two dwellings, but still needed outside help to keep it clean and tidy. The heating problems were enormous, and may well have been partially responsible for that elusive dewdrop during the cold weather. A man who would go to the extreme to avoid causing offence, the Rector, as we all addressed him, was nevertheless of strong principles and a power to be reckoned with if the law of right was challenged. Coming into my life immediately after Canon Caley of Westacre, he also went some way towards softening my strongly held views of church and state – with one aim in mind to keep the agricultural labourer in his age-old conditions of serfdom – versus the working man. We certainly never heard a sermon based on the oft quoted hymn lines of, "The rich man in his castle, the poor man at his gate, etc.", from Andrew Gibbbon. I'll say he only helped slightly to soften my lifelong suspicions of so-called servants of God, because there were many occasions in future days when I found myself at odds with ministers from various religious orders, and usually those on higher rungs of the church ladder. Still, I have always been a rebel, with or without a cause, and am unlikely to change now.

When the church fête came around the joke was touted that "Gabby" would be able to buy a new bike with the proceeds. Nothing could be further from the truth, of course. Mrs. Pitt, who, despite being a staunch Methodist, worked for the rector and on occasions he called at her house for some reason. On one such occasion her son-in-law to be, John Cully, was fooling around with a pair of lace-up corsets, and had them on when a knock came at the door. "It's the rector", whispered Jean, as her boyfriend tried to divest himself of the then modern-day suit of armour. Finally, giving up, he fled into the back garden before the door was opened to admit the clerical caller, who always had to stand inside with head bowed owing to the very low ceiling. All those left in the room were almost convulsed as they thought of John trying to untie the back fastening straps outside. If fat Max Borton, the neighbouring butcher, had spotted him in his predicament, John's life wouldn't have been worth living, for such an event would have spread through the village like wildfire. No one ever forgot the time when John was stuck in those corsets. Poor Andrew must have wondered why all the Pitt family were choking as he explained the reason for his visit.

On another occasion, Mrs. Pitt, who ran the welfare clinic at the village hall, experienced difficulties in finding a key holder on the afternoons the event was held. The village hall committee deemed her as not needing a personal key, even though her time between morning work and opening the hall left little space for key hunting. When the good lady mentioned it to Mr. Gibbon he suggested the problem be left with him to resolve. A few days later he produced a key, and with a touch on the side of his nose, made it clear the matter need not concern anyone but themselves. He wasn't a man to let voluntary work be hindered by local red tape. We just presumed he had arranged for another key to be cut from his own. But there, most of his little kindnesses were done very quietly, and the majority never came to light, the way that he liked it. He retired to Oxford in 1969, so I was fortunate enough to know him for ten years in the village, and to remain in contact with him as he worked part-time for Oxfam. I take great pleasure in recording what a fine man he was, despite being the butt of our harmless jokes at times.

As May of that first year advanced and the mink kits arrived, pink, naked and blind, it slowly and painfully became clear that the average litter throughout the whole number of females wasn't very high. Gillian and her father were obviously disappointed, although, with hindsight, there were almost as many animals as could be comfortably accommodated in cages and boxes produced in readiness.

The food supply was also unpredictable as the slaughterhouses tended to operate a first come, first served policy regarding tripe, lights and liver. Also, on very hot days, suspect items of food were offered, as no refrigeration took place before the items reached us. We had only a holding fridge at that time, so any surplus obtained had a very short shelf life before having to be ground up for the ducks. On numerous occasions Gillian had to sit at the back of Witney slaughterhouse, waiting for cattle to be killed, before steaming tripe came out the other end, the amount available depending upon the size of monetary tip offered. Hungry mink would have to wait for us to mince the food just brought in before they had a late afternoon or evening feed. This led to savage fights between well- grown kits still living together whilst waiting for new cages or boxes to be constructed. This living hand-to-mouth caused stress and unsociable hours for all concerned. This second problem didn't make much difference to me as, by living in, I had no family to consider, and could be available to help whenever needed. Occasionally it upset my Saturday afternoon plans, or a T.V. watching invitation at the Pitts' home had to be cancelled, much to Jackie's annoyance as she had set herself the task of inviting me on every possible occasion. Hardly a day passed without her arriving on her little, blue Raleigh bike to ask me to watch some programme or another. If the answer was "no", then she would return home in a not too good frame of mind; the answer of "yes" would send her back, as happy as a sandboy, pedalling furiously along the footpath, putting all other users at risk of being run down. As I watched, her mop of fair hair closely resembling a cartoon of the rising sun, could just be seen above the front wall. No brush or comb could tame that hair, and like Jackie herself, it certainly had a mind of its own. It was on evenings such as this, when work intervened, that I felt peeved, for I hated disappointing the little girl when my presence seemed to be so important to her.

Before the rush of growing mink ruled over our lives, I took a few days' holiday in order to return to Norfolk. This time the train journeys were enjoyable for I have always liked travelling on the railway. My family was very pleased to see me, and I spent the time recounting all the experiences of my new life. Of course, my mother took a close look at me to make sure I was not losing weight due to lack of food. Apparently I passed muster for no adverse remarks were made. The truth was I fared very well for food, as my Manor meals were augmented by a large number of tasty extras, pressed upon me when visiting Mrs. Pitt – so much so that I felt embarrassed accepting them all from a widowed lady who had to work all the hours God sent in order to support her family. The days passed quickly, and apart from visiting Aunt Ivy and Grandad Bumfrey at No. 9, Pretoria, I didn't go far. Grandad offered me a cup of tea from the old brown pot which he kept simmering on the side of his open range, but I declined on the pretext that I had already partaken of one at home. Grandad's tea was so black that even my RAF- educated stomach, accustomed to tea in all shades from grey upwards, couldn't take to it. A kind man was Alfred Bumfrey, but his teapot made all nieces and nephews quake in their shoes when a cuppa was offered from it. Cousin Maurice remembers it to this day, mentioning it in a recent letter. I did have a few words with neighbours, but somehow felt alienated, and when my longstanding mate, Leslie Lloyd, began moaning about conditions of work, I felt like screaming, "Why the hell didn't you stand up and be counted when I did". In the event, I said very little, but thought the more. My final thrust which, in the end, I couldn't resist, was to suggest he looked for another post if he was so hard done by, but I don't think he did. Like us all, we just have to moan sometimes, and let's face it, he wasn't footloose and fancy free like I was. With no domestic responsibilities I could walk from one job to another, and did just that, averaging no more than eighteen months in any one job, until after my fortieth birthday. Once the Soigné mud had been shaken off my boots, I didn't allow much dirt to cling to them after that.

As the weeks went by and high summer came, I found I missed my home much less, and began to live at Standlake rather than just lodge there. I ceased to feel uncomfortable in the Spilmans' company, and enjoyed alfresco meals on the lawn under the shade of a huge walnut tree. This was something we never did at home for main meals were always eaten at the living room table, probably because there was nowhere to sit outside. One could hardly take dinner sitting in the middle of a large vegetable patch. On the other hand, I had always enjoyed my packed meals outside, in all weathers, either under the hedge beside a wood fire in winter, or lazing in the shade during summer. The garden being walled was very private, and the only people able to view us were a few left on the top deck of the six o'clock bus as it trundled along from Oxford. The pets always joined our party, racing to get through the garden door first and causing some danger to the balance of those carrying trays. On one occasion the cat, which was renowned for her ferocious temper, walked sedately across the lawn when Cheena and Snippet barged through the door. In unison they decided to chase their feline compatriot, and sped across the grass. Instead of running away, their supposed quarry just carried on walking at the same speed, thus spoiling their sport as only a cat could. Cheated out of their intended chase, and fearful of those sharp claws, the two pursuers shot one on either side of her and braked sharply to end up looking rather silly trying hard to give the impression that chasing cats was the last thing on their minds. The very amusing incident left no doubt in we spectators' minds who was boss between those three. In fact, the pecking order went in reverse of size, with the much larger "spotted dog" coming in a very poor third.

Visitors from the higher echelons of village life often called as we enjoyed the evening sunshine in that peace of an English garden. Colonel and Mrs. Kirby Smith, Brigadier Goadby, or Captain Wilenkin might come to discuss British Legion affairs, although Flight Lieutenant Spilman never wished to use his retired military rank, whereas the first two gentlemen expected theirs to be used without question. When visitors arrived, I immediately gave up my chair and excused myself on some pretext or other, retiring to my room which overlooked the garden. Their voices would drift up to me, and I often marvelled at the numerous amusing topics apparently being discussed which, in turn, produced those loud "Ha, ha, hars", which seem to be a feature of retired servicemen's informal meetings. As the sun set and the evening cooled, I could smell the smoke from my boss's pipe, which was his constant companion. I also turned over in my mind how a man in his position made use of this appendage at crucial moments. If an answer to a particular question was required, and he couldn't form it quickly, his pipe would need a lighted match to be applied, and the time taken to produce the requisite number of puffs before conversation resumed gave time for the brain to regroup. This unique action by pipe smokers was used extensively to good effect, giving the impression that no embarrassing break occurred in conversation. I seriously considered the advantages of this ploy, and wished I had perhaps become a pipe smoker. Further consideration, however, told me the expensive and smelly habit wasn't worth pursuing just on that score alone, so I settled for the knowledge that when it happened then I was sure my opposite number was stalling for time.

On one stifling, hot July evening, just as I was preparing for bed, a knock came on my door. Hastily donning my dressing gown, I opened up and found Gillian there. It transpired that she and Judy, along with some friends, were planning to take their boat on to the Thames at Newbridge, and then go for a midnight river trip, and they wondered whether I would care to join them. Being a chap who always looked to sleep my allotted eight hours without exception, this would be a first. Quickly making up my mind, I dressed again and was soon helping to fix the boat trailer on to the Ford Consul. Away went our loaded car the mile or so to Newbridge, where we launched the fibreglass boat. Expert rowers quickly had us travelling downstream towards Bablock Hythe where I had first met up with that old ferry man. Through the half-dark of a midsummer night, we splashed along in fine style. Trailing my hand in the cool water was heaven, and I enjoyed this "new life" experience immensely until I struck upon the thought that I could not swim. After that the cloudy waters of "young" Father Thames didn't look quite so inviting. Visions of the boat overturning and my life ending in eight feet of water at midnight took some of the shine off my student-like excursion with these young bloods. On the other hand, if only my old workmates at Soigné could see me now, living it up on the river, they would realise there was more to life than the monotonous round of World War 1 memories, retold for the umpteenth time. As you may have guessed, the boat didn't capsize, even when I was persuaded to try my hand at rowing. Our path became decidedly more of a zigzag, but I slowly mastered the art without losing an oar, and eventually returned to my bed at four o'clock, having enjoyed the experience, and apart from a couple of gnat bites, unscathed.

Chapter 8

Back to School

As my seven months' temporary work in Standlake drew to a close, I began to have feelings of regret that I had to move on. If only this job had come up before I embarked on obtaining grants for further farming education I would not have bothered. The mink-farming bug had bitten me well and truly, and I felt my future lay in that direction, and not in general farming. But the die had been cast, whether I liked it now or not, and anyway my work with the Spilmans was still only on a temporary basis. There was certainly plenty of work to be done, but the financial returns weren't high enough to warrant a full-time employee as yet. So it was, with some trepidation, that I prepared myself mentally for a return to what appeared to be an extension of my school days.

During the short stay in Standlake I had made new friends, and got to know several local characters. Frank and Chris Douglas, who kept the grocer's shop, Florey's Stores, were two of the latter. Both men were typical, traditional grocers, with spotless, ankle length, white aprons, and the obligatory needle-sharp pencil lodged behind one ear. Many commodities were still served up loose, making the shop smell deliciously as only a corner shop could in those days. As with the grocery vans of pre-electricity times, they sold paraffin oil, and Chris would cross the road, his shiny, brown shoes sparkling in the sun, and draw a gallon or so from a hand pump over the holding tank in the corner of his orchard, where a large house now stands. I suppose it gave him a welcome breath of fresh air, and also allowed him a few minutes' gossip, away from the eagle eye of older brother, Frank. I got to know Chris quite well after we spent an hour or so together trying to recapture a loose mink which had entered their storehouse situated next door to the Manor grounds. Chris took the occurrence of this smelly interloper in his stride, but Frank wasn't too pleased, I can tell you; I suppose the strong odour from the farm, carried on the prevailing south-westerly wind, did little to improve his half day rest period should he wish to sit in the garden. Chris, who lived on the Abingdon road, was well away from it, whichever way the wind blew. Frank wasn't over-fond of the smell carried on our clothes, so in working hours we shouted any orders from the door.

Chris Douglas also kept a few bullocks, which grazed his orchard and the field opposite the Manor where the houses of Manor Crescent stand proudly today. These fields ran right through to the allotments, as did the gardens of Saddlers and its neighbours. I often saw the bullocks looking over their gate as I took letters to post early in the morning. Max Borton, whose butcher's shop occupied the front room of Pear Tree House, would be cutting and chopping meat as I passed. His huge Alsatian dog would bound up to the closed gate, making me jump, even though I expected him to be there. A growl from the unseen Max would take him back to his knuckle-bone outside the shop door. As soon as Lionel Bint stirred at the Bell, Max would slip across for a tot of whisky at the rear window overlooking his garden. Butchery was heavy work, and Max needed to keep his liquid intake and physical strength up to par. Max was reputed to sell two types of meat, first class for those who paid on the nail, and some less tender for those who waited for a final demand before shelling out. This was how it came to my ears, but as I didn't buy meat at that juncture, I would not swear by its authenticity. At any rate, Max always did the weighing and pricing, just allowing his wife to take the money. On Mondays this master butcher went off to Abingdon market where he chose his meat on the hoof, and was, I have no doubt, a welcome customer at the local hostelries.

I have made mention of Max Borton, together with Frank and Chris Douglas simply because they were larger than life characters, built to stay in the memory.

Another gentleman I met through an escaped mink was Jack Knipe, the farmer just across the road. He lived in a pretty, little thatched cottage, beside a track leading to his farm buildings. He met up with this fat, male mink shuffling along that track, presumably smelling out the local poultry. Having alerted us to his unwelcome visitor, he kept tabs on him until we arrived to tempt him into a box with raw liver as bait. Taking the easy way to get lunch, he entered our trap and was quickly secured with a metal slide. Jack had reached retirement age and well beyond, I would think. Cyril, his son, did most of the work now, ably assisted by Alice, his wife. It was only a year or so since Mr. Knipe senior had given up his local milk round. One of his famous calls on Monday mornings, as the washing went out, was, "Go on, Mrs., peg it up high". In her pre-school days, Jackie stayed with her Granny Pitt, whilst her mother worked. On one occasion Jackie was sitting on her little pot, and Gran had just perched on a bucket in the back kitchen – remember, the toilet was at the bottom of the garden. Open came the door, and Jack stepped in with the milk. "Oh well", said Gran, unfazed by his appearance, "you've caught us both on the throne this morning, Jack". What the milkman said in return is unrecorded, which may be a good thing in the circumstances, but apparently they all had a good laugh. What a shame that, on his death, an alleged family dispute caused the little cottage to be demolished and when the site was sold houses were built over it. The desecration of that thatched cottage, through no fault of Cyril Knipe, I hasten to add, caused me to revise my ideas of knocking down the old and replacing it with new in order to improve housing in rural areas. My own refurbished cottage has given me thirty years of comfortable living, and I wouldn't change it for the world, but steady on, I'm rushing away at too fast a pace.

Whilst on the subject of cottage refurbishment, I must mention one instance that caught my eye. Cyril Collins, who married a local lady, Noël Smith, had moved into the shell of a tiny cottage named Saddlers, next door to the already mentioned orchard of Chris Douglas. It appeared that the couple had moved from pillar to post whilst trying to remain living in their own village. At last, in desperation, they bought this tumbledown cottage where "Lonee" Florey had lived for many years. Cyril and Noël could be seen working at every possible opportunity, in an attempt to build a house around themselves and tiny daughter, Celia. It was a labour of love, and the end result, after literally years of sweat, was a very comfortable home with ingle-nook fireplace, combined with radiators heated by an oil-fired boiler, a good combination of ancient and modern. The front section had to be completely rebuilt, and Cyril was a familiar figure up on his scaffold making the most of fading light before setting off to the Mill smallholding to shut up his poultry for the night. Noël's brother, David Smith, had also worked hard on The Vines, another cottage further down High Street. David was a carpenter by trade and Cyril a boat builder who had worked on the river at Oxford in earlier days. My knowledge of local people didn't extend much beyond the confines of High Street, but there was enough of interest to hold my attention during my short initial stay.

Mr. Hill, whose cows grazed next door to the orchard, was a member of the Plymouth Brethren. He and his wife lived in Harcott House. Bert Johnson, whose son, "Sonny", ran a small engineering business had been a leading parish councillor. Mr. Webb of Lincoln Farm rode up and down in a large wheelchair propelled by two levers operated by his arms. Hedley Shepherd, the builder, along with Pat and Leyland, his sons, was known through Mrs. Pitt. These were a few residents further up High Street who were on the fringe of my acquaintance. The local bakery, situated opposite the post office, had closed on the retirement of Mr. Louis Tuckey. A large barn set behind now housed a flock of chickens. I especially remember them after Mrs. Pitt told of the time her dog rushed across the road and upset them, to such an extent that Mr. Tuckey claimed the shock put them off lay for a week.

In the summer of that year, 1959, a terrible tragedy struck the community when little Alastair Theobold was accidentally drowned in the river behind the rectory. It appeared that his mother had taken him with her as she did some work for Reverend Gibbon, and the little lad slipped her attention for a minute or so, with fatal results. His father, Charlie Theobold, who was also a native of Norfolk, I got to know well in later years.

So it was with a heavy heart I said goodbye to my friends at Standlake. The Spilmans had been good to me during my stay, as had Mrs. Pitt and her family. An open invitation was extended for me to come and work during holidays from college if I was still interested in mink.

A short holiday in Norfolk reunited me with my family and enabled me to help Dad get up his potato crop. Needless to say, it was a pleasure to work on a weed-free garden after attempting to find potatoes in a forest of undergrowth at the Manor. I had experienced great embarrassment there trying to explain away why my fork had pierced the only tuber worth saving on a root. Freddy's crop might not have been particularly heavy, but there would be enough to see the family through most of the coming winter. Mrs. Spilman's, on the other hand, might give a couple of boilings if the spuds were cooked in their skins.

Now clear of Soigné's cloying mud, the "Derek Bumfrey Road Show" set off once more, this time to Lincolnshire and the Farm Institute of Kesteven situated in Caythorpe village. Recent experiences of new surroundings did nothing to help or reduce the rumblings in my stomach and the lifelong "first day sick headache" wasn't long in appearing. Not only was I going back to school after a ten year gap, I was once more preparing myself to run the gauntlet of doing it alongside a fair proportion of farmers' sons. As if the experiences of their catty comments at Hamond's Grammar School hadn't been enough to scar me for life, I was putting my head into the lion's den again. Thankfully things turned out differently this time, and it was only a tiny minority who thought themselves God's chosen men of farming.

The Institute was housed in a large building, originally a country seat of an estate owner. Outbuildings and stable blocks had been turned into dormitories and classrooms. Younger members of the intake lived in the main building under matron's eagle eye, whilst we more senior students occupied dormitories adjacent to the house. Five of the "trusties" shared one billet, Jock Wallace, Graham Bolt, Brian Field, "Gilbert" and myself. With the exception of Gilbert, we had either done National Service, or worked a few years on the farm. Some of us had done both, of course. Gilbert was a coloured man who had come from abroad to learn British farming methods, and was a wonderful character, with the most perfect manners. He entered into all our jokes, even when sometimes they went against him. I have often hoped that civil war didn't break out in his home country and rob him of a chance to use some of the farming methods he strove so hard to master. Who of us could forget the unusual sight of a gentleman, with skin the colour of ebony, walking across a wet, Lincolnshire field, holding a black umbrella above his head? All our leg-pulling never stopped our friend from taking his rolled umbrella into the fields on showery days. Jock was, of course, a Scotsman, Graham was from Lancashire, Brian was a near local lad from North Lincolnshire, and I myself from Norfolk. Thrown in with Gilbert, we had a very varied agricultural background which was all to the good.

By far the largest number of students were on the General Agricultural, one year course. Three girls and two men (one of which must have been around fifty years of age) were on a poultry course. With respect, we called the veteran Mr. Cutler, and it must have been strange for him amongst all we young bloods where I was the "Father of our Course" at twenty-six. The work was split fifty-fifty between theory and practical. Our timetable was quite formidable at first glance, but designed to keep everyone on their toes both physically and mentally.

Each practical gang consisted of four students selected to give as near a cross-section as possible, based on age and experience. These working parties were allocated to a different section of farm work each week in order to gain an all round insight into the varied aspects of farming.

Working with cows, pigs and poultry meant weekend duties as well, whilst mechanised and manual sections gave us free weekends, apart from early Saturday mornings. The normal day began with an hour or so out at our practical sections. The only exception was when working with dairy cows when we had to meet head cowman, David Gribbon, at the dairy one hour earlier than normal for early morning milking. This did not go down too well with those natural lay-a-beds, and a half-mile walk in the cold and dark Lincolnshire countryside did little to encourage them to put their feet on cold lino' before 6 a.m. The only spur really was the double penalty of no breakfast and a dressing down by Mr. Treble, the head of animal husbandry and a champion of good, fresh, early morning air. Obviously late finishing at the dairy (David never allowed students to leave if one speck of milk was left in the pipes, or muck on the floor) meant they were late for breakfast, and that meal also had a sharp finishing time. Boy, was it a long time to lunch if that first meal had been cleared before you could rush to the dining room. Woe betide any last minute, frantic student who met up with Mr. Rowland or his deputy, Mr. Treble. By the time interrogation over the reason for your lateness had been conducted, classroom time was imminent, and one dare not risk a second rollicking in one morning. Not that I fell foul of the two most formidable lecturers myself, but the corridors often rang with their voices as they enjoyed tearing the ears off one of the younger students. Of course, my RAF experiences stood me in good stead as, compared with square- bashing and police training, this was heaven. I felt sorry for the youngsters who obviously hadn't been used to fending for themselves. They shot around like frightened rabbits, for a while at any rate, almost as I had myself in early National Service days. The only request was that we keep our beds and belongings tidy to allow cleaners free access to the billet. No kit inspection to fear, and we could walk on the floor and not slide around on pieces of old blanket, as in days of yore when on guardroom duty.

My biggest concern was the classroom, and whether I would be able to slot back into a learning groove. Probably this self doubt made me redouble my efforts to make as much information stick in the memory as was possible. An added spur was the thought of my paying by loss of earning power, and the need to be knowledgeable enough to recoup that financial loss in years to come.

Money was tight at that time, and I knew my small nest egg saved for extras outside of grant-paid board and course fees would soon disappear if I attempted to live the life usually associated with students at college. So I set my mundane course of action from the very outset. All my spare hours were used for private study, whether down in the library or in the billet, when everyone else had gone out. To my regret, there was no college football team, but the rugby team held sway, so I travelled to away fixtures with them, although I knew little or nothing of the rules of rugby. At least I knew my team's colours, and could shout when they attacked and groan when they suffered a reverse. This cost-free excursion helped clear my head of books, and helped me integrate with the other students in a recreational atmosphere. Later in the summer term I was able to act as scorer to the cricket team, which I really enjoyed. The only serious cock-up I made in the score book was my misspelling of a leading light's surname. The gentleman in question pointed out quite forcibly that his ancestral name was spelled "Horsfall", and not "Horsefall" as I had entered it. I could understand at once that an added letter "e" made a name of land owning stature into one only slightly removed from a person renowned for constantly falling from his mount in the hunting field. These small name misspellings mean a lot to we poor mortals who suffer it for a lifetime. I'm sure if my name had really been spelled with "ph" in the middle, everyone would have substituted an "f" instead of the reverse. That be as it may, I did at least know the rules of cricket, and enjoyed my position as official scorer to a not unsuccessful team.

The first week's practical work consisted of lessons on the basic principles of ploughing. Using an ancient Standard Fordson tractor and trailer plough, we set and used the implement, taking turns about. The sun shone on the dusty stubble field, and the afternoons passed very pleasantly.

Our instructor had come from full time practical employment into teaching, and not vice versa, so we received tips from a real agricultural background. To me, who had been kept from all mechanical operations which involved placing my behind on a seat whilst employed at Soigné, this came as a revelation. My first fumbling attempts at gears and steering must have been a revelation to the three younger members of our group as they had been born to the tractor seat. Perhaps, as the machine was antiquated, they had to reverse their modern ideas of power lift equipment, so that helped to even things up. In any event, we were all there to learn, and I made good use of my time. Ploughing didn't seem to equate to mink farming in any way, for my future was looking in that direction, but one never knew what might be of use in the days to come. I did find things mechanical difficult to understand, but with the help of my two engineering students, Jock and Graham on either side in our billet, I learned a great deal outside the classroom. To ask them questions came much easier than to ask an instructor in front of a full class. In return I could share my knowledge of animals and crops, so our exchanges were done without embarrassment on either side.

From the last remark you will have gathered that my nervous system was still gripped by a fear of hearing my own voice in public. This fear had haunted me from my earliest days, preventing me asking for clarification in class. My worst nightmare was re-enacted every week, on the one night when an outside expert came to lecture on his or her pet subject. At the end of each lecture one student was chosen to give a vote of thanks to the guest speaker. My constant fear was that my turn would come, and I would stand red- faced, tongue-tied, unable to make a single utterance. The gut twisting, weekly torture need never have been suffered, for as luck would have it, there were more students than lectures, and the dubious honour was not allocated in alphabetical order, so I was never asked anyway. I suppose if I didn't worry about one thing, two more quickly took its place. They say worry takes years off one's life, so on that score I should have passed away years ago.

We sat end of term exams before the Christmas recess, and to my surprise, I made a very reasonable hand of it. At least I hadn't lost the art of being able to tackle exam papers. This method had been well and truly drummed into our thick heads prior to sitting the Cambridge School Certificate at Hamond's Grammar School, so much so, in fact, that I still managed to finish first in an RAF police exam which I'd tried hard to fail. This time no such thought crossed my mind as I wished to gain my General Agricultural Certificate come the next summer.

After spending Christmas in the warmth of my family I was ready to go back to Standlake in order to renew acquaintances and earn a few pounds working on the mink farm. My journey back to Norfolk from Lincolnshire had been aided by a lift in Nobby Gribbon's car. Nobby, who was on my course, was the younger brother of David Gribbon, head stockman at Kesteven. Their home was just outside Swaffham, so I was fortunate enough to be dropped off at Pretoria free of charge. I hope I offered a little towards petrol, but Nobby being a very generous and open-minded chap, would have probably refused it anyway. Poor old Nobby had a lot to live up to as big brother, David, had been "Old" Treble's star pupil, and try as he might, it was impossible to win many accolades from his tutor. That situation made him one of us, if nothing else, but as I said, he was a very likeable young chap.

Dropping back into the mink routine was pretty easy. The pelting season had just been completed, although a few mink skins, or pelts as they were known in the trade, still remained pinned to drying boards, where they stiffened slowly before being despatched to the Hudson Bay Company's sales in London. The workshop where the gruesome task of removing the skin of freshly killed mink had taken place smelled as though skunks had been lodging there since I left in September. Mink are similar to the skunk, in that they have very active musk glands situated at the back which give off a pretty foul smell when mink are frightened and an even more lethal dose when a scalpel cuts those gland sacs in the skinning process. Musk is designed to retain its odour properties, and this I can assure you works very well. Being a new smell to me, it almost encouraged my breakfast to reappear when my nose first came in contact with it. I almost wished little Jackie would appear to recommence her spring cleaning passions of earlier days, forcing me to work outside. After a time I became more accustomed to the odour, and was able to resume my box manufacture in readiness for next season's mink crop.

The limited mink coat harvest had done little to pacify the bank manager on the business overdraft. Obviously, most younger females had been retained for next year's increased breeding programme, so apart from female culling and surplus males, the saleable produce had been small. No mention was made regarding my permanent return, but an invitation was offered regarding work for the Easter vacation before I set off back to Kesteven.

The winter term in the heart of rural Lincolnshire had very little to recommend it. The windswept fields felt the full blast of Arctic air. Setting off in mid-January for the morning milking, across frost-bound fields, before 6 a.m., brought back memories of square-bashing at Hednesford. Frozen pipes and icy concrete walkways held up production, leaving very little time for breakfast, although restrictions were relaxed slightly when winter was at its worst. The warmth of the piggeries and poultry battery houses were far cushier numbers than Mr. Treble's much vaunted, hygienic dairy, which, in his eyes, was the only worthwhile part of the college set up, putting any money back into the council coffers. The pigs and sheep he just tolerated, but the poultry unit, run by Mr. Cherry, was well below his lofty countenance. A difficult man to sum up was Mr. Treble, but he was a character nonetheless. Shirkers beware, for he would not tolerate slackness in any shape or form, and any clever student who tried to take the rise out of a farm employee was on the slippery slope to disaster if it reached the boss's ears. Tom Rowland may have been Principal, but it was the Treble who had all the practical understanding, and plenty of clout to go with it. His eyes and ears were everywhere, and we held him in awe and respect.

My work rate continued at a high level, and many a night, when the billet was on the chilly side, I went off to the library where it was warmer. The Herbert Jones cup, awarded to the top student at passing out, stood in a display cabinet, and I cast envious eyes at the names engraved upon it.

As I felt my finances were standing up well to the strains of student life, I allowed myself an occasional Saturday afternoon trip to Lincoln. I visited the magnificent cathedral, and sent home the obligatory picture postcard. I also frequented Sincil Bank, the home of Lincoln City Football Club then hanging precariously to their position in Division 2 of the football league. Their prize asset, Andy Graver, a centre forward of proven goal scoring ability, lightened our afternoons with his skill, and the tin-roofed stand resembling a school cycle shed in reality, echoed with applause when he hit the back of the opposition's net. When the highly elevated Middlesbrough came, they paraded an ever more lethal number 9 in the form of legendary Brian Clough, who scored twice in the visitors' 4 – 2 win. I remember he hardly chased the ball at all, but hovered around the Lincoln penalty area until a chance came his way, and then his finishing was lethal. It seemed as if he was saying to our local hero, "Anything you can do, Andy, I can do better". That, I suppose, sums up the football career of that never bashful Brian Clough when both player and manager.

Back to Standlake again, just after Easter, when tentative enquiries were made as to my future work plans. Would I want to resume a full time job with mink, and prospects of higher earnings as the proposed growth came to fruition? I had long since decided to return, if the opportunity arose, so plans were made for me to take up a post in July, when work requirement would be at its height. Filled with plans of a bright future, I returned to college for a final term, telling all and sundry I was fixed up for work after my course was complete. I never discovered the thoughts of Mr. Treble who had no time for those who diversified in farming, but who preached a gospel that centred on food production for the nation as its only commandment. What he would have thought of the present non- farming policy fed out of Europe to British farmers, I dread to imagine. His stout heart would have bled him to death.

Spring and summer out in the fields was again a lovely experience. Lambing in early spring, and field cultivations kept us all busy. I even felt that I would have liked to stay on as permanent labour, in order to share the student life permanently. I felt I would miss the comradeship much as previously when RAF service finished. But there, the die had been cast, so back to Standlake I was destined to go. Everything went along swimmingly until one morning at breakfast I read a letter from Gillian explaining that the kit average was again alarmingly low. This in turn cast a shadow over my planned return to mink farming. The sun suddenly went in, and my working world sank under a cloud blanket of uncertainty. Even so, my work at college had to continue, and sticking to the allotted task, I went into my final exams with hope, knowing I had done my best in revision and preparation,

The days between the exams and knowing our results dragged, as we just went through the motions of work. Everyone was itching to get home, and then on with new lives. The students had scanned job vacancies on the notice board, most of which seemed to be ordinary stockmen's situations, on a par with those held down by my father and grandfather, without a year's intensive training. Nothing caught my eye, so I just hoped my mink farm offer would be still open when I returned to Standlake. At last we had our results and, to my surprise at any rate, I came out as top student, and duly received the Herbert Jones trophy. I've got to admit, I was proud and felt a quiet satisfaction in having given quite a few farmers' sons a run for their money. The replica cup is one of my treasured possessions, and gets its clean along with my brass ornaments.

What are my memories from that year? Obviously all the most important things, like the Cadbury's chocolate roll wrapped in silver foil which came as a treat with Sunday tea; also the Sunday night when Nobby Gribbon drove us back through dense fog along fen roads, with deep, water-filled dykes on each side (we even ended up in a farmyard); finally, it must be dear old Gilbert, with his city umbrella, which was as black as his skin, walking across that muddy field on a wet winter's afternoon. We certainly saw life in Lincolnshire.

Before I conclude this chapter, I have to admit to one person I could not remember from college days. This chap was Barry Osborn, who will turn up later in my story, and very close to home. Sorry, Barry.

Chapter 9
A Home in the Orchard

Returning home from college towards the end of July I gazed out at the ripening corn on Swaffham Breck, and realised for a second year I would be taking no part in its harvest. Long, dusty hours in the barn, with all the cut and thrust of leg-pulling with Laddie, Dilberry, and Geoff Thaxton, were a thing of the past, and I felt a certain amount of regret that I would not be sharing it. Harvest work, in every shape and form, had always been fun since my inception at the age of nine as a holgy boy on those huge horses. Even before that, the long days spent rabbit catching with Grandad Eke or schoolmates had been intoxicating, and the peak of the year's activities. However, none of these happy memories could cover the bitter taste left in my mouth over the events which led up to my leaving Soigné Farm almost twenty months before. I avoided all but my close family, and even tried to close my ears to any happenings on the farm where both my brother and father still worked. Shutting out those enticing, happy memories, I resolved never to look back, but to press on in the new field that had opened up for me in a totally different environment, to shut the door on conventional farming, and put all my energies into mink rearing, even if the financial rewards were barely on a par with basic agricultural rates, the inadequacy of which had been argued over so vehemently both in trade union and domestic circles less than a couple of years ago

A year's college course, with no wages received, had been sweated through and just to take up where I left off financially was hardly progress; this situation I failed to mention to my parents. Even to myself, I hardly dared admit these facts, and felt that perhaps I should take a trip to the "funny farm", rather than to a mink farm. Call in the men in white coats to take me away!

Despite these slight misgivings, I had a gut feeling that the path before me would turn out to be the correct one, and having trod that way, I can now honestly say I did the right thing, for me at any rate. So, as soon as I could depart, the dust of Westacre was once more shaken off my feet, and that now familiar trek across England was made, this time carrying as much of my clothing as was possible, for wasn't I setting up home for myself?

After my return to Standlake had been confirmed, Dick Spilman bought a small caravan and placed it in the orchard. Helping me ferry my cases and kitbag down the drive, he introduced me to my new home. Strategically placed just inside the gate, opposite the mink and mincing shed from whence the prevailing south-westerly wind blew, my new home stood waiting for me. Left to my own devices I summed up the situation. The caravan was of a small, touring type, but large enough for me. The gas cooker was adequate for my needs, as was, hopefully, the tiny gas fire. All I needed now was some food, as I was to be self-sufficient in all areas except an occasional bath in the house. Taking a quick time check, I realised the shop was still only just open, and I quickly took off for Florey's stores. Just as I sped out of the gate, I met Mrs. Pitt steaming along the footpath.

"Can't stop", I said, "must catch the shop".

"No need", came the reply, "I was just coming to tell you I had got bread, milk, and other things for you, and to invite you to tea with us. Mrs. Spilman said you were coming today".

My first feelings were that I would have liked to settle into my new home at once, and set out to be totally independent, but such kindness couldn't be spurned, so hoping that Jackie would let me return home before dark, I took up her kind offer. After one of her delicious, cooked teas, followed by an equally tempting pudding, I was glad my planned meagre fare had been put on hold. After settling the bill for things purchased by the good lady, and promising Jackie a tour of my new home the next evening, I set off back in order to get myself shipshape for work next morning, as the need of money was becoming acute, to say the least.

The day had been hot, and recent dry weather had dried the mud around the mink pen. The ducks managed to produce a little patch at the rear of Gillian's mincing shed, but this failed to hold their attention, as my arrival seemed to be much more interesting. Approaching the step leading to my open door, with necks stretched out they conversed as only ducks can, apparently discussing this strange vehicle which had encroached upon their patch of orchard. Having been shut up all day, the caravan was like an oven, so the first task was to open all windows and also the roof light. Having done that, my next thought was to explore the cupboards which I found contained an assortment of plates, cups and saucepans, as well as cutlery in a bag. Someone had given thought to my proposed bachelor existence, for an antiquated but functional tin opener had been included.

After my initial tour of inspection, and the packing away of clothes, I lay back on the padded seat which would double up as a bed, and took stock of my situation. The evening sun cast shadows across the orchard, and everything was peaceful. I was king of my own little castle, had my wireless and books, and could please myself when I ate, slept, went out or came home. At last I was a free man, or as near to that as was possible. I would revel in living alone, no problem there, for I had always enjoyed my own company, and I was embarking on a job that was a challenge without being too taxing on my delicate nervous system.

It took me some time to realise that, during my musing, the lone fly, which had followed me into the caravan, had now been joined by a host of friends, and at the present rate of addition my tiny home would soon buzz like a beehive. Added to this slight inconvenience was the smell wafting in on the evening air from the general direction of my near neighbours, namely the mink. How short had been my blissful existence, far from the madding crowd. By beating at my unwelcome guests with a rolled-up newspaper, and drawing the curtains, I managed to keep control of pest infestation, but the smell remained as the airless evening dropped into twilight. Here was a problem to trouble my sleep, and mar the first morning of this new job. Perhaps I won't mention it at the outset, and maybe I shall get used to the tainted air after a short time of indoctrination.

The caravan was still like an oven, so having made up my bed, I settled down with a minimum of covering, and tried to drop off. The strange and unaccustomed sounds, a squeak here, and a rattle there, came plainly to my ears through the curtained but wide open windows. Eventually I must have dropped off, only to wake in the early hours literally frozen with cold. When the outside temperature dropped, the caravan, which was, after all, only a tin box with no insulation properties, lost its heat rapidly, leaving my uncovered body almost open to the elements. Hastily closing windows and skylight, I found a couple of blankets and settled down again. Never having had experience of caravan living, there was a lot I had to learn about insulation, or the lack thereof, in vans of that era.

Waking early to another bright morning, with promise of more hot and dry weather, I was very concerned to find the clothes left out the previous evening felt distinctly damp, and condensation glistened on the walls. Visions of being struck down with rheumatic fever caused by damp clothes or beds came instantly to mind. Hadn't Mother preached the gospel endlessly that any form of dampness around the body was to be avoided at all costs? Why, she was so paranoid on the subject that it could almost be construed that she would want to air a flannel before allowing us to wash with it. Hastily lighting the small gas fire, I aired my underclothes for a short time before putting them on.

Not having any distance to travel for work, I had plenty of time to prepare and eat my breakfast of cornflakes followed by bread and marmalade. It was a joy to step outside into warming air and meet Gillian at the big gate. I felt I had experienced before whatever jobs were planned for this first morning, so no hidden terrors lay in my path. The noisy activity coming from the mink cages intensified as the occupants became aware of human presence through our voices. Without doubt, the first job on the agenda would be morning feed. Kits were fed twice daily, as their fast growing bodies needed constant food, and anything less resulted in vicious fights breaking out, possibly with fatal results. So it was out with the four-wheeled trolley, to be loaded with four trays of food ready prepared the previous afternoon, and away into the first alleyway. With two trays on the front and two at the back, we worked away, one on each side. Batches of hungry kits jostled and fought to be first at the heap of food deposited on the cage top. Even if those obligatory fish boxes had been left off, the waiting starlings would have needed to be fast to steal anything. Those kits were voracious eaters, and the food disappeared almost as fast as we spooned it out. There was no time for conversation between we two feeders, but in any case, Gillian was never a great talker, especially early in the morning. Her concentration was directed at the condition and health of her mink, and my eyes had to be skinned for any signs of distress on my side. Despite neither of us being great conversationalists, we worked easily together, without any uneasy silences, and often shared radio programmes when doing repetitive or monotonous jobs, so we were a good team, and enjoyed our long hours working together.

The next task was, of course, the watering. This operation gave great enjoyment to the youngsters who rushed to be in pole position at their water cups in order to get a refreshing head wash as the liquid swilled in from our watering cans. Some kits would roll upside-down under the waterfall, and get a wash that way. To them it was all good fun, and I must say it gave me much amusement to watch their antics. The slightest strange noise or action would send them hurtling into their box with enough force almost to rip it off the retaining hooks. Then, one by one, a little head would appear, followed by a lithe body, as the suspected danger receded from their mind, and the most adventurous came out to investigate, eventually creeping to the cage end. I could have watched them for hours, but pressure of work forbade.

It was apparent from the outset that work would mainly consist of, and revolve around, feeding of the "five thousand" – not quite that number of mink, unfortunately, but enough to keep we two busy for seven days a week. The reference to the miracle connected to feeding of five thousand wasn't slipped into my story just by chance, for often, because of the uncertain supply in the food chain, we felt a miracle would be needed to stretch the rations around. Obtaining sufficient supplies seemed to be one long, continuous headache. Slaughterhouses in Swindon, Witney and Oxford were haunted, badgered and begged for tripe, liver and lights. Huge bullock livers, bearing growths of pus, arrived after being condemned for human consumption. These abnormal sections were cut out, and discarded, and the rest was cut small enough to feed into the tiny mincer. Tripes were washed thoroughly, then sliced into strips before being gently coaxed through our machine, which was grossly inadequate for the task expected of it. Everything seemed, and in fact was, painfully slow, taking precious time from other essential jobs. The fish frames crackled, liver spat back its blood-laden liquid into any unsuspecting face and tripe repeatedly wound round the worm and blocked the mincer. Such was life under the scorching midday sun as we toiled to produce enough food for the afternoon feed programme. Every greasy surface and utensil had to be scoured, using tepid water from the house. With the Aga running very low, in order to keep the kitchen temperature bearable in summer, water heating was a problem. By the time Mrs. Pitt had drawn a goodly supply to cope with the aforementioned washing up mountain, there was little left for our use. Tempers tended to get slightly frayed on occasions as we struggled with totally inadequate and outdated equipment – and never more so than when poor Gillian sought to solve the hot water problem. With commendable forward thinking, she left two kettles to boil on the Aga hotplate for washing the mincer. Carrying her precious, very hot water down in a bucket, she stood it down on the shed floor – unfortunately behind me – as I dismantled the machine. Stepping back, my foot went clean into the bucket, filling my shoe with water of an unusually high temperature. This sudden shock sent me hopping around, screeching like a banshee and clutching at my foot. The shoe flew off at the first attempt, but my thick, woollen sock not only held a large quantity of hot water, but also refused to be parted from my throbbing foot, causing me to continue my war dance. Eventually, by propping my tortured body on a sack of meal, I managed to remove the offending sock, which was doing a very effective job, such as might a hot poultice on a boil. Gently examining my scarlet, throbbing limb extremity, I was relieved to see a lack of blistering, for luckily, I suppose, the liquid had lost a little heat on its journey down the drive. Nonetheless, my pain and injured pride were by no means helped by my workmate, who heaped hot coals upon my tortured self by blaming me for spilling her precious hot water.

"Bugger your hot water, what about my foot?"

"You shouldn't be so clumsy", was her unsympathetic reply, "and there's no need to swear, either".

All that from a slip of a girl, an army sergeant couldn't have been more ruthless to a wounded soldier in the trenches. For a moment the atmosphere crackled, and my new world could have exploded and ended before it had hardly begun. Instead, we both began to laugh as we saw the funny side of my gyrating around, bellowing and clawing at my foot, and anyway, no permanent damage had been done. Neither of us commented upon the added chore of trying to wash our greasy machinery in the replacement lukewarm water from the kitchen tap. Peace was restored, but my foot was damned sore.

I fear, and not for the first time, I am getting ahead of myself. On my second evening in the caravan, Jackie arrived to carry out her tour of inspection, sailing in on the proverbial little, blue bike, which, in time-honoured fashion, she dumped down on the drive. Making observations well beyond her eight years, she noticed the flies immediately, and the smell only a few minutes after. When young lady visitors remark on these things, it's high time one treats them seriously. After offering her services to do my shopping on Saturday mornings, she departed, presumably on more urgent business. Likely targets would be Jean and John, who were possibly trying to enjoy a T.V. programme in her absence. Jill and Bert had married during my time away, and now lived in a rented house on the Abingdon road.

After the departure of my friend and advisor, I walked off across the orchard to review the possibility of a better camping ground. I knew from a winter's experience that parts of the ground flooded after heavy rainfall, and these areas would need to be avoided. To the south of the mink run slightly higher ground ran on to the field hedge, so this should remain dry, even in February. Also, the prevailing wind coming from the south-west would carry the mink smell away from my van. Would it be possible to tow the caravan across the rough orchard to the site, one could only ask. When the subject was broached next morning, the boss said he would try that evening, whilst the weather was fine and the ground dry. With the help of man- and woman-power pushing from behind, the operation proved successful, and my home sat on a rough, green lawn bordered by ancient apple trees and a few nettle patches. This was heaven on earth, I considered, as I sat by the door watching the ruby-red sun go down behind Mr. Hill's tall, thorn hedge. The only drawback I could think of was my increased distance from a water supply, but I could always carry some back when leaving work. It didn't occur to me that my rush for progress, the main reason for deserting Norfolk, had pushed me in to a situation akin to that of my father when he carried drinking water from High House Farm to our cottages across the meadow. What price my kind of progress! Perhaps I would have consoled myself by thinking that sometimes one had to go backwards in order eventually to make progress. My mother would have considered me mad, a penny short of a shilling, or a good ounce short of a pound.

In the early hours of the morning I was rudely awakened and tricked into thinking I had moved my van into an earthquake zone. It was rocking in the most alarming manner, causing the crockery to rattle and me to shake with it. What on earth could it be? Opening the door with some trepidation I soon found the culprit. Judy's horse had found a new rubbing post, or at least a second one to add to the mink run corner. After shooing the wretched beast away, I climbed back into bed, knowing full well a wire fence would have to be erected around my abode before another night's sleep was attempted. There is a deal of truth in the saying, "There's no rest for the wicked, and little for the righteous either".

With Jackie dutifully doing my shopping every Saturday morning, and her mother taking in my bread when Constable's roundsman called from Bampton, my basic requirements were well taken care of. It puzzled my errand girl, when she came armed with her little, blue-covered order book, why I always ordered stewing beef from the butcher's for Sunday dinner. The truth was hidden in the fact that I only knew how to cook stew, and had little choice in the matter. She was also very amused at the way my Norfolk accent pronounced the word, "stew". I suppose it came out as "stu", which was far removed from the B.B.C. English spoken by the true residents of Standlake (only joking!). They didn't realise I had arrived to "edicate" them. A bottle of green-topped, raw milk was left daily for me by "Rocky" Johnson, who had taken over the milk round when Jack Knipe retired; Jack had delivered with churn and measure carried on his pony and trap, I believe. Rocky was brother to Barb Nichol, the previously mentioned poultry plucker, who could often be seen cramming along on her bike with dead chicken or duck heads hanging over the side of a wooden box on the back. They were off to the bungalow in Green Lane where a huge heap of feathers out the back showed where the lady of the house did a brisk trade in poultry defrocking. Rocky, whose real name was Cyril, and his wife never failed to get their milk into the village from Black Bourton, whatever the weather, even resorting to tractor power when deep snow blocked roads in winter. They were two "salt of the earth" characters who became good friends of mine over the years.

For the first few weeks of my full time return to the Manor I was left alone to get on with mink farm work. No odd jobs came from the house, thank goodness, for truthfully there was no spare time. There was neither enough shed room nor cages for the overcrowded mink families, and no spare boxes to place on the cages even if we'd had them, anyway. Hand to mouth we went at everything. Make do and mend was the order of the day. Come the winter we will have all the time in the world to make equipment for next year. That was the only thought we had to keep us going. Part-time help was advertised for, but very little was forthcoming. Bert and his father worked on Saturdays, in a vain attempt to keep the water out of the slate roof, but this precarious and dangerous job was like trying to seal the holes in a sieve with darning wool – repair one patch, and disturb two more. The only solution would have been to strip the whole roof, felt and re-slate with very expensive Cotswold stone slates. Being a listed building, no cheaper materials could have been used. Bert senior was all for giving up, but his son refused to be beaten, and kept on trying to defeat the wet. Andrew Rance came for a time after school to help water the mink, do some washing up and small, odd jobs, but the bulk of work fell on to myself and Gillian as we struggled to keep afloat. I was always promised that I would be repaid for any overtime I put in with time off when things were quieter, but it was difficult to see when this might be. Eventually, I had an extended holiday after Christmas, but of course I could have done with extra money, but if it was there, which I doubt, it wasn't forthcoming, and I was too gullible or wrapped up in the job to press for it. Despite all the drawbacks, I really enjoyed the work and challenge, and so beavered away just as if I had a financial stake in the place, which of course I didn't and never would have. John Culley used to query my long hours, and question whether I was being taken for a ride. As all my trade union ideas and ideals had been put on the back burner, I was deaf to any of either John's or Bert's veiled warnings that I was being used, and I worked on the doubtful principle that you can't do too much for a good master. Experience eventually told me this ideal very rarely works in practice, which is a pity, for I did enjoy my work at this juncture.

As the days shortened and the weather became less clement, my halcyon days of living in an orchard paradise became a thing of the past. Squelching across the sodden grass, in fading light, to a cold caravan, with no hot meal until I produced it, wasn't quite so enjoyable as was lounging outside in warm, evening air whilst watching the sun sink slowly in a blaze of glory, promising another dry, sunny day to follow. Divesting oneself of muddy boots, without trailing slime all over the limited floor space, was a work of art, but where to hang wet, outer garments to dry was even more of a problem. Steam created by cooking and drying hung around the ceiling, causing runnels of moisture down every wall. Clothes showed signs of mould in drawers and cupboards. On dry, breezy days I could safely leave the windows open to facilitate a drying process, but as these conditions were few and far between in November, I began to fear the dreaded rheumatic fever might strike me down. The tiny gas cylinder supplied was grossly inadequate for constant use, being only designed, as was the fire, for holidaymakers. Also, I dared not leave the fire burning at night, thus waking to a freezing atmosphere as temperatures dropped. A combination of a low pressure, gas bottle and a heavy frost meant the fire wouldn't light, and there was no hot water. By dinner-time a slight rise in temperature meant a release of gas, and a hot drink was possible. A replacement gas cylinder was available, just as long as the boss remembered to call at Coopers of Oxford, in St. Ebbes, when he went to the colleges where he had drinks dispensing machines, another arrow to his bow. Several times he managed to forget my refill, leaving me on tenterhooks as to whether the existing cylinder would hold out. It seemed to me, at times, I not only raised fur coats, but lived very like a trapper in the outback of coldest Canada. This bed I had made for myself was pretty hard, but there was no turning back. Life at Westacre hadn't been good enough for me, and there was no way I would admit defeat and crawl back home, although of course my parents would have welcomed me with no recriminations.

Towards the end of November the mink had grown their thick, winter fur, and the time to harvest it had arrived. We had watched as the faded summer hair slowly fell away to be replaced by full-coloured, bottle-brush fur with a beautiful sheen. Animals looked twice the size, and our only problem was to prevent them fighting each other and ruining their new coats with bite marks, for many were still three and four to a cage. As I had never been at Standlake whilst this pelting operation was taking place, everything was new to me, but excitingly so for a change. Work was to be centred in the workshop where two rocket-shaped poles were set up, one quite a bit larger than the other. These were to accommodate male and female pelts as they are called, once removed from their owners. A large drum occupied one end with half its barrel solid, and the other half covered with small, mesh wire. A latched trapdoor gave entry into each compartment. To complete the equipment, two sizes of slatted, wooden boards, with solid, wider ends, were on view, and I presumed they too were sized to accommodate male and female pelts. All was set up in readiness for harvest, in a vastly different way, and at a time of year very alien to the harvests I had known on Soigné Farm. But, like all harvests, it appeared that every available minute must be geared to gathering the crop. Six days, Monday to Saturday, had to be used from crack of dawn to burning the midnight oil in order to catch the winter fur at its very best. Nothing could wait beyond Christmas, or else the prime look would be gone. Lashings of clean, wood shavings were tipped into boxes in order to clean off the grease from new fur. Showers of these shavings were flung out through pop holes and on to the floor as the animals burrowed in their fresh bedding. Great fun was had by all, and the shed floor soon looked pristine with its new covering. Mink love to be entertained, and this process certainly did that for them, and it gave us some laughs as well.

The shavings came home in large sacks carried in the horse-box towed behind Mr. Spilman's Ford Consul. This model was a notoriously bad starter in damp weather, and many a morning saw us pushing it along the road outside the Manor. I hasten to add, the horse box was always attached after we got the car started, for boy, was that wretched thing heavy to push. It left three of us gasping, at great risk of cardiac arrest and in need of oxygen masks to recharge our lungs, by the time it had spluttered into life. If all else failed, Bill Saxel was summoned from the garage to put jump leads on, but of course, at added expense. Our lungs and muscles came cheaper.

So we leave the mink happily playing in their sweet-smelling softwood shavings, not anticipating the imminent approach of the grim reaper.

Chapter 10

Harvest of Fur Coats

As I believe one famous cook once said when preparing jugged hare, first catch your hare. Well, the same could be said for pelting mink, first catch your mink. Easier said than done, I'm afraid, even if he or she is already in a cage.

Gillian had been round the previous day carefully selecting a dozen or so well-furred animals on which to start our work. The first of these gentlemen obstinately refused to enter his nesting box, however much we scratched the rear side in order to attract his attention. A trip around the outside of his cage by me did nothing to alarm him, as it was intended to do, and only resulted in his climbing up the cage end to get a better view of this strange shooing and blowing human – not a good start to a busy day, and that was an understatement. There was no other choice but to move on to the next victim who was conveniently curled up, asleep in his box, which was a wonder after all the scratching and rattling we had done further down the shed. Quickly slipping a metal slide between box and cage, we lifted off the box, and by keeping a tight hold on the slide, kept the tornado of tooth and claw safe inside. The next operation was to transfer the mink from box to examination cage. This long, metal, trap-like cage had a false bottom and a portcullis- type entry at one end. The portcullis was lifted to allow the animal access, and then lowered quickly once the mink entered and before it could turn around, for they are so versatile they can turn in very limited space. By lifting the metal floor to gently squeeze the animal, a close examination could be made to the very root of the fur. If any old summer hair is left, causing discolouring of the pelt, then back they go for a week or so to finish off growing that winter coat. After blowing into the fur, Gillian confirmed her opinion of yesterday, that all was well, so off we went for the next one.

After filling our four examination cages, we then had to render our four animals unconscious, and to do this we held each individual head inside a jam jar containing cotton wool soaked with ether. Of course, mink do not volunteer to stick their heads inside jars of ether, so once more we had to catch them in thick gloves, and hold the wriggling, twisting, squirming victim until they went to sleep. The neck was then broken by pushing back the head with a gloved heel of the hand. All this time-consuming work. for two people of course, took place inside the mink compound, and it was inevitable that an escape took place from time to time and a muddy mink had to be recaptured and returned to the cage for cleaning before the operation could take place another day.

The bodies were laid out on a wire frame, and then transferred to our workshop where operation number two took place before the mink stiffened up. A cut across the pelt from inside each back leg to the tail virtually released the pelt, and usually, for me at any rate, punctured the two scent sacs situated near the base of the tail; this covered my hands in a foul smell designed to repel enemies by its intensity and persistence. By cutting the four paws with secateurs, in order to leave them on as part of the pelt, this work was relatively easy. The pelt, kept inside out, and with its fur next to the rocket-shaped pole as mentioned in the last chapter, was stretched and held down by clips on its rear paws. Now came the tedious job of scraping away considerable surplus fat, which the animal had laid down naturally to help it survive a hard winter had it been left in the wild. Great care had to be taken in this very tricky but essential operation. Excess fat left on the pelt meant it would not dry properly, and would end up feeling thick and of poor sale quality; too much pressure on the metal scraper cut the hair roots, causing damaged hair to fall out in later operations. At first I found myself taking so much care that my output was painfully slow, but by degrees practice began to make perfect, and after another season my speed and quality were up to par.

After the first batch had been skinned and scraped, we went through the process with the next consignment, and as you can imagine, the whole thing was very slow. Just add the food preparation and feeding programme to be dealt with daily as well, and you will see the problems we had in that first year of my participation. How Gillian and her father had managed previously, I don't know, although of course numbers would have been lower, with mainly culling only taking place. My having to learn the job didn't help either, although being able to take on food preparation and feeding, thus leaving Gillian and her father on the days he was there to pelt full time, speeded the work. Obviously, as the number of mink killed increased, my work in support became less, allowing me more time in the relative comfort of the workshop. It was quite an attraction at the end of a raw December afternoon to leave the fast-darkening orchard and repair to a lighted, warmer, if foul-smelling, workshop. Gillian had her wireless for company, and we tried to keep up with any interesting serials being broadcast at that time.

My meals were pretty chaotic during this period as work necessarily continued well into the evening, for time was of the essence. Mrs. Pitt worried herself sick in case I wasn't feeding myself properly. The smell attached to my working clothes prevented me entering the village shop, and Frank Douglas decreed it best if I shouted my orders from the doorway. His staff were always very obliging, and ferried my few groceries needed in mid-week to me outside. One thing did strike me as curious, and that was the small fact of the money changing hands was seemingly sweet-smelling to Frank's otherwise keen and delicate nose. When a later mink farm temporary employee, Hank, took two steps inside the shop, Frank became so agitated that his needle-sharp pencil shot from behind his ear and embedded itself in the pound of butter being prepared for a lady's order. As for the rest of his staff, they stood paralysed by the shock, and almost swooned before the expected smell hit them. I remember Hank used to do it on purpose just to upset our resident shop owner, and always succeeded. How lucky I was to have my own little errand girl to shop for me on Saturdays, and how thankful Frank and his staff were to fulfil that order for her. Yes, Jackie was nothing if not reliable in her self-appointed duties, and never failed to collect my order. On one occasion, when her mother needed to take her to Oxford on the Saturday, she didn't think she could go because of my groceries. Only after it was pointed out that Friday afternoon, when school finished, could be substituted did she withdraw her objection to the proposed trip. That is what you call dedication to duty, and in one so young.

Once more I fear I digress from the main theme of my story which, I believe, we left as I withdrew to the comparative comfort of the workshop after a day of raw temperatures and frozen fingers. Just before daylight finally faded the last batch of mink were killed off, thus allowing work to continue under artificial light. After the day's consignment of animals had been pelted and degreased on the poles, their pelts were placed, skin side out, in the covered side of the large drum also housed in the shed. This section contained hardwood sawdust which, as the drum was turned by hand in early days but by a slow- turning motor in latter years, dried any fatty tissue left on the skin. After a short period the pelts were removed, turned fur side out, and with a change of sawdust, returned to the drum for the same action to be taken. Eventually they were transferred to the wired partition for a final, steady revolving, in order to shake small, adhering particles of dust from the fur. It should be noted that the drum needed to be large enough and revolve at the correct speed to allow the pelts almost to reach the top and then drop the maximum distance, before the action was repeated.

Mrs. Spilman supplied a cup of tea around 5 p.m., and enquired as to the proposed time her two work persons would require tea. Usually they tended to work on until all the pelts had reached the sawdust and drum stage before stopping, and I continued with them, even though it had long passed my official finishing time. Two facts of life kept me there, even if overtime was not likely to be paid. The first was the workshop, with its very small but comforting electric fire, company and wireless making it slightly better than a cold caravan, and secondly I was learning all the time, which I enjoyed. Even when tea was taken, the work was not finished, for Gillian at least, as the day's pelts had to be "boarded", that is stretched and pinned by staple gun round the bottom edges on those slatted boards previously spoken of. Often, to release a sufficient number of boards, pelts processed a couple of days before needed to be unpinned first. These had been upstairs in a spare bedroom drying out slowly, and now appeared as flat, board-like specimens looking very far removed from either the bottle-brush thick coats of a live animal or the much sought after stoles or full-length coats of the rich and famous. When fully dry our longwinded and tedious work was done, all the rest would be in the clever hands of the furrier, but not until our harvest had been shipped to London and through the auction sales at Hudson Bay Company headquarters, which, to say the least, sounded much more exciting than the cold, muddy orchard through which I found myself plodding home after my long, smelly day at the sharp end of fur production.

Nevertheless, I had enjoyed the experience once my conscience had overcome the killing of animals on which such care, in the animal husbandry sense, had been lavished over several months. I don't suppose animal welfare activists would understand the seemingly unfeeling attitude of those of us who kept and cared for animals with the sole object of killing them for some form of market as an end result. Not that I would in any way condone the necessity of keeping semi-wild animals in captivity just to supply fashion houses with fur for ladies with nothing better to do than parade in front of cameras displaying to the world that they are filthy rich. Far better the ladies in question put on a thicker dress, with a much less plunging neckline, to keep warm that way, thus allowing mink to wear their coats in the wild, preferably in North America and not turned loose in England where, with no natural enemy, they can wreak their own ruthless brand of killing on defenceless wildlife. For, take it from me, Mr. Mink is no saint in the wild. A marvellous animal to watch and to pit one's wits against, but it is the most ruthless killing machine the natural world has ever produced and one that kills more for pleasure than for food.

To me the mink gave hours of interest with their tricks, antics and bright, outgoing characters, coupled with sheer ferocity and determination to match anything pitched against them. In defence of any farmer, be he fur or otherwise, it must be pointed out that no animal will produce meat or fur to a first class degree unless that animal has been cared for, fed well, and kept warm and healthy. Any other course would be counterproductive, and no farmer could financially stay in business for long using any other methods. As for me, I just found a job which I badly needed on an existing mink farm, part of a worldwide accepted industry in the late 1950s. Today I would not want that job, and I feel the trade has no place in modern life when synthetic materials can be produced to cover all necessary forms of fashionable clothing.

Unfortunately the story will not end here for the introduction of mink into this country, for whatever reason, will have a lasting and possibly catastrophic effect on resident wildlife where there have been accidental escapes or animals blatantly released into the wild.

None of these deep, debating thoughts entered my tired brain as I followed my dim torch beam across to the dark caravan. Let's get the gas fire lit and some belated tea on the go. Due to my very primitive washing facilities, namely, a drop of hot water from my kettle in a bowl, the smell of mink musk pervaded myself and the van as a whole. Even though I had an open invitation to visit the Pitt family, I felt it both too late and in poor taste to carry such an awful smell into their tiny, homely cottage. I felt myself to be a self- imposed outcast, just as long as the pelting season lasted. At the best of times, fishy smells were difficult to discard, but even to my nose they smelled like violets compared with the present one.

For over a month the only person I met socially was my faithful errand girl who would have come with a linen peg on her nose in order to deliver my tiny grocery order on time. My mail of course was delivered with the Spilmans', usually a weekly letter from home with the statutory messages, "Make sure you eat well this cold weather", or, "Air these clothes again before you put them on", the latter included with my laundry parcel. If only my mother could have seen my scrabbled together late meals and condensation running down the caravan walls! How well I was taking note of her warnings, but what could I do, short of surrendering my independent stance and returning home. Pride made me stick it out, for was I not a Bumfrey, stubborn as a mule and twice as awkward — my mother's description of her husband on more than one occasion, and true at that, for both him, myself and even more so brother Michael.

Loneliness, however, did begin to get me down, although after Christmas, when the workload fell off, John Culley invited me to go to Headington with him to watch football, the local team still playing in the Southern League. We picked up Uncle Dod, Mrs. Pitt's brother-in-law, at West Street in Oxford, and often his son-in-law, Peter Heath. It was enjoyable even if some of the football was rudimentary. Dod, who was a very quiet man of slight stature, and originally from Suffolk, used to get quite irate if the home team passed the ball back towards their own goal, much to our amusement. On one occasion he was so excited over a crucial Headington goal that he threw caution and his cap to the wind, and the latter landed several rows down towards the front, much to the surprise of a young couple who were using the event to hug one another enthusiastically and snatch a quick kiss. Quite a section of the crowd enjoyed a laugh as the missile was handed back up to its, by now embarrassed, owner. The incident reminded me of the time a large leek left the hand of its Cardiff City owner in a quick burst of excitement and landed in the region of my right ear. This was at Carrow Road, Norwich, whilst an F.A. Cup tie was being contested.

Despite my present football entertainment being played at a much lower level than that of Norwich in Division 3 South of the Football League, which I had been used to, it proved very enjoyable in good company. We dissected the game, in the custom of all fans, as we sat in George Street waiting for Jean to finish work at Renmore's. After dropping off Dod and Peter in West Street, we made for Standlake where Mrs. Pitt always invited me to tea, and then John would suggest watching Match of the Day on T.V., so loneliness in the caravan was averted for Saturday.

Sometimes I would go to church on Sunday evening, but not often in the winter as it was so cold in there. Mrs. Pitt tried to persuade me to go to chapel, but that didn't appeal either. Occasionally the Spilman family would go to St. Aldates Church in Oxford and invite me to join them. The services were quite good, given in a warm building and a lively atmosphere. I still read any and all mink farming publications avidly, and of course had my wireless, which also went with me in the daytime if work patterns allowed. The mink seemed to enjoy the sound when it sat on the back of my food trolley as I slowly worked up the shed with their feed for the day. They were only given one feed during winter months, and that a limited one, as we tried to slim the animals down to the required size they would be under harsh, winter conditions normally experienced in the wild, where lack of food would force them to live off stored body fat laid down in good times for this very purpose. We found, by experience, that our earlier efforts of slimming were not stringent enough to encourage female egg production or to stimulate males to work in March. These facts were vital in producing a good kit average over the whole female herd. Fat males preferred to sleep, bulky females produced single or twin kits and had very little milk to feed them. These were the kinds of tricks we only learned by the time the bottom fell out of the fur trade, due mainly to world wide over-production, shades of present day problems.

In addition to entertainment from my wireless I sometimes had, in holiday times, a human passenger on whom there was no on/off switch – Jackie decided it would be nice for me if she sat on the trolley whilst I did the rounds. With a continuous flow of conversation, my little fount of all knowledge kept me on my toes mentally in order to keep up with her. The mink even paused in their feeding to take a quick look at this joy rider sporting a mop-head hairstyle, giving verbal vent on a subject dear to her heart at that present time, whether it be a coming visit to sister Gill at the top of the village, or some imagined misdemeanour on John's part the previous evening when he wanted to watch T.V. instead of keeping her company in some game or other. Yes, between us we put our own limited world to rights on many occasions. To her credit Jackie always kept her hands well away from box bottoms and cage tops where mink noses poked out just waiting to snap at an unsuspecting finger which, in a child's case, would have meant a quick and painful amputation of the digit.

Around that time we saw quite a lot of the village school children who, under the guidance of Mr. Snelling, their headmaster, were making a scale model of the Manor. Several visits saw them with rulers and paper, taking measurements in order to construct their project. A superb job they made of it, and we were invited to the school in order to view their handiwork. An additional visit was made, almost certainly at the instigation of Miss Jacqueline Pitt, in order to see the mink. Before entering the run very strict instructions were instilled into the little angels by their teacher on the dangers of putting hands and fingers near the boxes or cages. Imagine my horror as I saw one little girl about to put her nose to a knot hole in the side of a box with the lady occupant just waiting to seize such a delectable morsel of human flesh. A quick grab at a tiny shoulder saved the day before a pretty little face was disfigured for life. I suppose she imagined that, as fingers and hands were well away, noses didn't matter. The very thought of that incident is enough to give me nightmares.

A less traumatic incident occurred when another little girl tentatively poked the tip of her handkerchief through the wire box bottom, and then, to her horror, watched it disappear in double quick time. After running down the shed to tell her teacher, she couldn't remember which box the handkerchief had disappeared into, so the trophy remained with its new owner. Weeks later we found it in a rather dilapidated state, tucked up the box corner, looking very slept upon and far short of the pristine condition its original owner had been used to seeing it in. As I have said before, the mink held on to anything that ventured inside their cage be it starlings' legs, fingers or handkerchiefs. Nothing came back after being seized by those razor sharp teeth.

Most of my time during that first winter of permanent labour on the mink farm was spent in the comparative luxury of the workshop. As the mink numbers were down to just breeding stock, Gillian minced and fed on most days, which allowed me to work full time on new boxes and cages in readiness for next season's kits. We had a small electric saw, and a special circular cutter for making entry holes. The only real drawback to a speedy production line was dismantling army ammunition boxes, which were so well constructed that most of the side panels split rendering the wood useless. This exercise really was counter-productive and very frustrating to boot. Even so, our pile of new boxes grew steadily, and the outlook for next season began to appear promising.

I recall one very frosty February morning, with some freezing fog keeping visibility down to about forty yards. Judy came flying back down the drive leading from the orchard to report the not unusual fact that her horse, in company with Susan Walker's was missing. I was promptly co-opted to a search party which set off through the orchard and out towards New Road. Keeping well spread out, we progressed over the main road and into flooded, and to me unknown, fields. After smashing through continuous sheet ice I began to realise why the name Standlake came into being, for it seemed as if the village did stand in a lake, certainly after a very wet winter. Eventually, as the sun broke through the mist, and after sloshing through what seemed like miles of ice and water, we located the two runaways. They too seemed to be fed up with their waterlogged surroundings, and waited patiently for halters to be put on. Then, splashing along behind the two girls, their hooves soon filled the rubber boots of their owners with icy, muddy water. It wasn't until later, when the flood water subsided, that I realised we had waded around those flooded fields that ran directly down to the River Thames, with no idea, on my part at least, where field ceased and deep river began. How easily a non-swimmer like myself could have disappeared into the depths. Perhaps the moving water had remained unfrozen so that its presence would have been obvious if I had been close to it, but the unpleasant thought of drowning passes through my mind whenever I see the flood plain as a sheet of water. Not harbouring these thoughts at the time allowed me to enjoy this unexpected break from box-making, especially as my boots weren't filled with icy water.

Another excursion, and for a whole day, was a visit to the Hudson Bay Company's fur warehouse in London. With the final batch of mink pelts packed carefully in the boot of the Consul, we set off for the capital in much more comfortable conditions than when I hitched a lift in the draught-ridden ex-RAF truck. The pelts were to be entered in the monthly auction, and would be the last pay cheque of the harvest. At the warehouse they would be labelled, graded and then put up for sale in large batches, and bid for by furriers who would then begin the process of manufacture. The visit conjured up visions of trappers in the frozen north of Canada bringing their furs into the trading station by sled. It was not quite the same bringing them by Ford Consul, but a mite more comfortable I suppose. There were furs of every description to be seen, and the staff were very friendly and ready to explain things as we were shown around. I must say my employers did everything to make my day out enjoyable, which went some way to repaying all the long hours I had donated towards the end product being sent to world auction.

After leaving Hudson Bay we drove into the East End where it had been arranged we could see for ourselves the next stage of mink coat manufacture. From the scene of world centre fur sales, we seemed to descend into Dickensian conditions, where a small, Jewish gentleman greeted us in what appeared to be a back yard establishment. Expecting to meet Fagin and Bill Sykes at any moment, we followed him inside an old shed which contained a number of low tanks. Soaking in some foul-looking liquid was what appeared to be old socks, but amazingly turned out to be mink pelts. Shock! Horror! To think those beautiful, luxuriant pelts that we had so carefully and lovingly cleaned would be treated like this sent shivers down our spines. It was unbelievable, but as was explained to us, the skins had to be made supple again before they could be used. To my amazement they had to be cut into very narrow strips before being sewn together in such a way that the nap of the fur lay correctly for human adornment, which apparently was very different to that for which the fur was originally designed. Working our way through the various stages of manufacture was certainly an experience, and explained to a degree why the price differential between fur at the farm gate and in the furrier's window was so great.

Back in the workshop it was difficult to realise that we were part of such a worldwide business, but it had been nice to see beyond the mundane, everyday work. Our efforts to prepare for the coming season seemed to be progressing well, at least in the box and cage department. Fine days were now used to work on shed extensions, and in fact we had filled the existing protected run. The need to extend was obvious, but money being tight, the expense on metal stakes and wire and tin baffle tops, was a problem. This being before the agricultural law enforcing the safe fencing of mink came into force, it was decided to risk escapes and extend with only a two strand wire to keep horses out. This kind of irresponsible action became quite widespread among the mink farming fraternity, and led to feral mink becoming a problem as escapees fled to the river where breeding took place the following season.

The one real problem likely to hamper the plans for extension came in the food production area. It had been painfully obvious that the tiny mincer could, in no way, cope with more mouths to feed at the height of our season. The hand to mouth method of obtaining food was going to be an even bigger problem. In winter slaughterhouses could hardly give away tripe, but at the height of summer, when we were desperate, only a dribble was available. A substantial deep freeze was required to store and hold surplus supplies. Blocks of frozen fish could be bought relatively cheaply direct from ports, if bulk loads were taken. The one big drawback was that larger machinery needed three phase electricity, which had to be paid for. Installation was expensive, and apparently an overdraft had to be sought from the bank manager. This was the business watershed when serious decisions had to be made. Although financially I was not affected, through my job prospects I was very much involved. Much midnight oil was burned as Gillian and her father mulled over the options open to them. Gillian had spent time in Scotland studying methods used on huge fur farms there, and had gained valuable knowledge over the years. To expand into a farm of viable proportions, investment had to be sought. Possibly the thought of taking a partner with money to invest crossed their minds, but Gillian was so single-minded about her objectives of where she wanted to go and how to get there, I'm sure that idea didn't get very far. The thought crossed my mind that, if a new man was brought into management, then one employed man might get the push, thus saving a wage – mine to be precise. Things became very unsettled for a short time, mainly because of conjecture on my part rather than hard facts. Serious looks on management faces have always given employees a sense of unease.

I must presume the bank manager became convinced the business was viable at that time, and released the capital for three-phase electricity to be installed. On this basis we looked forward to a new season with great optimism. Smiles once more became the order of the day as days lengthened and March came round once more.

Chapter 11

Taking to the Road

One important event I failed to mention in the previous chapter was my taking to the road again, behind the wheel of a motorised vehicle. You may remember I took three driving lessons in King's Lynn before leaving Norfolk, as part of my personal crusade to lift me out of the Soigné mud and mentality, and to give a wider job prospect in the process. Unfortunately, the lack of finance and willpower had quite easily allowed me to slide back into my non-mechanical world, and all thoughts of becoming one of the country's fast growing band of car drivers had been left on the back burner. Because the mink diet consisted of fresh meat and fish, which, under our present set-up needed to be collected almost daily from local outlets, a van driver was in constant need. The Spilman family could provide three drivers, which was quite sufficient when they were in residence, but the very fact that those three were in one family meant they couldn't take a holiday together. On the rare occasions when they did go off for more than two consecutive days, a relief driver for the ex-RAF truck had to be bribed or cajoled from amongst their friends, who quite naturally jibbed at the thought of visiting the quite gory, not to say smelly, backyards of slaughterhouses, even if I was back home to unload their rather unusual cargo.

So it was decided, rather hesitantly by yours truly, that driving lessons should be booked once a week at the British School of Motoring in Oxford. The plan was for me to drive the van to Oxford, with my new "L" plates firmly fixed front and back, under instruction of one or other Spilman – whichever one had business to do in the city. Usually Gillian either went shopping, or collected offal during the hour of my lesson. Sometimes it was both, and in that case I drove to East Wyke Farm, which housed Alden's somewhat antiquated slaughterhouse, just off the Abingdon road towards east Oxford. The system worked very well as it gave me a feel of the vehicle on relatively quiet, country roads, as we took the scenic route via Appleton and Cumnor before joining the main Oxford/Swindon road at the top of Cumnor Hill. Let me explain that handling a machine, which moved by mechanical power, did not in any way come easily to me, but the world had moved on from horsepower in its original sense, and I had to move on too, albeit almost kicking and screaming. But, as the instructor pointed out on several occasions as I sweated cobs getting a tiny Morris 1000 through the fast-increasing traffic, if you can drive in Oxford you can drive anywhere. After numerous narrow squeaks with undergrads, on bone-shaker bikes or stepping off pavements whilst in deep, theoretical discussion between lectures, I began to understand his meaning. Those dual controls fitted to the School car saved many a promising academic career from being cut off in its prime, and me from losing my driving licence before I'd progressed from provisional. Thankfully I had a very competent and understanding instructor who, I'm sure, often despaired as my nervous disposition prevented me from remembering the basic principles of driving drilled into me on a previous lesson. The man had the patience of Job as he cajoled me towards that dreaded test. How I wished my driving had commenced in war time when tests were suspended, thus allowing some of the death-defying car manipulators I had known in Norfolk to take to the road without being over sure as to which side of the road should be adhered to.

Eventually, after an hour long lesson, during which time my nerves hardly allowed me to know left from right, the dreaded walk to my instructor's car, with a stranger clutching a clipboard, seemed to me akin to the condemned approaching the scaffold. An added burden was upon me, due to the Spilmans having arranged a holiday, which would require me to pass, thus enabling them to leave a "competent" driver in charge. The minor theoretical part of the test was no problem, but the practical side went quickly downhill after a jay walker stepped off the kerb just as I prepared to turn left into a side street. At least my emergency stop was successful on that occasion and did not have to be repeated under artificial conditions, but the shock of almost knocking the lady over, through no fault of my own, meant my confidence, if I had any to start with, was fast draining away. Obviously my failed certificate indicated that more practice was required, which was, in reality, a very kind way of describing my pathetic performance. I think the poor old examiner would have developed writer's cramp in listing my faults, and been late for the next appointment as a consequence. So, with my tail very much between my legs, I resumed the seat in the old truck to trundle back to Standlake, with mud-spattered "L" plates still in place. Again, another poor Standlake dupe had to be found from amongst the Spilman fraternity and persuaded to visit slaughterhouses on their behalf – a good way to lose friends, should you ever need to do so.

A re-test was immediately requested, and lessons resumed over the next few weeks. Having to change instructors just before the test, due to my original man striking out with his own business, didn't seem, on the face of it, a great help. Add to that a Friday afternoon slot to take it, when traffic would be at its worst, and "the grim reaper", as the strictest examiner was known, to be my executioner, things looked grim to say the least. Despite all this apparent downside, everything went well, and my pass certificate was one of life's great achievements for me. The fact that I almost ended my life, by failing to put my arm out whilst intending to turn right off the top road, was of little consequence, except to an unknown driver who was about to overtake me at the time. His sharp braking and subsequent foul language both saved us and relieved his frayed nerves no doubt, but such small and inconsequential incidents could not dampen my euphoria. I had at last obtained success in a mechanical field, even if I still had no idea what went on under the bonnet of the machine I had been licensed to drive.

Being reserve driver meant that, on a few occasions, my world extended beyond the confines of the Manor grounds. A trip into Witney or Oxford meant a break from the workshop, although I seemed always to be rushing in order to get back and not disrupt the flow of box or cage production so necessary for the coming season. One quite amusing incident arose when the Spilmans needed to borrow a small roller to flatten ground, which was destined to become lawn, outside the kitchen window. Mrs. Pitt, who was a mine of information through working at several houses, arranged with a Mrs. Ingham for the loan to take place. I was roped in to collect the roller after tea, but needed guidance on exactly where Mrs. Ingham lived. Starting our old truck, I waited for Mrs. Pitt and Jackie to be my guides. Imagine my surprise when the former arrived, pushing her bike on which she intended cycling to our destination. Jackie had no such ideas, and quickly piled into the front seat with her fair mop of hair just visible above the dashboard. She then disclosed that her mum so mistrusted my driving that she would rather cycle than risk her life with me. What didn't add up, though, was that she let her most precious little daughter ride instead. Jackie had no worries, and would have ridden to London if the roller had been based there. We have laughed many times over the incident, and Mrs. Pitt replied, "Ah, I thought you might turn us over". Luckily, her aversion to my driving did not last over long for later I hired a Morris 1000 car for three days and drove her and Jackie to visit their relatives, as a thank you for all their help and kindness to me since my arrival in Standlake.

Mrs. Pitt's elder brother, Bill Day, lived at Highworth, in a bungalow behind the Plough Public House. Now Bill liked his pint of beer, and nothing short of the world ending would move him homewards without having the proverbial "one for the road". When word was passed along that his sister, from Standlake, had arrived to see him, the remains of his pint were downed in a gulp, his trilby hat rammed back on his head, and Bill was on his way, amid cheers from the regulars. "She's got Bill under the thumb", was their reaction to his fast-disappearing posterior. Bill was very fond of his sister, Irene, which was painfully obvious, as he was prepared to give up good drinking time to be with her. Despite being fond of a pint, and sixpence each way on the horses, he was a good-hearted countryman, very kind in his way, and quick to realise his sister had been experiencing a hard time since the loss of her husband. Bill and his wife, Sally, were very homely, and the latter made a very nice cup of Camp coffee, served in very thin china cups.

Then, on to Swindon we went, where sister Else lived with another Bill – Keen by name, and keen by nature. He had huge allotments and would load our car boot with all types of vegetables and pickled onions, as well as some flowers. Yes, he was a keen gardener and bowls player along with his son-in-law, Ted Leighton, a policeman by profession.

By the time we had also driven to East Leach, a very pretty village on the edge of the Cotswolds, to see brother Sid and wife Ada, to Oxford to see sister Bet and husband "Dod" (he of hat-throwing fame, previously mentioned), and then to Wokingham to see sister Win, the three days were up, and like Cinderella, our coach had to be returned. With the long list just given, I still left out brother Ben, also in West Street, Oxford. Mrs. Pitt was one of thirteen children, so her family was both large and well spread, leaving some still to be visited on future occasions.

In the event, I enjoyed the experience of seeing the Oxfordshire countryside for the first time, escaping with my ally, Jackie, and being always ready to try out nearby swings when family talk became boring to our more adventurous spirits. Yes, being the proud owner of a driving licence had opened up a new world for me, and for my two friends as well, which was even more rewarding. Today we all take car riding for granted, but for people like us then, having lived in a bus and bike world, it was a definite novelty.

As 10 March approached, all plans for the mating season were put in place. Gillian had produced a large-scale plan of her proposed programme to match male and female in breeding lines. All animals were named individually, and this name was combined with parental information on a white label stapled to their box. Obviously, each colour mutation had to be preserved, and inbreeding avoided where possible. As the age of computers was still a long way off, all the mating possibilities had to be worked out by longhand, and this was quite an extended job, but not too uncomfortable a one when undertaken in a warm office on a raw, winter's day. On the other hand, the practical side of this intensive and vital operation was fraught with frustration as each spitting bundle of female refused the attentions of her planned mate. It seems that most lady mink carry the idea of playing hard to get a mite over the top. The plan was always to convey the female to the male cage, in order to give its incumbent the advantage of playing on home ground. When released into the cage, madam would fly around like a thing possessed, giving the larger and slightly less mobile male no chance to get near her. The big decision now was to ascertain whether she was really trying to play hard to get, or whether she wasn't yet in season. If the second option was indeed the case, a deadly fight could well ensue, and if left unattended could result in a bloody battle and death for one of the combatants. The difficulty stemmed from the fact that the prelude to copulation between these fiery animals was never in any way "lovey-dovey". The male would grasp the female by the scruff of the neck and drag her around, which was in a way understandable, after she had spent some considerable time spitting in his face, biting him when possible and shrieking at him from the topmost corner of the cage. Less dominant males occasionally shrank from their duties in the face of such aggression, deciding to opt for a quiet life and curl up for a sleep. When this happened, as it occasionally did with a highly bred male on which you had pinned hopes of improving stock quality, then theoretically prepared programmes went to pot. Backwards and forwards went boxes all day, amidst the cacophony of shrieking females, howling March winds and grinding of teeth as obdurate animals upset the best laid plans of mice and men. Copulation could be reasonably rapid, but usually seemed to last for hours. Then, just as we had undertaken some other tricky task, the pair would break up and a fight to the death could ensue. This time the male could be very nasty, wishing to rid his cage of the love of his life in order to have a well- earned snooze. Quickly removing the metal slide covering madam's box entrance, one hoped she would flee for cover, and enable us to take her back home. All details were then recorded, for she had to be returned to the male in, I believe, ten days' time; this was the time her mating cycle would return, and if, for some reason, the first attempt had failed, she caught on at the second one. Those twenty days in March called for great expertise, patience, hope and dedication, for the whole year's enterprise depended upon getting as many females mated as possible, for there was no second chance. Some females never took a mate, after repeated attempts. Towards the end of our campaign we abandoned the prepared chart, and put them to any male who had the stomach to fight on, but even our Casanovas gave up in despair, their looks telling us they could not mate with a harridan hanging from the ceiling.

At last the season was over, and Gillian retired to the office, with her battle-scarred, much-changed, dirty and scuffed chart, to record the eventual matings. I relaxed, as the battle-weary males were moved from the centre of the shed out to their summer quarters, well away from their erstwhile wives who needed peace to gestate their kits, our eventual harvest come the end of the year.

Preparations for the kitting season have already been outlined in a previous chapter, so there will be no repeat, but bear in mind the need for quiet and isolation during the mink confinement, even though essential tasks had to be carried out. These tasks involved expansion, for which three-phase electricity had been installed by S.E.B. engineers. Following this installation, two large, concrete bases were needed to floor a huge deep- freeze unit, and a concrete-sectioned mincing shed. Bert Coombs and his father duly arrived to set up frames and levels on the chosen sites inside the orchard gate, opposite to the mink run; Sands and Gravels, whose diggings almost surrounded the village, shot a huge load of mixed sand and ballast as near as was possible; bags of cement came from Stephensons, the Oxford builders' merchants, and with the help of a cement mixer, barrow and muscle-power, the large expanses of concrete were laid on a fine April Saturday.

This was my first experience of the builders' world, and little did I expect to be involved in it, up to my ears, before the decade was out. On this occasion my contribution took the form of barrow man, which was about as low down the labouring scale as a greenhorn can get. Even so, a great deal of sweat soaked my shirt before the day was out, for Bert was no slouch where work was concerned, and kept that old mixer running hot, not to mention Mr. Coombs senior and yours truly. Needless to say, the ever-inquisitive ducks had to try this new, flat surface to see if swimming was at all possible, causing a slice of ex-RAF parade ground language from a sweating Bert, but apart from a set of cat's dainty paw prints, the dry concrete of Monday morning was beautiful to behold. A contract firm of deep freeze engineers constructed the new food-holding store. Shortly after, a local firm of sectional concrete garage manufacturers erected the mincing shed, complete with large, wooden, double doors on the front. A large mincer, electrically driven, took pride of place, with a tap, hose for cleaning down and a reject bath for food washing. What an improvement. In fact, it all seemed too big for the small amount of food needed for our present breeding stock. Its advantages came into full view when July's rapidly growing and ever-hungry kits made feeding an all day occupation.

All these operations, with their associated noisy comings and goings obviously needed to be completed in the intervening month between mating end and female confinement. The schedule was tight, but all was peaceful by 25 April. As the next week or so would be our slack period, I usually took a week of my holiday. There appeared to be a "sod's law" policy at work in that, as soon as we closed the normally open sheds with the clear plastic sections, the weather decided to turn up the heat with an unusually warm, dry spell. This may have been uncomfortable to those little animals with fur coats and distended bellies, but to me, with holiday plans, it was a bonus. My trips home to Norfolk became less frequent as I settled into my new life, and this year in question I hired the car, as recorded earlier. Either way, I seemed to click with very pleasant weather.

On the occasions when my employers took a holiday en bloc, I moved up to the house where the two dogs, Cheena and Snippet, as well as the cat, could be looked after quite easily, and the beloved Aga kept refuelled. It was on one such occasion, when sleeping in the rose room – so named by the girls because of its rose-patterned wallpaper – that I met up with the Manor ghost. Having been well primed by Judy as to that particular bedroom and its spiritual inhabitant, I suppose my sleep was rather tentative on that first night. Having checked security on outside doors, and made up the Aga, I left the two dogs in their respective baskets and retired for the night. Being on the road side of the house, and in a strange bed, meant that sleep didn't come easily to me, despite having had a strenuous day. After tossing and turning for quite some time, and opening my eyes furtively at every creak of the old house, I eventually over-compensated by sleeping heavily. Suddenly, something struck my chest, causing me to go rigid with fear, and I was certain that the Manor ghost had got me. The apparition on to which I eventually fixed my terrified eyes was gruesome, to say the least. Looking down on me was a long, spotted face, with lolling tongue. Two large paws pressed on my chest as Cheena, the Dalmatian, carried out her idea of an early call. It appeared the kitchen door had not been closed properly, allowing the dog to nose her way out, to climb the stairs and enter my open bedroom door. After getting no response from my slumbering figure, she had resorted to thumping my chest with her forepaws. She was quite heavy for a ghost, and it took me some time to gain strength enough to galvanise my muscles and remove her from my torso. It required many deep breaths before shaky legs carried me downstairs, in order to shut her safely behind the kitchen door and resume my troubled sleep. Having met such a solid Manor ghost, I had no wish to encounter the more ethereal version, and spent the remainder of the night with head covered and door tightly shut. If ghosts can float through doors, at least I never saw it, but my experience with the spotted dog spoiled the hoped-for pleasure of sleeping in a real bed for a week. For once I was glad to return to my cramped caravan. The appearance of a modern Manor ghost became quite a talking and laughing point for a few days after that.

The eventual kit count was not as high as was hoped for, but the numbers justified the need for larger food storage equipment. The tiny, pink, blind babies rapidly became ravenous, growing families jostling for pole position as soon as the food trolley came along on its twice daily rounds. Mothers of very large families – some had up to eight hungry offspring tugging at them – were removed to save them being sucked to death. These families piled one on top of the other to sleep off their meals before returning to play and have mock fights. It was when someone forgot the "mock" part of the battle that re-housing had to be carried out. Like all young animals, they grew better as a family unit just as long as bullying didn't start. Mother would lay the law down in no uncertain manner if their rough and tumble disturbed her well-earned rest. Hours of entertainment could be had by watching their antics, for they looked such lovable and soft creatures, the kind of pet everyone would like to own. Handsome is as handsome does, when applied to them, and it wasn't long before tooth and claw became the order of the day and little teeth held fast to any flesh or cloth within their range.

The year continued on a par with the previous campaign, still with food shortages, despite our new freezer-holding capacity. The problems came with obtaining sufficient fresh food to use for immediate consumption, let alone to build up a reserve. Even with frozen fish blocks in bulk from Great Yarmouth, the percentage of tripe and offal from local slaughterhouses was not sufficient to cater for our increased numbers. Small, local mink farms had sprung up in the last year. Mr. Marchant had one just outside Crawley, Major Brown had one at Finstock, and a second establishment in our village was being considered by Major Nicholls, and so it seemed as if mink farming had become a line for retired military personnel. The last-mentioned gentleman had bought Stones Farm, and was constructing sheds and cages in a pasture at the back. His plan was to buy in ready- prepared food from us, of which we had little enough to spare, although a contract was undertaken. Livestock sales were also hoped for in that area, before the next breeding season when farming in earnest was to begin. My employers also gained some free labour from Major Nicholls in exchange for training in mink husbandry. Very welcome it was too, and from a very pleasant and genuine man, always smartly turned out despite the ever-present muck and mire associated with mink farms.

The large-capacity mincer and equivalent mixer made food preparation certainly bearable, if not a pleasure, during the heat of mid-summer, which coincided with the height of voracious eating by our charges. Every vestige of raw material, brought home in the horse-box trailer, was seized upon and mixed with an over-percentage of fish offal, and then rushed along the shed aisles with hungry noses pushing through the wire on either side. No need to cover food in order to protect it from starlings, as it was gobbled down before they had time to settle.

The nightmare, from which we had hoped our huge freezer would save us, still haunted us quite regularly. With tinned pet food just entering the minds of entrepreneurs, tripe and other offal bought from slaughterhouses looked to be on the wane. Where could bulk, cheap feeding constituents be obtained locally? Once more the outlook for expansion seemed bleak as autumn set in, and the pelting season came ever nearer. Was the time for folding the operation and getting out completely being forced upon us? Fresh food was the lifeblood of the mink industry, and that was why so many large farms were concentrated near white fish ports, with an easy and cheap source of food. Standlake, in the Midlands, and about as far from the sea as is possible, suddenly became the wrong site for the fur trade. Serious expressions became the order of the day as management wrestled with this seemingly impossible problem.

Just by chance, Gillian and her father got the inkling of an idea. Chicken processing plants were beginning to appear, as this type of meat became more than just Christmas fare for the man in the street. By driving on beyond Swindon, to Wootton Bassett, the boss obtained a small quantity of offal, and discussed the possibility of buying in bulk should it prove viable. Having already to travel as far as Swindon twice a week for his laundrettes, the few extra miles would be relatively negligible as regards cost and time expended. On his return we viewed the liquid mass of heads, feet and entrails without undue enthusiasm. The boss, however, was full of the idea and was sure a long-term solution to food problems was at hand. We were coerced into trying various mixtures on the mink who seemed to enjoy it. Our main concern was how to obtain a consistency stiff enough to stay on the wire mesh tops of cages. By adding more bran and some extra ground chicken feet, we eventually came somewhere near what was required. This revolutionary idea kept the wolf from the door and enabled the Manor Mink Farm to rumble on into the next season. As the numbers of mink decreased with pelting, and food intake reduced to a trickle of October requirements, the extra trip to Wootton Bassett seemed unnecessary, but, as a link needed to be kept, a small quantity continued to be collected, much of which ended up as minced duck and chicken food. Freezing didn't seem justified on the grounds that special trays would have to be bought for the freezing, and, anyway, a surfeit was obtainable at all times. So, a good percentage of chicken offal went into the food, and any surplus tripe was frozen and stored.

None of our steps forward were ever without two steps seemingly backwards. In the middle of the next mating season it was learned of a case where capon cockerels' offal was fed to mink, and the hormone implants given to help fatten the birds (which were still active within the birds) rendered male mink sterile. Although pretty sure no such large heads had passed us in our processing, and supported by word from the plant manager, everyone sweated a bit until the new season's kits began to arrive. Just to add to our protracted worries, the first arrivals seemed to us to be later than normal, but we eventually put it down to "sod's law", and our nervous systems.

One character I must mention is Hank. What his surname was, I can't remember, that is if I ever knew it anyway. No matter, but Hank appeared from somewhere at a time when labour shortage had reached an acute and desperate situation. I believe he was of Canadian extraction, and may have had some experience of mink farming, but after half a day in his company I needed to take fairly large pinches of salt with his ever-expanding tales. He had nowhere to live and Mrs. Spilman wisely had no intention of supplying lodgings, however desperate her husband's labour shortage. Eventually, he threw himself on the mercy of Reverend Gibbon who allowed him to sleep up over a stone-built garage in the rectory grounds. Living rough didn't seem to bother him as all those feeling sorry for him gave sustenance where they could. As for me, my sympathy for his situation cooled rapidly under the onslaught of grossly exaggerated tales, which poured into my ears during work time. On the first occasion he failed to arrive for work, I was prevailed upon to seek him out, just in case he had died of exposure during the night. Eventually I gave way to pressure, and entered the garage. Even though my nose was accustomed to rarefied smells, it rebelled at the stench of vomit and alcohol. I soon retired and left my erstwhile workmate to his own devices. His affinity to the bottle produced scant sympathy from me, and confirmed my opinion of him from the start. Mrs. Spilman would have removed him from the payroll on the spot, but her husband was a softer touch, and Hank – give or take an odd day or two – continued there until Christmas when pressure slacked off and numbers of mink decreased. The final nail in the coffin came at Christmas when Hank pressed his own self-destruct button by presenting the daughters of the house with scanty undergarments as presents, all gift-wrapped. The lady of the house was not amused, and issued an edict on the spot to the effect that they must be returned immediately. Only Hank would have had the audacity or stupidity to stir such a hornets' nest for himself, and I doubt if he reigned long after that little episode. He was a character, if nothing else, and life would be very mundane without people like him crossing our paths.

Another more local man, enlisted to work with mink, was Terry Knipe, who lived – and still does, in fact – near the top of Rack End. Terry was very pleasant to work with, and handy in the workshop where cages, boxes and other mink paraphernalia still needed to be produced in order to keep up with expansion. Having Terry there allowed me to spend more time actively involved in mink husbandry where my heart and talents lay.

Gillian spent quite a slice of her time visiting the large Scottish mink farms, and dealing with increasing office duties, whilst being able to leave her beloved mink in my hands following methods which, through her own by now quite extensive experience, she felt to be correct husbandry.

Unfortunately, there was just one fly in the ointment which was a shame, as at this period life was very settled and relatively smooth running. Terry and his bed had such an affinity that his body was very loath to leave it in the morning. I'm sure that on several occasions it was the voice of Mrs. Pitt, sent expressly from the Manor, that eventually prised him from the sheets. Yes, Terry was a good mate to work with, once he was through those gates, and of the very varied employees I shared work with he was the easiest and most pleasant. Being a born and bred countryman like me helped, of course, for we shared interests. Terry was also a keen photographer, developing his own pictures in a dark room set up in the cottage. Mink, being very photogenic, gave him plenty of scope for his hobby. As I said, this period, although we did not know it, was the calm before numerous storms destined to rock the boat of life, for me at any rate.

Life must go on, as mine did, but another chapter is needed to hold the next episode.

Chapter 12
Storm Clouds Gather

With the advent of chicken offal as a regular source of supply, food problems became less of a headache, which improved life in that working hours became much more uniform. However, seven-day working was needful at the height of our season, which meant that either Gillian or myself spent practically the whole of Sunday at work if we took weekends turn about, or half the day if sharing the work. Either way, the age-old problem of stock feeding resulted in a treadmill kind of existence slowly taking hold.

I was back to the position my father had been in for many years of his life, and one which I had vowed never to get myself into. As a result of this constant feeling of a repetitive round of work, my temper became shorter, making problems normally faced as challenges into mountains to climb. It's at times like this when bouts of frustration either cause accidents or bizarre incidents. Taking the first example, the resulting accident was entirely my own fault. After a few months' use, the belt from the electric motor to our mincer began to stretch causing slipping to take place when in work. By using a substance called belt-stick, adhesion could be regained, but really this was only a short- term solution. The options were either to reposition one of the machines, or to buy a new belt which could solve this annoying problem. After several complaints by both myself and Gillian, neither option had been taken up by the boss. Constant application of belt-stick caused a build up of adhesive on the flywheel. On the morning in question, which incidentally coincided with an important football match at Oxford, the build up caused the belt to fly off. In a fit of pique at being held up on a busy morning, I snatched up a sharp, pointed knife and ham-fistedly set about removing the hard lump of adhesive. Within seconds the knife had slipped off the obstruction and into my left hand, between thumb and forefinger. Feeling very sick, and reeling backwards, the first thoughts to enter my head were, "Oh God, I shall miss the match this afternoon". Obviously one must get one's priorities right, and the most important thing came to me first. After a trip to the doctor, an injection and copious bandaging, I made the match, despite all the advice of not to go being showered upon me. Standing behind the goal in London Road, my hand ached, I felt sick, – even sicker when Oxford lost – and on reflection I knew it all to be my own fault. My mother's oft repeated words came back to me with clarity, "Your temper will land you in prison one day, my lad, you see if it doesn't". Looking back now, from an even longer distance, I hold up my hands to say, "But for the grace of God, there languish I". My hot temper, when under control, has, on occasions, been an asset, but when out of control it could lead me to disaster.

The second instance of temper, under great provocation, was hilarious, for me at any rate. I was working at the bottom of the orchard extending sheds, and under some pressure due to overcrowding. The timber was wet, and the saw badly in need of sharpening, or better still being replaced completely. After attempting the impossible task of cutting wet wood with a blunt saw, with its closed teeth jamming up on every other stroke, my temper flared. Wrenching the offending tool from the wood, I flung it as far as I could behind me. When I looked up, to my surprise, I saw it high up in the hawthorn hedge surrounding the field. Well, I had to laugh then as I contemplated whether a blunt saw had been better than no saw at all. When Mr. Spilman arrived a few minutes later I enquired whether he had another saw. Looking rather nonplussed, he enquired the reason for my request. Where was the one I had been using? With a grin, I explained its poor state of health, but when he wished to examine it, I had to point out its present position. His eyes shot out on stalks, and then resumed normal service. It was his temper that flipped when I told him I had thrown it up there because it was useless. Without doubt, I added these extra words, ".like the rest of the tools I'm supposed to use in this God- forsaken place". To me, the situation was so funny that involuntary laughter took over, and increased as he blew his top over my sacrilegious abuse of his saw, and the firm's tools in general. On this occasion his usual good humour failed to take over, and we worked in prickly silence for a while, struggling with a replacement saw which, if anything, was worse than the one still hanging well above reach in Mr. Back's hedge. If he or Jack Laitt had been working that field they would have been reporting flying saws to the Oxford Mail. How long it hung there rusting, I don't know, but I vowed never to get the damned old thing down.

Dick Spilman reminded me quite often of Willie Thaxton from Soigné days. Neither fell out of temper, as a general rule, preferring to smooth over confrontations with a jovial observation, which tended to blunt any barbed or sharp attack I was attempting to launch at them. This worked very much to their advantage, leaving me wrong-footed and feeling cheated out of an air-clearing verbal battle.

These small "family" upsets were only shower clouds passing compared with the black storms which threatened Mrs. Pitt in her tiny cottage. A pair of cottages were wedged between the butcher's shop, Pear Tree Cottage, and the grocer's shop, Florey's Stores in the centre of High Street. Mrs. Pitt and her family had lived in the Stonesfield slated one, and George Cox in the thatched one. These very old habitations were fast approaching the stage at which they were classed as "condemned". No refurbishing work was contemplated as demolition and replacement still carried the day at that time. Nowadays, a foot high stone wall has to be returned to a habitable accommodation if it began life as a house. The early 1960s saw new buildings replacing history, using ghastly, reconstructed stone only one step removed from the concrete block. The cottages in question were owned as part of the Douglas empire built up over the years when £100 would buy a row of houses. In previous years, when the sitting tenants were offered the chance to buy, they couldn't raise 100 pence before pay day, let alone £100. So, those with enough capital stepped in, and who can blame them? Rented out at affordable rates, but which were not sufficient to allow repairs to be done or modernisation to be carried out, these properties fell into ever-increasing disrepair. The cottage occupied by George Cox, a gentleman with a wooden leg, I recall, was in a grim state with sagging thatch from which foul, blackened water poured, both inside and out, when heavy rain fell. He moved out and immediately a building firm, who considered themselves part of the self-appointed village hierarchy, ripped down the old building whilst, as it appeared to observers, making every effort to shake the life out of its neighbour which was still occupied. Poor Mrs. Pitt was naturally concerned and very unnerved by this bullying tactic which was seemingly designed to force her to move. Large holes were left at the end of her back kitchen as beams attached to the partition wall were yanked out. These bully boy tactics raised my hackles, I can tell you, although technically it was nothing to do with me. Her son-in-law, Bert Coombs, certainly let fly at the perpetrators of this action for, like me, he was ever-ready to take up cudgels on behalf of the weak against the strong. In reality we were powerless to do much, apart from fix some tin sheets over the holes, but even then wind could blow dust into her food preparation area. The trouble was that the skins of those involved were too thick to feel any remorse for treating a widow with a little girl in such a callous manner. My trade union leanings, which had been dormant since close contact with "the other side" by living at the Manor, began to surface again. I quickly realised how easy it was to become brainwashed by living and working in different environments. Having been hypercritical of union officials dining with employers, and Labour Party M.Ps living the life of Riley after elections, I had almost fallen into the same trap. Just in time I knew which side of the divide my place was, and my attitude towards those employing me hardened quite considerably; and when those who thought they had a God-given right to be on Councils, or to rule by wealth alone came into my sights, they were knocked down whenever the chance arose. From that point on I fear I became more and more of an embarrassing liability, despite being a labouring asset, to my employers. Having to listen to conversations from the opposite point of view whilst at work made things worse, and I often boiled with indignation, but managed, miraculously, to keep my trap shut, but oh, the effort involved. In this I have a lot to thank Terry for. That part of the Knipe family were of my political persuasion, so at least we could air our own views when working together.

For a time after this things settled down again at work. The house situation had little to do with the Spilman family, except for the fact that Mrs. Pitt, who worked for them, was so worried, and expressed her wish not to leave the centre of the village and move up on to the Council estate if she was offered alternative accommodation – and such a move was very likely, bearing in mind my reference to those who held posts as councillors for Standlake. If you consider the position of the former Council estate, and its distance from the centre of the village, you will understand that a veiled policy of ethnic cleansing was under way as working class villagers were re-housed well away from their self-elevated, so-called lords and masters. It wasn't until fairly recently that a second small block of elderly folks' bungalows came in the village itself. How three bungalows near the green were allowed in, I don't know, but perhaps as long as they weren't paupers living in them, then no effect would be felt on market prices appertaining to mansions round about by the influx of three elderly couples. Suddenly it seemed as if scales had dropped from my eyes to reveal the fact that here, just as in the community I had left, there was friction, and power struggles were taking place. It also became clear, as the years unfolded, that I would become very involved in fighting for what I considered right against wrong, but I would stress that those rights and wrongs were only judged in my opinion. Others may have seen things from a totally different angle, and why not? One cannot condemn others for setting themselves up as God, and then don that mantle oneself. Just because I'm always right is not my fault (joke!).

Jean, Mrs. Pitt's eldest daughter, arranged to marry her longstanding fiancé, John Culley, in November. They had managed to rent part of a large bungalow at North Leigh, so had decided to take the plunge into the murky depths of matrimony. A very excited Jackie was chosen as one of the bridesmaids on the big day, to be held at Standlake Church.

One Sunday, a few weeks before the event, I had come over the fence between the orchard and cottage rear garden, and was repairing something by the shed. Jackie, who was always around on such occasions, began climbing the apple tree to fill time before Sunday School. Doubtless, she was already dressed to go, and when her mother looked out of the back door, she was ordered to descend and refrain from such tomboyish behaviour. Immediately the door closed, up the tree went her ladyship, again in rank defiance of the last order. Bang, out she fell, and not being of fairy-like proportions, landed heavily on one arm. Trying not to give vent to loud howls until the scene was set to her advantage, she scrambled up and immediately persuaded me to perjure my soul by supporting her tale of having tripped over a stone. What choice had I, except to be supportive of my ever-trusty errand girl in her hour of need? Having got the tale right, she let out a mind-numbing cry, in the sure conviction that her fall over that wretched edging stone had resulted in a broken arm. Her mother, after casting a searching glance at the gyrating offspring and my red face, decreed there was no such damage, and condemned the by now snivelling wench to Sunday School. Our concocted story held good, under severe interrogation both as individuals and in tandem. In fact, we were almost hailed as innocent victims when it was discovered a day or so later that the arm was broken and plaster had to be applied. This very fact brought a fresh shower of trouble on to the fair mop of Jackie's head. This time, sister Jean piled in by declaring that "Our Babe", as Jackie was known in the family, could not possibly be bridesmaid unless the arm had healed and that awful plaster been removed before the big day. Luckily, Jackie's hero status at school took the sting out of that one. Mr. Snelling, her headmaster, drew a tree on it, and others scrawled on any clear spaces available, which made Jean even more adamant that no mucky old thing like that would be allowed to mar her wedding photos. All's well that ends well, and the offending plaster of Paris came off just in time, so my much-maligned errand girl was back in the frame for the big day.

The weather was unkind, even for November, as the cold wind, carrying lumps of sleet, blew across from the open north side by the Church. Jean's heavy bride's dress got muddied at the gate, but it was a happy family day, ending with a reception organised by her mother with help from local friends, in the old village hall. I remember wiping up with Nellie Taylor and Ada Rose, whilst those who could, danced the light fantastic.

When Jean's vacated room was offered to me as a place to lodge I decided, with the onset of winter imminent, to give up my idyllic caravan home in the orchard and avail myself of the offer. To get back to good home cooking and a warm fire was a glimpse of heaven. Unfortunately, I had to sack my errand girl, but I could compensate by being available to play board games on a regular basis. The caravan had served its purpose, but was a poor substitute for a house, even one with gaps in the end wall of the kitchen. So began an alliance which Mrs. Pitt and I shared for almost forty years, despite speculation, rumour, insinuation, and downright wicked lies as to what our relationship was. At the end of the day it was our business, and will always remain so. All I will say is that it will never be my fortune to find a more reliable, genuine or constant friend if I live to be a hundred. Many times it was destined to be that we two were against the world, and the world had no chance of winning.

Just prior to the wedding preparations I bought my first car, or at least Bert arranged it all for me. Where I should have been without his friendship and support, I hardly dare think. Anyway, he was working for the Luxicars garage group, run by the Jewson brothers, Peter and Stanley. Bert had been building for them at Abingdon, and had spotted a second-hand Morris 1000 in good condition, in their showroom, priced at £500. Having no bank account, I had to draw that sum from the Post Office in cash. Setting off in Bert's car on Sunday morning, we clinched the deal. Imagine the salesman's face when I pulled this wad of notes out of my pocket. In those days it was certainly quite a sum to carry around in a jacket pocket. If Bert hadn't been known to him, he could well have imagined we had robbed a bank. Being the proud owner of a shiny, black limousine gave me a new credence, even if I had no more idea than the man in the moon about what went on under the bonnet. Housed at night in the mincing shed, it meant I had to drive it out every day to enable us to work, but I have always favoured some form of garage to keep my vehicles under cover, even if a car is the last thing modern householders would think of putting in their garage.

I fear that, under the pressure of the pelting season, my temper grew shorter, and I became very difficult to understand and work with. In hindsight I feel some sympathy with my employers of the time. It really was a mirror situation of my last days at Soigné when I almost wished upon myself a situation in which I could press the self-destruct button in order to seek pastures new. Eventually, on Christmas Eve, I engineered and argued some point of principle over which neither I nor Gillian would back down, and I resigned on the spot and walked out. If my memory serves me correctly, it snowed heavily on Christmas night, or on the day itself. Heavy snow on the plastic roofs of the mink sheds could prove disastrous, owing to the weight. Looking out over the back fence I saw Gillian struggling to clear the danger, with some shed roof sections already sagged in. Donning my wellingtons, I went to assist a comrade in distress.

"Hello", said a surprised, but obviously relieved ex-employer. "I thought you had left us."

"Well, I've decided to come back as you appear to need a hand."

Off we went, working in tandem, as we had done so enjoyably over past years. By using a home-made, wooden implement, shaped like a large rake without teeth, the snow was gently dragged off the roof, much to the delight of the mink who were always ready for a new and interesting game.

At the end of an exhausting, but different type of Boxing Day spent snow-scraping and pipe thawing, we retired without another word on our big fall out, and allowed normal relations to carry us into the next year.

I think it was just prior to this particular Christmas that Jackie's famous, or infamous, little, blue, Raleigh bike suddenly disappeared, much to her consternation. Funds being very tight meant it had to be sold in order to buy a bigger one for her Christmas present. Some hopelessly inadequate tale had to be concocted to cover the mysterious disappearance, I'm sure. On the great morning, a small parcel was there for Jackie to open. Inside were front and rear cycle lamps, with a note dreamed up by Bert, which read, "Sorry we couldn't afford the bike, but here are the lights to go on with". Even when the new machine came to light, its proud owner was unable to ride it for weeks. Treacherous roads and heavy snow made it impossible, and I'm sure the young lady had no wish to court another broken limb so soon after the apple tree incident, although to wait was very frustrating.

Unusually heavy snowfall for the area made life very difficult at the mink farm. Blocked roads shut off fresh food supplies from Witney slaughterhouse. We could not get to them, and farmers were prevented from getting their cattle to slaughter, anyway. Wootton Bassett might well have been on the moon with its chicken offal, for all the chance we had of getting there. The blocks of frozen food held in reserve now had a drawback, due to the simple fact that day and night temperatures were below freezing, so there was difficulty in thawing them out. A tentative suggestion that a short spell in front of Mrs. Spilman's kitchen Aga would help fell on unsympathetic ears. We did manage, but life was far from easy, and almost permanently frozen pipes made things even worse. Constantly lugging cans of water from the house to fill drinking cups, which became ice blocks in minutes, was soul-destroying, to say the least. Severe winter conditions make animal husbandry hard work, no matter the type of livestock involved. The only ones enjoying it seemed to be the mink themselves who were actually in their natural environment. Their thick fur stood straight out making them look twice their size and black, beady eyes shone with health as they scratched away at drinking ice blocks with a fury only they knew the reason for. Desperate starlings risked life and limb in an effort to pinch food, which the cage incumbents defended with renewed vigour and great enjoyment. For them, life was enlivened by all the increased activity; our frozen feet and fingers were of no consequence.

Meanwhile, Jean, in her fresh marital bliss at North Leigh, was suffering frozen pipes for the first time. In a burst of frustration, she was recorded as saying, "I wish I'd never left Standlake; we never had frozen pipes there", to which her equally frustrated husband, John, replied, "No, of course not, your water supply was down in the well". The laugh that followed averted a crisis, and saved Jean running home to mother, which could have proved difficult through six-feet drifts appertaining at the time.

There had been an occasion in the past when Jean found herself with too much water in Standlake. A terrific night time thunderstorm had raged over the village, knocking out the electricity supply. Jean, her mother and Jackie were upstairs without any form of light, so the former volunteered to go down in order to get a torch. Gingerly feeling her way down the stairs, what a shock she had when her bare foot went into a flood of cold water lapping the bottom step. Wading around, searching in vain for a torch, she was instructed from above to feel in the sideboard drawer for a cigarette lighter. This she found, but no amount of grinding at its wheel would produce a spark, so the three castaways sat on the stairs waiting for dawn and subsequent rescue. Frank and Chris Douglas came to see how things were, and after a briefing via the upstairs window, they received the door key and opened up. Out came a flood of muddy, black water, causing the two rescuers to take hasty, evasive action. The heavy rain had run off the rotten thatch next door, bringing a black scum with it, and run down the path and under a poor- fitting back door. First filling the kitchen and then the lower-lying living room, a close- fitting front door stayed its progress, causing it to rise until it lapped the bottom step of the stairs where Jean's dainty foot had come into contact with it. Luckily, the front room had a step up, and so escaped the stinking mess left behind when the flood drained out into the street.

There was no insurance to cover flood damage in those days, so I suppose Mrs. Pitt's indomitable spirit and the close family support that working people had and needed then, saved the day. Ever resourceful, the little family had battled on after the death of their breadwinner. Mother swept the chimney by using bean canes tied together. The two older girls staggered down the garden, carrying the big lavatory bucket between them in order to empty it into a freshly-dug hole. The laughter that began to erupt half way down the path hardly helped, as their smelly burden slopped dangerously near to their legs. When we old fogeys look back, with rose-coloured spectacles, to the good old days, endless grind of the manual side of life is often blotted out. Perhaps it didn't do us any harm, but muscles did ache, feet blistered and raw hands smarted. Despite all these things, that little cottage was never without a warm welcome and offer of refreshment. Bert, when he returned from National Service, gave great help. Mrs. Pitt always regarded and treated him as a son rather than son-in-law, and no better man ever walked this earth, as I was to find in all the years he remained my friend. His untimely death from cancer, at the age of 54, left a gap in all our lives no one will ever fill.

Just to hark back to those days when everyday life was hard and money in short supply, the very fact that almost everyone was in the same situation produced a togetherness, and one for all and all for one unity in trouble and in joy. People next door were neighbours, and not just near-livers, as became the order of the day when most ordinary folks wanted to be seen outdoing those living roundabout. What a sad loss to village life. I will not say my observations are universally true as I myself have excellent neighbours, but still in a modern pattern, which is the only way younger people can know. I must still say that I would exchange the two or three car per house situation for the rusty bike and stick- carting perambulator era, although perhaps I would draw a line at well water and bucket lavatory. I suppose all through the ages people at my time of life would wish to retain some sections from their past, whilst keeping advantages of the present.

It was around this time that Eric Kharl came to play with Jackie. One afternoon they were in the front room when Mrs. Pitt glanced up in time to see Eric about to sit on her fine-meshed fire-guard. She requested that he desist from this as it would get bent. Almost immediately, Eric plonked himself down on it. His by now irate hostess leapt up, and gave him a cuff on the shoulder for blatantly defying her. With some haste Eric made for the door. "I go home now, Mrs. Pitt", said Eric, and made off at speed. Jean reprimanded her mother, being of the opinion that Mr. Kharl would return and complain about Eric's chastisement. When a knock came at the door they all feared the worst. The knock only heralded the return of Eric, with a short, terse statement to the effect, "I come back now, Mrs. Pitt". His angelic face portrayed to the world a false picture for, in less than five minutes, I looked out of the back door just in time to see his retreating figure speeding down the garden path carrying an axe which he had obtained from the shed. Whether he planned revenge by beheading the small daughter of the house, I didn't wait to find out. After relieving him of the offending weapon, we took turns to watch this playmate Jackie had taken under her wing. We have often laughed about Eric, the axe man.

To return for a moment to that very cold winter which I believe was the worst and longest-lasting in this area since 1947, my car had to be started and run out of the mincing shed every day. The reverse procedure, in late afternoon, soon bled the battery of power after two cold starts per day with no restorative journey in between. Cranking the cold engine soon lost its charm, so eventually it was left outside, unfortunately directly under overhead wires whereon crowds of starlings sat daily, their resultant droppings covering my poor car. Freezing almost instantaneously made removal impossible, and despite dire warnings of acid contained in them which would eat away the paint, I had no choice but to leave it until a thaw set in, which happened just before mating season rolled round once more.

The Arctic conditions had been a great help in slimming our breeding stock down to the required dimensions.

My next trip to Norfolk was special, due to the fact that I had a car, for the first time. Much polishing had taken place after the initial removal of birds' mess, for I wanted to make a good impression on my late workmates. I'm sure my little car didn't cut much ice with them, and you would have thought I would have learned my lesson after preening around before, making a fool of myself by falling off the back of Ron's motorbike in RAF days. I shrugged off the lack of interest by declaring to my mother that one day I would return with a car stretching the length of Pretoria cottages. Poor fool that I was then, far from appreciating the important, simple things in life that have real value. Remember, I was still out there making my fortune.

On the plus side, I took my mother for a ride along the North Norfolk coast. It was a rough, rainy day, but the wild sea, viewed from the comfort of a car, was something to enjoy. We had fish and chips in newspaper on our laps, and drank from a flask. Just a few thoughts were given to Dad and Michael working outside in the wind and weather, and we made sure we were home in time to warm the house and prepare a hot tea. No day off for them to ride out, even if the prodigal son had returned on wheels. There was no red carpet for the black sheep of the estate in those days. I felt alien to Westacre.

Work at the mink farm continued on a peaceful basis, although a constant gnawing in the background disturbed my peace of mind as pressure was being put on my landlady to get herself removed from the cottage. Although eternally thankful to have missed the severe winter in a caravan, my present lodging was precarious. Mrs. Pitt was almost distraught at the thought of leaving her little home, so cosy in its familiar way, and handily placed for her work. Private renting at affordable prices was coming to an end, except for the council properties. For her own personal reasons she had no wish to live on the extreme edge of the village, and even less incentive to move to another one. Every avenue seemed to be blocked off. Rev. Gibbon gave what help he could by suggesting a large, mobile home, to be placed in the rectory field, but there was no help from the church as the land belonged to them, and the idea was flawed on many counts, anyway.

Eventually I took the problem up with Mr. Spilman, as both I and Mrs. Pitt worked for him. I suggested a tied cottage be obtained and rented to me, so that we both had a home. The idea was met with very little enthusiasm, although, in all fairness, I don't suppose he could pluck the necessary money to buy out of the air, any more than I could. He did take us to look over a property at Rack End, which was in a worse state than where we were. We also looked over a much larger house, which had been home to Sonny Johnson and his family before they moved into the new bungalow beside their garage and workshops. Although larger than we needed, it was much nicer, and I could see poor Mrs. Pitt furnishing it in her mind's eye and becoming optimistic that the day had been saved. Unfortunately, nothing came of it, probably the price was too high and our hopes were dashed again. To add to the family worries, Bert and Gill were also being forced to move on, as their rented house on the top road was being repossessed. As a strange twist of fate, Bert bought the cottage in Rack End which we had been shown over a few months previously. Being a tradesman builder meant that he could do work on it himself, and with the untiring help of Gill and some labourers, including a clueless me, he made Copanda Cottage into a very comfortable home. But more of that later.

When the second property suggestion fell through, I felt very frustrated, and deeply sorry for the lady who had struggled so hard to revive her life after the death of her partner. Finally, I laid my last card, which turned out to be, it seemed, only of very low value. I put it to the boss that either he found me a house, or I would seek other employment. As usual, I did this with no thought or forward planning as to what the next move would be if my gamble failed. As had been the case at Soigné, my bluff was called and, as I would never give way in a crucial situation, I left, removing my car and parking it in front of the surgery, and taking my labour to be toted in pastures new. I left with anger in my face, for I felt betrayed after all the work I had put into building the farm up from its earliest days. In my heart was a great sadness, for I loved the work and most of all the animals, and I knew I would miss them more than anything else.

Chapter 13
Into the Retail Trade

Have you sometimes felt that you have lived through situations in your life before? Well that is just how I was experiencing things as I sat at the table in Mrs. Pitt's cottage. The fire of battle had died within me as I took stock of what sort of fool I'd been this time in taking on the undoubted superior strength of an employer, single-handed, although I had banked on the fact of Mrs. Pitt also working for the Spilman family as being enough to tip the scales in our favour. But the gamble had failed, in the short-term at least. Now we still had no house to move into, I had no job, and with Mrs. Pitt also determined to cut her work ties at the Manor, less income for her. How often had I preached to others the common sense maxim, never to give in your notice until you have another job to go to. Depending solely on that Friday pay packet to live should din into even the thickest skulls such a basic understanding. Just how thick was mine, you may well ask.

The one great thing about burning all your boats, and blowing up all bridges, is that, as you cannot go back, you must go forward. After two cups of tea we both felt better and able to think constructively. Mrs. Pitt was adamant about leaving that huge pile of dishwashing to some other poor soul taken on in her place just as soon as she had organised herself. She felt sure that both Mrs. Gibbon at the rectory and Mrs. Ingham in Abingdon Road would extend her hours with them to cover those about to be lost. This did indeed prove to be the case, making our withdrawal of labour from the Manor complete.

My situation didn't, on the face of it, have such an easy solution, but as soon as the Oxford Mail arrived at the shop we checked down the long list of situations vacant in an effort to locate something suitable. Everything my eye surveyed seemed horribly alien to me in employment terms. Setting my capabilities on no higher a plane than labouring, and completely ignoring my educational achievements at both school and farming college, it was no wonder most situations were passed over. The name, rather than the type of work, caught Mrs. Pitt's eye. The son of a person, for whom the good lady had worked before marriage, was seeking a man for duties at a large, new shop he ran in Cowley Road, Oxford. Hoping to be remembered, and so help me to gain preference, she set off with me to Oxford. The gentleman did, in fact, remember her with warmth as a very good friend and cook when he was a boy, but unfortunately the post had been filled, and no more vacancies existed. End of story, but at least we had tried.

A couple of days later I spotted a likely opening with the Co-op in Cowley, where an assistant warehouseman was required. Now, without a word of exaggeration, the jobs vacant column was never without a requirement from the Oxford and District Co-op. Even allowing for it being a very large employer, this did seem to indicate a very rapid turnover of labour. Notwithstanding, I set the nose of my Morris 1000 towards its birthplace at the top end of Oxford from us, and eventually pulled up at the newly- constructed Cowley Centre. It looked very grand, I must say, with the Co-op grocery flagship at the head. Mr. Currill, the manager, called in Mr. Piper, the assistant manager, to help him look me over. They were very pleasant, and were obviously relieved to interview someone of moderate intelligence for a change, offering me the job without asking for references – of which I had very few. I did offer to supply some, for I knew Rev. Gibbon and Colonel Ingham would support my honesty, if not my control of temper. Work would be on a different pattern of five days a week from Tuesday to Saturday inclusive, and with late opening (a new innovation) on Friday. My spirits sank momentarily as I thought of losing my Saturday football matches, but it was a sacrifice which had to be made for the good of the cause. The only reservations my two prospective employers had was the distance I had to travel, but I soon assured them I owned a reliable car, so that point was set aside. The only other point they tentatively raised was a strict condition of employment being to belong to A.S.D.A.W., the shop workers' union. No problem for me, a member of the agricultural workers' union, since a transfer could easily be arranged. How interesting to belong to a closed shop situation which I had heard so much about, where strength of union members made life fair for all. Although I enjoyed my days at Cowley, I didn't see any union strength protecting individuals from the vagaries of management. Having been introduced to the warehouse manager, I was booked to return and start work on Tuesday morning at, I believe, 8.30 a.m., finishing at 5.30 p.m.

For the first few days I hardly peeped into the shop itself. Our domain was contained in the basement, and all incoming goods were taken down via a lift from the loading bay at ground level. I did eventually discover the upstairs emporium had separate sections for wine, greengrocery and delicatessen, as well as the normal grocery gondolas which were self-service. All very modern, although some of the vegetables had a very sad, second- hand look about them. We second class citizens from below ground wore grey, warehouse coats and, as servants of old, weren't welcome in the shop after customers were admitted. Strangely though, we were required to be at the doors for 5.30 p.m. to lock them on the dot, and make soothing gestures to any irate customers who had just missed the cut-off point, and to usher out the stragglers left inside. I suppose our grey coats gave us an air of security guards, without the additional expense for uniforms.

My below stairs boss, whose name I cannot recall although I should be able to, was very much a working man who got stuck into tasks with a will. As I was hewn from the same stone we got on well together. Any idler around was liable to get the proverbial kick up the arse from "Prin", as his nickname went outside his hearing, though for what reason I never knew or tried to find out by asking him. It was quite a novelty to disappear inside on raw, November days, our only contact with the outside being to look out at it from the cover of our unloading bay. For the rest of the time it was all strip lighting in our underground cave. This, I began to believe, was not good for our health, despite its warmth on those miserable, winter days. I had one cold after another during my stay there and put the cause down to the lack of fresh air. Being used to working outside, I missed that environment. On all but the coldest days, when I ate my sandwiches in the staff canteen, I went out to my car and ate there. This also enabled me to read without the constant gabble associated with communal eating places. On Fridays, with extended hours, I treated myself, on Mrs. Pitt's insistence, to a meal at a little restaurant run by an ex-football league referee. The walls were full of photographs taken at various events in his career. He also served a good lunch at a reasonable price.

Having Mondays off, and on only a low rate of pay once travelling expenses had been deducted, I set about finding gainful employment for that day. Mrs. Dobbs, who ran the Standlake post office, had a row of derelict cottages running back alongside the post office building, with gardens behind Lock's Cottage. A bungalow now stands on the site, but then the gardens were cultivated by the Dobbs family. Frank Dobbs, being a rep for Libbys, was understandably not terribly enamoured with the heavier side of gardening, so his wife set me on to tidy and autumn dig the area. Digging all day is hard work, and as I actually hate gardening despite having had to do at least some all my life, I suffered a fair bit in order to boost the funds. The constant dripping of my nose from continuous colds did not help, but having experienced this whilst bent double over a sugar-beet hook in Norfolk, it didn't cause me to slacken effort. The thought of Mrs. Pitt scrubbing and polishing huge floors, as part of her efforts to keep the ship afloat, banished any thoughts of self-pity. Mrs. Ingham also had plenty of gardening that autumn, and other odd jobs as well. Some large boughs, fallen from a horse chestnut tree, were to be sawn into logs, which was just up my street, especially on a frosty morning. Taking my own folding, wooden sawing horse, I naturally left it in an open shed in order to finish the job the following week. Imagine my annoyance in finding it vandalised by some idiot who had sawn it in halves. I suppose they thought it funny, but somehow I didn't. As Bartletts, a building firm from Witney, had been working there, I blamed them, whether they were guilty or not. John Culley, Jean's husband, who drove their lorry, took up my case and got me a much improved model made up in their carpenter's shop. After being a leading prankster in my misspent youth, I wasn't quite so enthusiastic over taking a dose of my own medicine. I believe most people around me thought it amusing, but I didn't, so perhaps age was catching up with me and my sense of humour was changing accordingly.

On into the new year my employment carried me. Luckily no serious weather conditions prevented my getting to Cowley. Severe conditions, such as the previous winter had thrown up, would have scuppered the whole delicately balanced way of earning my living, and I was very conscious of that fact. I never went anywhere near the mink establishment, although I did get snippets of information from Terry, who still hung on there, but with less enthusiasm than when we worked together. It appeared two men had been taken on to replace me, both being mink experts from the north. If my source of information was to be believed, the word "expert" should be contained inside inverted commas.

We were unable to make any progress as regards re-housing, although Mrs. Pitt continued to approach any possible property owner in the hopes of success. Many offered sympathy, but no one came up with a concrete solution, so the situation became more acute with each passing month. Buckets were strategically placed to catch roof leaks, and rags were stuffed into cracks to keep out the draught where the soft, internal wall originally between the two cottages had been left open to the elements. Short of poisoning the well, every effort was made to force her from the home in which she had raised her family. All was done in the name of progress, or rather to make more money for those who were already well-endowed financially, though rather less well off in human feelings – and this by neighbours of many years' standing, which quickly makes a mockery of my affirmation of loyal neighbouring in past years before the ink is dry. In true Count of Monte Cristo fashion, I vowed revenge on those who put that poor woman through such a mental hell, and, without the strange twist destined to happen later in my life, there is no doubt that retribution would have been wreaked, and probably on the very edge of, if not outside, the law. Since those days, on every occasion I sing the harvest hymn, "Come ye thankful people, come", their faces swim up before my eyes as the third verse reaches, "Give His angels charge at last, in the fire the tares to cast", and I wish them to roast for ever in the fires of hell. No commemorative seats or committee rooms given to the village will ever erase the sight of a brave lady hiding her tears from those around her, and putting every effort into keeping a home for her daughter. Of course most of this nasty business was kept out of sight as much as possible. When you run a business, and like to sit in the front pews at church for big occasions, one must keep face. Add to that a seat on the council, and you would like others to view you as God's gift to the village and not as a soul wished into the fires of hell. Nothing has ever changed my view, especially not the threat to take court action over an allegedly unpaid bill for 12s/6d. discovered when the business closed. Both parties knew the bill was paid, but as no receipt could be produced, the solicitor was instructed to proceed unless a payment was made. Yes, I suppose we should have expected such action from a man who boasted of travelling to Abingdon expressly to bank his farthings when they ceased to be legal tender. There are some things in life one can never forget or forgive, and unfortunately or otherwise, my memory is very good and forgiveness not very forthcoming to the living or to the dead.

As the winter days receded my journeys to and from Oxford became more pleasant as I saw more hours of daylight. Having discovered the manager, Mr. Currill, was a keen Oxford United supporter who disappeared every Saturday afternoon of a home match, I persuaded him to let me attend a couple of very important cup matches against higher class opposition. Everyone was friendly at the store, and although I was in an alien environment, life was very pleasant. One of my tasks was to take the secretary to the bank on occasions, using my own car, for which I was rewarded with 2s/6d. petrol money. I also helped collect money and orders around the new estate of Blackbird Leys, which was under construction at that time. Once or twice I covered the Littlemore round when the normal collector was unwell. We received the money for the previous week's groceries, and took the customer's order book back to be set up and delivered before the weekend. Each cardboard box was labelled and delivered on a van from the group transport depot on Osney Mead trading estate. The order department, also below ground with us, was run by a fierce lady who terrorised everyone, including Mr. Currill who always sent his deputy, Mr. Piper, to quell any riots which broke out from time to time. I can hear her now, roaring at the luckless deputy, "Where's that bloody Manager, why doesn't he show his face down here?". "Because he's got more sense", Mr. Piper would mouth towards us as he made a hasty retreat. She had a heart of gold, I think, but I was never quite sure.

I tried my hand on the delicatessen counter, resplendent in a white coat and pristine apron. Trying to look efficient, and feeling far from it, I cut cheese, served ham and worked the bacon slicer. Most customers knew what they wanted, which made life relatively easy for me. Mr. Currill, or those above him, decreed that, for our size, we were not selling enough bacon, so a special offer fortnight was advertised, and a specialist bacon man from the Kennington branch would help us to increase sales. Mr. Currill, carried away by his enthusiasm, ordered more sides of bacon than would normally have been the case for six months. Hoping to make a good impression on the visiting expert, he set me and his sister who was normally in charge of wine sales, to practise our boning skills in readiness. Well, by the time I had removed the bone from fore hock, the centre of the joint was just a jammy mess, which admittedly was hidden when the whole was tied, but reappeared when a customer required only half the piece. Needless to say, my knife work was painfully slow.

On the fateful Tuesday morning I kept myself gainfully employed down in the warehouse, clad in grey coat. It wasn't long before the flamboyant voice of Mr. Piper floated down, "Derek, you are supposed to be up here. Get your white coat". With the speed of a condemned man, I elevated myself by one floor, as commanded. Jack Luckett, the expert, was a large man with an artificial leg. As after-effects of wounds sustained during World War 2, he had eventually lost his own leg. A very cheerful man, but one who would brook no messing around, he was on to his task at once casting a critical eye upon our preparatory efforts for his display. As quick as lightning, he cut up a side, de- boned and tied joints, sliced rashers and had a display ready almost before the first customer came through the doors. Thinking he had enough for a whole day's selling, I couldn't believe my ears when he instructed me to fetch more from the cold store. All the time he worked, a continuous stream of bacon-lore, dos and don'ts, assailed my ears and was sincerely meant for my assimilation. Higher and higher piled the joints, and with every addition my eyes grew wider, though I dare not utter a word to the effect that we had enough there to last the fortnight. Then Jack began his sales pitch. There was never any doubt in his mind that every person who entered the store would have bacon in some form for tea, even if they were of the Jewish faith. He exhorted everyone to visit his counter, he gave out such mouth-watering recipes for bacon-this, and bacon-that, we were drooling from the outset. It is wonderful to stand and watch a tradesman at work, and Jack was certainly that. He loved his product and had every confidence in what he sold. My puny efforts, when left in charge whilst he enjoyed a well-earned cup of tea, wouldn't have moved that mountain in a month, but even so he never put me down, giving encouragement by saying practice makes perfect. We didn't clear the whole display for Tuesday was our quietest day, but Jack sold most of it. My thoughts were that Mr. Currill would expect me to continue this level of selling after Jack had departed a fortnight hence, for he was prone to wild expectations like that. For all Jack Luckett's enthusiastic encouragement, I knew my heart was not in the job, and longed to be working outside again.

At any rate it was a privilege to work with Jack, and as you can see, I didn't forget the experience, and still remember that he preferred a fore-hock joint to the best and much more expensive gammon. There spoke a man who knew one end of a pig from the other!

A very large living van had been stationed inside the Manor drive, up near the orchard gate, and had been put there very soon after I left. Rumour had it that Mr. Spilman had recently bought a bungalow, "Maerda" (a dream, backwards) built for the late Bert Johnson in High Street, and now to house the mink farm manager, as I believe he termed himself. I didn't know him or his assistant as I distanced myself well away from the establishment, but even then I still seethed with anger every time I thought about my alleged shabby treatment six months before. The circulating rumour over the bungalow did nothing to soothe those feelings. My judgement was along the lines of things going swimmingly well at the mink farm if the manager warranted a house with the job.

One evening in May, I was cleaning my car on the surgery forecourt, where I parked it overnight, when Gillian Spilman came out of the Manor and down the road towards me. I doubt if we had passed more than a nod to each other since my departure from the mink farm, so I just turned my head to continue with the job in hand. To my surprise, she stopped and came in at the entrance, just a gap between two cast-concrete walls. Our opening exchanges were somewhat stilted and prickly, especially on my part, though quite why I don't know for we personally had no disagreement and had always enjoyed each other's company, both in and outside work. The one previous argument between us had only lasted one day before we teamed up again to battle against the ravages of snow. All very platonic, I would stress, with caring for mink our common interest. The long and short of Gillian's mission was to persuade me to return to work with her as things were in a poor state of organisation, to say the least, and the manager was on his way back up north, leaving the bungalow for me to move into, should I want the job. Not wishing to appear eager enough to snatch her hand off, I made a great show of being extremely happy where I was, and needing to think it over at length. It was arranged that I would meet her and her father the next evening to give my decision and talk terms, if applicable.

Returning indoors I was rather dazed by the sudden and unexpected turn of events. Obviously a return to work at the Manor would solve our crucial housing problem, but was I selling my birthright for a mess of pottage? Having lived in a tied cottage for most of my life, I knew at first hand their plus and minus qualities. It was very nice to live rent free, or on a reduced rate as part payment for work, but lose the job and you were out on your ear. Knowing my track record of falling out with employers by being unable to control my tongue or respect authority, it would be a big gamble. In the end we decided there was no choice really, and I liked the work which I was good at. Mrs. Pitt admitted she would not like to return to work in the house, and I pointed out there was no need to even worry about it. The bungalow was given to me as part of my job, and did in no way commit my housekeeper to domestic service. As you can see, we would now change our arrangement in that I would be the householder, and she my housekeeper. My lodging days were over, or would be if I took up the Spilmans' offer.

The next evening's meeting was quite amicable, and I had no difficulty in accepting the wage rates and conditions offered, which were much better than my original ones. We shook hands all round, and I was destined to return to mink farming as soon as my notice expired at the Co-op. I was very sorry to give that notice and leave such a friendly group of people. They wished me well, and hoped I was making the right move. I had no doubt where my heart lay, and just hoped I wasn't going back just to solve the house problem. The Spilmans had made their bed six months before, and had found it rather lumpy and highly expensive. Now I was making mine once more, and this time I wouldn't be able to get out of it, lumpy or not.

I suppose one episode that took place before we finally moved out of the old cottage should have put us on guard regarding tied houses. A family, with six school age children, was turned out of their home by the man's ex-employer. As both men were members of the British Legion, we fellow members pleaded that in no way should this situation arise within such an organisation. After having the necessity for the eviction explained to us by local officials, ex-officers of course, we were even less convinced of its morality. As Brigadier Goadby pointed out to me, when he came especially to the mincing shed in order to shut me up, just because it happened to be an ex-officer owning the house, and an ex-private being evicted, it made no difference to the case. That was how the law worked, and we must abide by it. His bloated, overbearing attitude really made me see red at a time when I had the sharp, pointed, tripe-cutting knife in my hand. With a burst of rage, I roared at him, "The law says I must not let the wind out of your fat gut with this knife, but I shall be very tempted to do so if you don't bugger off", and with that I drove the knife into the thick, wooden door with all my force. His puce face blanched, and he lumbered off down the drive at a speed his legs had not carried him for many a year. As I cooled down my first thoughts were, "That's done it, I shall get the sack even before we've moved into the bungalow", but, strangely, I heard no more of the incident. My mother's prophetic words came back to me, "Your temper will land you in prison".

On the day of the eviction, the younger children trailed past on their way to school. They told Mrs. Pitt they didn't know where they were to go home after school. "Mum couldn't tell us 'cos the men are coming today." They were quickly assured of a welcome at her house, and were to come there. Well, the men did come to carry out the letter of the law, as bailiffs are bound to do. All the furniture, what there was of it, sat on the roadside until barn storage was offered by a sympathetic villager. Some children slept at Mrs. Pitt's and the others with Granny Pitt who lived opposite the Green. Both were widows whose husbands had seen war service. At least half-a-dozen Legion members, including myself, relinquished our membership and returned our badges to the brigadier in protest at the refusal to help a member in distress. Retaliation came in the nicest possible way when Mrs. Pitt lost the little extras accorded to Legion widows, because the powers that be decided she must be cohabiting with me, and so put herself outside the rules. That was petty thinking taken to the extreme, but, as Bert so bluntly put it, "Bugger them and their blasted charity". Eventually the evicted family were re-housed at Bampton, but not before they went through the trauma of being parted for too long. We in the N.U.A.W. had fought long and hard for the abolition of the tied cottage, but the thorny problem had been put to the back of every Labour government agenda, and of course never even reached the ears of the party supported through the years by farmers, landlords and the landed gentry.

A young man, hailing from the north-east of England, remained living in the large caravan, and worked on with me. He was quite an outgoing chap, and a good worker. My return coincided with a very warm spell of weather. In the first week we received two huge loads of frozen fish blocks, and although handling freezing cold material between a refrigerated lorry and deep freeze, we sweated cobs. The driver couldn't split the blocks, so we produced a long, metal crowbar. At the end of the operation we stood watching as the vehicle disappeared out of the gate, and then we suddenly remembered the bar still on the lorry. The boss was not at all pleased at the loss when I reported it. When we did the self-same thing with another bar on the second load, even we questioned our combined sanity, and I had to drive to Leighs in Witney to purchase a replacement. It cost me £2.10s., but it was worth it just to keep the boss off our tired backs. I still have that bar today, so it outlasted its predecessors by quite some margin.

Work proceeded at a pace within the confines of the orchard, very much as in other years, but with a larger number of animals there was hardly time to draw breath between feeds. A semi-automatic watering system had been introduced, although there was still need to locate bone dry cups where blockages had occurred. Immediately tea was over Mrs. Pitt and I set off for the bungalow. Ably disrupted by Jackie, who was very anxious to prove her skills at painting, we scrubbed, rubbed and redecorated until tired limbs could be pushed no more. The wonder of getting hot water from a tap, or water of any kind for that matter, was a novelty for us as householders. A flush toilet, bath, washbasin, sink, airing cupboard – all these mod cons had been so sadly lacking in the cottage and we revelled in them. Mrs. Pitt admitted to always wanting to live in a bungalow, so it seemed as if all our dreams had come true when we moved in. There was a nice lawn and flowerbeds at the front. These were rather overgrown, but some hard work soon brought them into line. My car could be parked on the front end of a substantial, brick- built shed and we even had a pigsty beyond that. A large kitchen window looked out over a medium sized vegetable garden and away across grass fields at the rear. A beautiful row of tall elm trees stretched away towards Horn's Way, making a shady resting place for Cyril Knipe's cattle on hot, sunny days. This was certainly a wonderful answer to anyone's prayers. When later we found that the very ornate fireplace threw little or no heat into the room, however large our fire, we resorted to having an oil stove at our backs. Our shoes going green in the cupboards was a mite distressing, but these drawbacks were a small price to pay. At least we had a watertight roof over our heads at long last.

We were in our element, Mrs. Pitt keeping the house spotless and providing us with lovely meals in her large kitchen. I brought a wheelbarrow load of mink manure home with me each day to enrich the garden where I produced a marvellous crop of vegetables. After building some cages, I kept rabbits for breeding and eventually for the table. Laying-hens had a run in the corner, so we enjoyed fresh eggs. I even bought some mushroom spores and attempted to grow them in the dark pigsty, using mink-run compost as a medium. This, however, was one of my less successful ventures, and we never even raised one mushroom each; the two specimens that we did raise had to be divided between three! I constructed a corrugated iron lean-to over my car without planning permission, as one did in those days if no one complained. It was a wonder the aforementioned Brigadier didn't bring me to book as he set himself up as chief planning officer for Standlake, and if any building work offended his eye, he set out to get it removed or changed to his approval. He was quite a power within the village, and did, on one occasion, suggest there were other villages I might care to move away to and live within. As I did not wish to be part of the unofficial ethnic cleansing scene, I declined his suggestion.

Teddy, the new mink farm man, volunteered to make me a wooden unit to fit in an odd corner of the kitchen. He was a very handy carpenter if, as it turned out, exceedingly slow. By enjoying a cooked tea every evening that he came to work on it, he obviously thought an extended job would benefit him and pay well for his labour. Eventually our patience wore thin, and I threatened to knock it up for firewood unless he completed it, which he then did in double-quick time. He made a good job of it eventually and his handiwork is still doing service for me today, although in a different kitchen.

Before and during this period of blissful living by the Pitt/Bumfrey alliance, Bert and Gill Coombs had been battling away at a mammoth task in order to turn that poor old house in Rack End into a secure habitation. As previously mentioned, they too had to get out of their rented house in a hurry. There were certain strict conditions laid down by the mortgage company, one of which was that he had to construct a soak-away sewerage system within six months, and make various other basic improvements. The previous owner had also been under these restrictions, but had seemingly given up in despair, thus losing his mortgage. Bert took up the challenge, he and Gill working like slaves to dig a trench down the very long rear garden, lay pipes and then excavate two chambers needed for the system. Water continuously ran into their workings as they got below river level. The Windrush, which ran behind their garden, would be nice for fishing if ever Bert had time, but was a curse at that juncture. Pumps were rushed in as Bert and his enthusiastic band of amateur helpers poured quick-setting, expensive cement mix into the holes to make a base. Sheer guts and determination won the day and never have a young married couple worked harder to pull themselves up by their boot strings than those two. The system was finished, tested and passed within the stipulated time, and one part of the family had their own ground to stand on, although a mind-blowing amount of work remained to be done with very little money to invest in it. Eventually the one-for-all, and all-for-one bond got them through, with a lot of sweat, a moderate amount of swearing, and a fair percentage of laughs as a bonus.

Westacre Cricket Club 1960, the mates I left behind. Back row, left to right: C. Durrant, G. Creed, Gerald Andrews, Peter Welham, Michael Bumfrey and Derek Curl. Front row: Brian Reynolds, Colin Deasley, Roger Taylor (Captain), John Thaxton, Roger Reynolds (Scorer) and Terry Eagle.

Westacre Cricket Club 1965. Back row: Michael Bumfrey, J. Sandle, Derek Curl, D. Walpole, Gerald Andrews, John Thaxton, P. Wright and Albert Reynolds (Umpire). Front row: Tony Abel, B. Russel, A. Biddle (Scorer), Brian Reynolds, Colin Deasley. Note the well worn pads!

Fred Brewster at work in the now defunct Westacre Sawmill. Wot! no goggles, mask or gloves! Wot! no health and safety inspector.

The end of an era! Rats Hall Barn just prior to demolition. Note the electricity pylon which could have saved the hamlet a few years earlier.

National Union of Agricultural Workers, residential course at Esher in Surrey c 1957. The auther 4th from left back row, next to the larger than life, Brother Edgar Pill. N.U.A.W. President and M.P. for North Norfolk, Edwin Gooch, centre, front row.

Bob Brewer at the head of the victorious Aston Darts Team. Far right: N.U.A.W. District Organiser, Charlie Brown c 1970.

Caythorpe Court, home to Kesteven Farm Institute 1959/60.

"Jock" Wallace and Brian Field take a night cap.

The refurbished stable block, my home for nine months.

The Golden Balls public house, Brighthampton, Standlake, recently demolished for housing.

These thatched cottages just off Standlake Green were demolished to make way for Yew Tree Bungalows. But not before my friend Bert Coombs was born in the far end cottage 1st June 1935.

Days when Standlake ran on real horse power. This display was possibly in a field backing on to Malthouse Farm, Brighthampton.

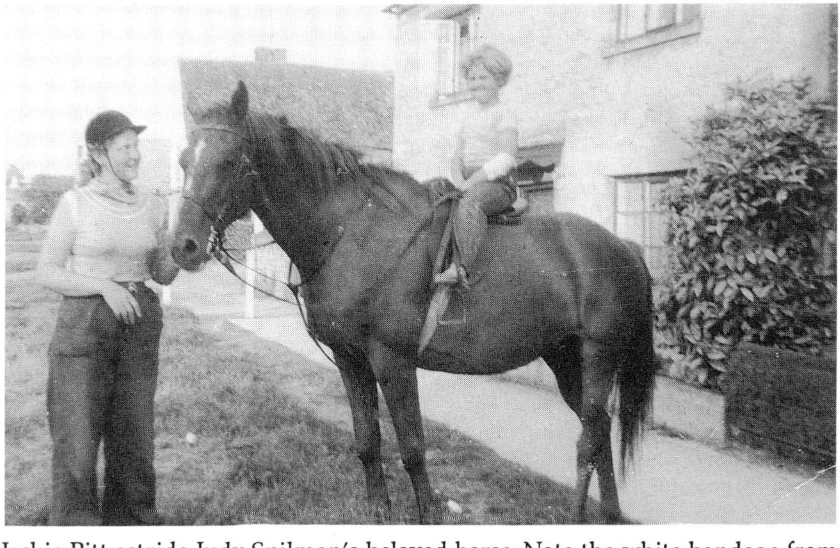

Jackie Pitt astride Judy Spilman's beloved horse. Note the white bandage from yet another injury.

Jackie Pitt (left) with elder sister Jean on the occasion of Gill's and Bert's Wedding, 1960. Gillian Ralph is in the centre.

Jackie Pitt equestrianised . . .

. . . and mechanised in front of the old house in High Street Standlake 1955/56.

My little errand girl Jackie on her way to collect the weekly shopping order.

Jackie Pitt with sister Gill and her fiancé Bert Coombs, outside the family home in High Street, Standlake.

Gillian Spilman at work in one of the long mink sheds.

The author assisting Gillian to remove the clear plastic side panels as temperatures rise in mid to late May.

Handling mink with thick leather gloves.

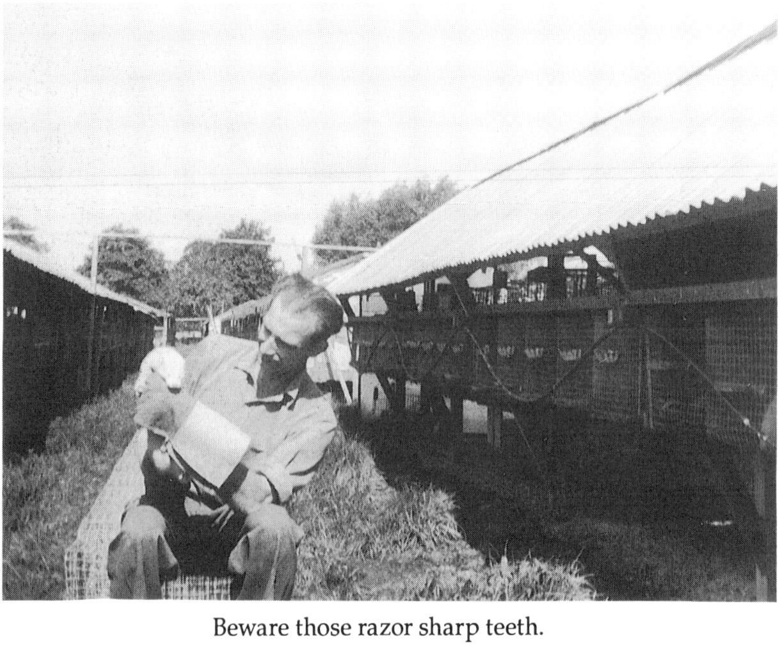

Beware those razor sharp teeth.

Fun and games with my tame female mink, without gloves.

Mink kits in playful and inquisitive mood.

A far cry from the efficient vicious killers they grow up to be.

58 Rack End, Standlake in the mid 1990s, a far cry from the original no. 2 Rack End of the Mid 1960s.

Man and Dog shed builders in snowy 1967.

Latter-day entrepreneur, breeding rabbits for meat.

A proud Mum, Irene Pitt on daughter Gill and Bert's Wedding Day.

Forklift driving at Stephensons of Oxford 1984.

Fun in the garden with Yvonne Coombs, nephew David and niece Carolyn Bumfrey.

The happy family day when my erstwhile errand girl Jackie Pitt became Mrs. Michael Probert.

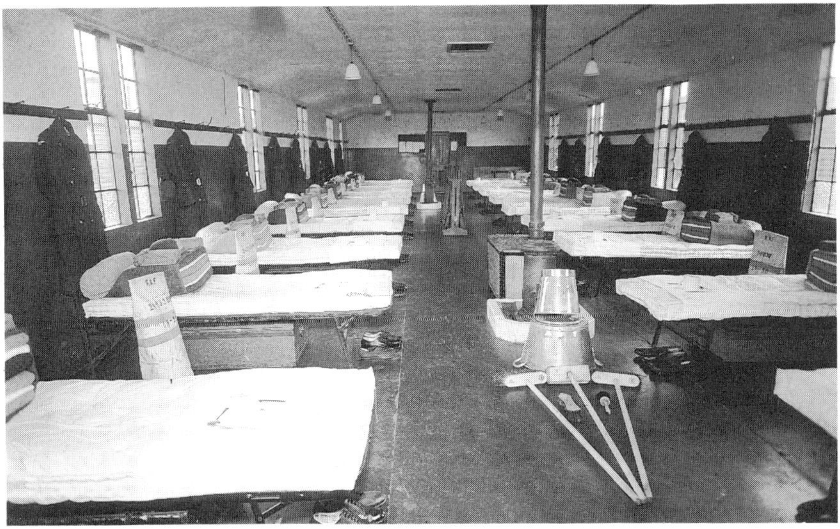

R.A.F. memories revived outside R.A.F. Feltwell. Above: the dreaded billet inspection, Hednesford 1951.

R.A.F. Police on parade, left to right: Sgt. Mann, Cpl. Mills, Station Adjutant, Cpl. Stanton and Cpl. Bumfrey, Feltwell Norfolk, 1953.

Westacre School and House, closed c.1950.

The "Wooden Hut", Westacre, now an estate office.

Westacre churchyard, family and friends – at rest.

The Historic Pedlar of Swaffham, carved by my late woodwork master, Harry Carter

The original Hamonds Grammar School, Swaffham.

Uncle Will's stable after 40 years of neglect. A large drinking tank originally stood by the door, Soigné Farm, 1997.

Entrance to the old horse and bullock yards where Will and Gipsy plied their trade.

Where now the pride in Modern Farming, my first visit to Soigné Farm for almost 40 years.

Rust and decay in all around.

Modern Farming implements.

Stables of yesteryear.

The corrugated iron bungalow was home to a family in the 1940's

It stands beside the A1065 just outside Swaffham as a stark reminder to some of us of the "good old days".

Duchess with the tip cart at Darkwood Farm fetching home firewood.

Returning from a summer time wagon ride with Ian Victor-Smith in the driving seat.

Back with horses, chain harrowing a pasture at an open day near Gloucester.

Ian Victor-Smith's Boxer and Punch taking a well earned breather, it was warm and I needed one as well.

The love of horses still brings with it hard work, brass cleaning for instance. The author outside Darkwood Farm Stable.

Or haymaking when the sun shines.

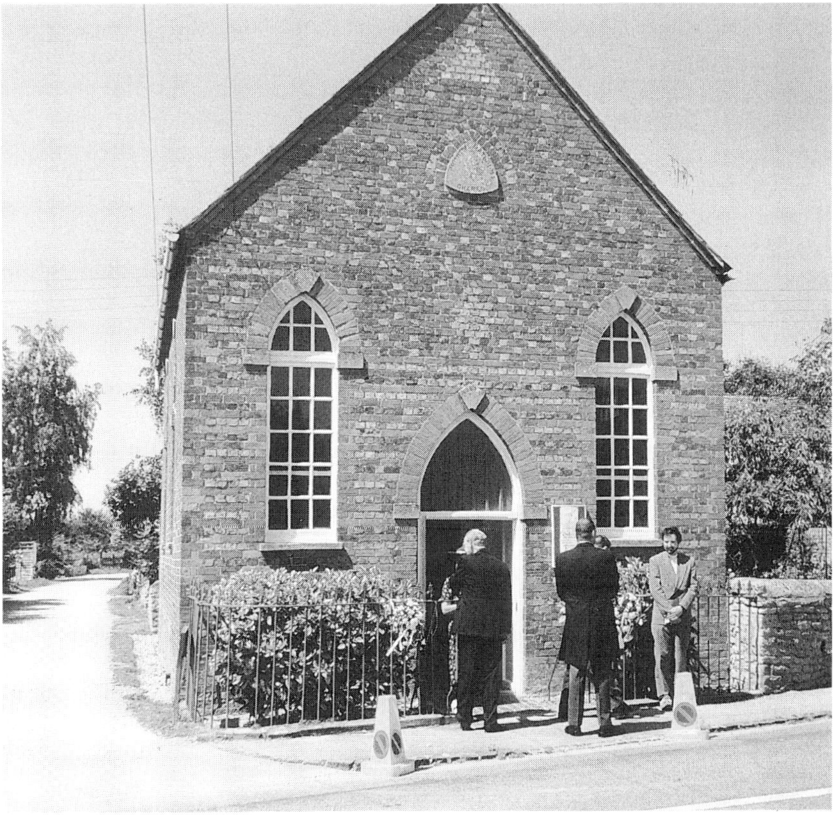

Waiting for the bride, Standlake Chapel's first wedding in 133 years.

The two hillbillies the author with Mark Probert as Norwich City fans who have "never seen a farmer on a bike", Christmas Party, 1998.

Chapter 14

Out of the Frying Pan and into the Fire

As I sit here on a New Year's day, looking back over almost forty years, and bearing in mind the last chapter recorded, there would seem to be a large amount of bitterness still left in my mind about those days. To write a true story of one's life, warts and all, it is very necessary not only to include your own warts but also those of other people, and let's face it, we all have plenty of those for life would be pretty bland without them. I count myself fortunate in that, by and large, this poison, built up over a number of years by repeatedly feeling the rough edge of life, has been drained away by influences from friends who always sought to see the best in people and who were not quite so prickly as myself. But to tell my story with real feeling, for the time being some more murky water must be stirred and bitter feuds uncovered, but hopefully not rekindled. As for my threatened revenges, well, as quoted in that wonderful play, Major Barbara, two black eyes do not make one white one. Anyway, I never really had time to get round to them.

We seemed always to be busy, working away at something and with no time to sit for hours watching T.V. Every vestige of daylight was precious, and was often extended by a light in the shed. After being one of the many helping with Bert's sewerage project, I began to enjoy getting involved with the ongoing work when long hours at the mink farm allowed. He built an extension on the back of his cottage which had to be a rather unusual shape owing to projecting pieces of neighbouring properties, his being a middle cottage in the row. We rushed over to Grove one weekend to rescue a roof of clay, handmade tiles, before the property was bulldozed down the following day. With these prizes he re-roofed the cottage. What a dust we raised in stripping the old, crumbling tiles off before felting. It was whilst we were creating all this mayhem that Gill's bike mysteriously disappeared. Having come down the street from one errand, she left her machine propped just inside the gate whilst statutory mugs of tea were made for the dusty gang. Wishing to go out again, she returned to the front only to find her bike missing. Coming to an obvious conclusion that one of us had hidden it, she began to harangue us for wasting her valuable time in childish pranks. When eventually we convinced her we had done no such thing, which took a while before she believed us, the mystery deepened. It was some time later, and after a considerable disruption to our work schedule, that a teacher from the Mulberry Bush special school returned the machine. One of their boys had run off for some reason, eventually being picked up in Eynsham, having procured a lady's cycle on the way. Of course, the much-relieved lady owner blamed Bert and his assembled labourers for not noticing the theft from their elevated position upon a scaffold. We could have pleaded dust in the eyes, but to our credit we just claimed to be too busy for gawping about.

During this period of roofing fever we also re-slated the end cottage for Mr. Townsend. I recall John Culley falling through a rotten rung of an antiquated ladder we were using. John, who always had a very slight, nervous shake, was even more shaken up. Mr. Townsend did go on, and rightly so, decreeing it should be sawn up for the fire, but, as we had no other means of reaching the scaffold, it soldiered on. This was before health and safety regulations came into force to help prevent we D.I.Y. pioneers from killing or maiming ourselves. Nonetheless, it was great fun, with Bert leading from the front, cap on one side, stripped to the waist and brown as a berry in summer. Fags went round like sweets, though not for me, gallons of tea quenched parched throats, and Gill's home- made cakes soon disappeared. Our leader was always on the lookout to upgrade anything in his property that was removable. On one occasion he accidentally cut through a pipe from the hot water tank, drenching himself and everything below in forty gallons of only lukewarm (luckily) water. To record the words his wife uttered, and names she called him whilst baling out the kitchen, would scorch the paper, so we will gloss over them. As an interested observer I found it quite an amusing spectacle, but kept my smiles to myself as I helped to mop up. At a much later date he had just driven a nail through a central heating pipe as Jackie's new boyfriend arrived to be introduced. After standing with his finger over the spouting leak until draining took place, it was a miracle he eventually married Jackie with a brother-in-law around like Bert. In reality, and joking aside, he was a wonderful man, and no family should be complete without one like him. His enthusiasm, which allowed him to attempt any task and succeed with most, was addictive. It helped to annul my fear of tackling even the simplest building job, although I had advanced somewhat from my Norfolk days when knocking a nail in straight would have taxed my limited skills.

Just one more story of the scores connected with Copanda Cottage. As mentioned, Bert was always on the lookout for any article going cheap which could be used to upgrade things in his home. In the first year or so he changed the living-room fireplace twice. When a closed-in Parkray stove, designed to heat water as well as normal duties, came along he could not resist the offer, and for a third time the semi-ingle-nook chimney breast was opened up. I clearly remember laying in the back of that opening trying to connect one of the joints, whilst Bert levered the heavy stove in an attempt to square it up. Dust and sweat caked our faces, as the connection just would not start. "Bert", I gasped, with my lungs full of long-dead ashes, "if you ever decide to change your fire again, let me know so that I can leave the country". If he made any other heating changes, he didn't tell me. This, however, was one of the happiest times in my life and, as it worked out, Bert would return my help a hundredfold in my yet another hour of need just around the corner – well, just down the road, to be exact.

I must not rush on, however, for life all round was enjoyable. We relished living in our bungalow. We three sat up until the early hours at the General Election to see Labour sweep to power. Mrs. Pitt regularly attended chapel, inviting me to go, but I was always too busy – shades of my father who, if you remember, was so vitally needed to milk cows that he could not attend my younger brothers' christenings. I never heard any reference to my own, so perhaps it never happened, though I doubt that somehow.

It was in this period that I attempted the impossible in trying to tame a mink. We had often played with kits for a short time until they became rough and began to use their sharp little teeth a mite too much, thus drawing blood. I chose a little, brown female from a nondescript family, and housed her alone. She was handled without gloves as many times a day as was possible. Often she slept in my pocket for hours at a time. Her favourite spot was deep in a leg pocket on the front of a pair of ex-army trousers I wore. It was a favourite trick of ours to engage visitors in conversation, and then gently poke her awake. Imagine the look of horror on their faces as a little, brown head with pink nose and black, beady eyes, suddenly popped out into the light. They thought at first it was a figment of their imagination. She was very well behaved, and never disgraced herself in my pocket or about my person as she ran around my neck, and often in summer had a trip around my open shirt, above the waist I would hasten to add. Tales of ferrets in other people's trousers were one thing, but mink inside mine was a party trick I never contemplated, thank you. The little creature remained tame for almost the year round before to me the novelty wore off, and her breeding instincts caused me to resume the norm and keep at least a glove between her teeth and my hands. She never returned to full integration with her fellows and was semi-tame, and in no fear of being pelted. At Christmas, Mrs. Pitt had a mink tie, and Jackie a hair band made from home-produced fur, which were much-appreciated presents from Gillian. Judy had a mink stole as part of her going away outfit after her wedding in New College chapel, an event we were privileged to attend as guests. Yes, life was good and our present position seemed almost worth all the trauma of the past couple of years.

Jackie and I have good cause to remember the morning when news of Winston Churchill's death came through. Mrs. Pitt was suffering from a bout of flu, and had, for a wonder, decided to take advice and stay in bed. We two deputies had taken over breakfast duties and were preparing to cook ourselves eggs and bacon. As the announcer read the news over the radio, we were of course shocked, as was the whole nation. Off we both went to carry the details to our stricken comrade, as if she hadn't enough to contend with herself. On the return journey through the bungalow our steps quickened as fear gripped us. There was a fire in the kitchen. We had left the pan with fat in it on the electric cooker and it had caught fire and was making a good job of changing the colour of our kitchen from sunburst to murky black. Seizing a cloth, I flung the pan outside and opened doors and windows.

"What's going on out there?", questioned a croaky voice from the bedroom.

"Nothing Mum", lied Jackie, quickly closing the internal door and thus preventing the smell permeating the whole house.

Needless to say, we abandoned all thoughts of cooked breakfast, needing all our time to clean walls and ceiling before our temporary invalid rose to find us guilty of negligence and perjury in covering the crime. When the truth came out, as truth always does, we were again accused of colluding to pervert the course of justice, as we had been over the apple tree/broken arm situation. In our defence, we pleaded that we did not want to cause her concern whilst indisposed, and that we had made a valiant attempt to restore the kitchen to its original condition. On the question of restitution regarding the ruined frying pan, well, "we" had to dip into "my pocket" and buy a new one of equal heavy duty standard. Winston may have led us to victory in the war, but he caused us some hassle with his passing.

One memory from Jackie's illustrious past which she recalls was in the low-ceilinged, old cottage, where Mother was preparing food on the living room table. One imagines Jackie had been causing trouble, and as a last threat her exasperated parent grabbed an empty milk bottle to make a mock gesture of hitting her with it. Instead it crashed into the low strip-light tube above Mrs. Pitt's already bursting head, sending shards of glass everywhere including into the food being prepared. Whether the extravagant gesture had the desired effect in silencing the rioting child, I don't know, but the memory has stayed with her ever since. Much the same effect on memory happened with Mark, Jackie's son, many years later when he had a mini-riot and succeeded in upsetting his Nan's jigsaw puzzle.

Quick as a flash, her walking stick made contact with his fleeing behind, registering a moment he never fails to recall when misbehaviour is mentioned. Jigsaw puzzles were treated with great respect after that, at least when Nan was doing them.

An unexplained wasting disease seemed to be on the increase among mink on most farms. The popular theory was that dirty boxes used year on year helped spread this affliction, so steps were taken by Gillian to clean the place up. Steam-cleaning techniques were used on large establishments, but were expensive for smaller units. We decided to set up a long, narrow tank of water on bricks, and heat the water by means of a Calor gas burner underneath. The boxes were then boiled, thus softening the grease deposited by mink fur, and allowing it to be scrubbed off by hand. The whole set up resembled something designed by Heath Robinson for the devil's workshop, but it was relatively effective. We spent many winter days scrubbing and repairing boxes. Teddy was good company, always regaling me with some tale or other. He had a little, grey van, which he used to go into Witney one evening a week to take lessons in the Catholic faith in preparation for marriage to a young lady of that religious persuasion, still at her home in the north-east. On his first visit he had addressed the lady who answered his knock as the priest's wife. His limited knowledge of Catholic priesthood was soon expanded by the man in question who curtly told him of his celibacy, the lady being his spinster sister. A good start, Ted!

We all went together to the fair on Witney Feast night. Arriving in daylight, we parked our cars a few yards apart, and went to enjoy ourselves. When we left the bright lights of the fair, in pouring rain, and tried to find our vehicles in a large field without the aid of a torch, the real fun began. My car, being black, was a no hoper, whilst Teddy's grey van wasn't much better. Eventually, after much cursing, interspersed with fits of the giggles, Ted fell over his van more by luck than anything else. By the help of his headlights, we located the Morris, and climbed aboard. I think we had more laughs blundering around in the dark than we did at the fair.

Our light-hearted life was unfortunately destined to be too good to last, and when the axe fell it knocked all our lives off balance and our plans for six, as the saying goes. When Gillian broke the news to me that the mink farm had to close down by the end of the year, I was totally gutted, as she was herself. It just wasn't paying its way, and with the over- production of mink pelts depressing prices on world markets, the outlook was bleak. The only hope her father had was to pelt out the whole stock and cut his losses before the financial situation became even worse. Ted was to go, just before his proposed wedding after which, I suppose, the young couple had planned to live in Oxfordshire. To say I was devastated was a gross understatement. I stood and looked around contemplating all the work we two, Gillian and I, had ploughed into this venture almost from day one. Every shed, cage, box, and animal held a personal touch, and now it was all to go. It just didn't bear thinking about, and for the moment I could only think of the work side of things.

It was later that the whole picture came home to roost. No job meant no house. Within eighteen months of grasping a saving straw on the sea of life we were being cast adrift once more. Our happy time had been short-lived, but at least we could hope all was not lost, and that I would be allowed to rent the bungalow. My tentative enquiries on this subject were met with equally evasive answers.

Suddenly the pace of life changed. From looking forward to a busy pelting season and planning which animals to keep as breeding stock, there was now no future. An abyss, dark and threatening, lay beyond Christmas. We went about our work almost as robots. Nothing had purpose any more. At home spirits were just as low, and I felt somewhat responsible for leading my two friends into the awful hell of the tied house syndrome about which I, of all people, should have been aware.

Without enthusiasm plans were made to begin the final harvest. The closedown advertisement brought some other farmers to buy selected animals, in order to improve their own stock. In the main we just took the animals as their fur became prime, until all cages, except for the last one, became empty. My pet remained the sole survivor, and lived on in the garden at Maerda, with a cage on legs as her home. Gillian offered to get me a job with a large Scottish farm, but I was not for moving away.

Major Browne, who had a smaller concern at Finstock, was keen for me to join him, and after considering whether to continue in a trade fast becoming uncertain in its future, I agreed to his terms. The distance to travel was less than my jaunt to Cowley, although Finstock lay on the other side of Witney. Situated on the very edge of the Cotswolds, it was very picturesque, the mink farm nestling in the bottom of a steep valley. Major Browne and his wife ran the farm, with one full-time, young girl, Judy, and a part-time, married lady, Sue, as well.

It seemed very strange at first to work in a capacity where I was not virtually in charge. My first days there were taken up in organising the box-cleaning tank, which had moved with me from Standlake. I had nothing to do with the animals at all as the youngest assistant did all feeding. After all boxes had been put through the sterilising treatment, my next assignment was even more removed from the animals I had been hired to care for. This involved erecting a post and wire fence around an adjoining hillside pasture in which cattle would be grazed. Visions of long gone days at Soigné came to mind, when Leslie Lloyd and I dug the deep hole for that notorious gate post. The limestone subsoil took some shifting, but my long, iron bar, purchased in such haste from Witney after losing two in two days on frozen fish lorries, came to my aid. Another help was a bag of cement which we mixed with gravel to hold the posts firm. I wondered what Barney Hooks and his Norfolk traditionalists would have said to that modern short cut. It was nice to be out in fresh air, and on grass as well. The view from the top of that field was magnificent, and chats with an elderly gentleman, who farmed a very small holding next door, were illuminating. I found later that he still cut his corn with a binder, which filled me with hope of seeing it all happen when August came round.

When I did eventually get my nose inside the actual mink pens, I noted, with some apprehension, the amount of food being given out to the animals. Often, old food had to be removed from cage tops before new was spooned on the next day. From our experience at Standlake this should never have been necessary when pre-mating measures were being taken to slim the animals. As no such policy was seriously undertaken here, the young feeder had no reason to appear cruel, in her own eyes, and restrict the intake of food during cold weather. On the few occasions when I fed, half the allocated food came back, and I was the centre of quizzical looks, which silently questioned my suitability to do the job. I felt very uncomfortable and in limbo. Despite this, the company was cheerful, and Major Browne a genuine gentleman whose word was his bond.

The shed layout consisted of one, long, open-sided building, with cages on each side of a central walkway. A higher, and much wider, second shed lay at the bottom, where the ground widened out. This resembled, and in fact was, a type of Dutch barn, with several rows of cages, with quite restricted light in the centre. A brick-built mincing shed, and deep freeze store stood at the entrance to the sheds, and a second building held dry food and was our lunch shelter. In severe weather my biggest worry was the journey out of the valley and up on to the Charlbury to Witney road. Often, heavy snow at Finstock had turned into rain at the lower levels of Standlake by the time I eventually reached home.

My Sunday working had become quite a rare event now, which gave me more time at home. Unfortunately, the bounce had gone out of our lives as any forward planning was only temporary. I paid a rent for the bungalow, but this was only an interim measure. No rent book was involved, and it remained a tied house, with me under notice to remove myself as soon as possible. There was no question of my new employer providing housing. He had no property, and anyway, I would not have moved to Finstock for a trade that was on the decline, or to another tied property. The latest bite was one too many, and I had no intention of being bitten again.

If a word or two of explanation on tied houses are needed, then let me explain. Throughout the agricultural world farmers almost always provided their men with a place to live. Single men often lived together in a communal bothy, or as lodgers in the farmhouse itself. This, of course, I had done myself when I first came to the Manor. Married men were given cottages, at very low rents, as part of their contract of employment. This system worked well to a degree in that workers could move from village to village, house to house, farm to farm, with only personal possessions to remove. The big drawback came on the worker's side, for, in the cases of death, injury or disagreement affecting the breadwinner, thus breaking the labour contract, the incumbent technically became homeless. The owner required his house for another replacement worker, that worker required a house, and the law was very firmly on the owner's side. This situation led to many sad and unsavoury evictions, such as described earlier. The N.U.A.W. had fought hard and long for the abolition of this very feudal system, but with no government backing. Slight changes to the law meant that, by appearing in court and being supported by a Union lawyer, one could gain time to find alternative accommodation, but never a complete justification for staying in the property because that was against the law as it stood. At least the owner couldn't take the law into his own hands and evict families whilst the bailiffs had to be issued with a court order to move in. All this I knew only too well, and had drilled into me when I had the distasteful task of meeting with my ex-employer in order to pay rent monthly.

Although we explored every avenue, nothing turned up, apart from a council consideration of possibly re-housing Mrs. Pitt and Jackie, but my position, as a would-be lodger in those circumstances, was not an allowable option. All this before any alternative housing had been offered. Mrs. Pitt, to her credit, decreed that we would either sink or swim together, thus closing that avenue of escape. As the weeks passed and the impasse continued, feelings between myself and Mr. Spilman became, understandably, more strained, until eventually I was summoned to attend Witney court to defend my case of unlawfully occupying Maerda, which was fast becoming a nightmare – perhaps one way of describing "a dream" backwards. Major Browne was aghast, and would have gladly paid a higher rent to me as part of the job, but no, the law must continue on its way until myself and my belongings were out, even on to the roadside if necessary.

A kind person, not removed a hundred miles from the other side and living in secure accommodation, so comfortably said to me, "Don't get involved too deeply with it; just leave it to the solicitors as it's nothing against you personally". I suppose that is what the judge thought, as the two solicitors made a show of fighting each other in court and then, at the lunch adjournment, almost linked arms to go off for a pint. From those observations I held no hopes of success, and was not surprised when his most learned upholder of British law which is founded on the age-old principle of he who has the most money and influence always wins, gave Eric Wallis Spilman his lawful right to his bungalow in two months' time.

On the very few occasions of late that I had blessed the chapel with my presence, I sat looking up out of the window suggesting to God that the only solution was for me to win a substantial amount on the treble chance football pools, which I did every week. With this proposed money, won by divine guidance, I could buy a house, and we could live happily ever after. If God really was on the side of the oppressed, as was suggested by the droning voice delivering a sermon, then what simpler solution did He need. Now, with only eight Saturdays' fixtures left, the jackpot was urgently required. But, if ever the Bible quotation, "My ways are not your ways, and My thoughts not your thoughts", a quotation which, at that time, I had never even heard of, came to bear upon a human problem, then it was now.

Smarting with humiliation after my setback at court, which came on an official document dated 27 July, 1966, giving possession of Maerda, High Street, Standlake, to Eric Wallis Spilman on the 27th day of September, 1966, I was ready to fight the bailiffs with whatever I could lay my hands on, and probably the axe earlier recorded in the hands of Eric Kharl. Don't then, for one moment, think I had turned all religious, for I felt nearer to rebels such as Wat Tyler and Robert Kett, as I was pushed more and more into a corner, and was prepared to fight to the end by whatever means, in an effort to keep a roof over myself and my two friends. When a human is pushed to the limit, as I was, there are no two sides to a question, and certainly no right or wrong. I don't believe the reason for my late employer wishing to regain his property was in any way vindictive, for he wasn't a vindictive man, but I was in no mood to even contemplate his side of the equation. The battle lines were drawn now, and there was a distinct probability that blood would be spilled, and not only in the metaphorical sense.

Well, if God really did mean to take a hand, as I firmly believe He, or whatever divine being who looks after us did at that time, He moved in a mysterious way, His wonders to perform. The following Sunday afternoon I was in the garden, having refused Mrs. Pitt's offer to join the tiny chapel congregation, when Alice Knipe called in. She told me that earlier she had been down to their orchard field at the bottom of Rack End and, by chance, met the doctor who owned the semi-detached cottage known as No. 2, Rack End. It was used as a weekend retreat from his working home in London. It appeared he was contemplating selling in the near future. Our critical situation immediately came to Alice's mind, and without further ado she returned to tell me about it. Hopping into my car, I sped to Rack End, parked in the grassy recreation field, and quickly sought out my quarry. Entering the garden, for want of a better word, for it was head-high in grass and weeds, I could hear voices, and eventually found two men enjoying tea in a clearing half way towards the tall trees at the bottom. I explained about Mrs. Knipe who, as it turned out, we both knew well, and the Doctor confirmed the fact that he wished to sell. The price was to be £2,200. I promised to spend the coming week checking financial possibilities, and he suggested I obtained the key from his neighbour and have a good look over the property at my leisure, before deciding to make a serious bid. Thanking him for his helpful suggestions, I retired to consider and discuss the momentous opportunity which had so suddenly come my way. Mrs. Pitt, who had returned from chapel to find me missing, was as gob-smacked as I was at the turn of events, and set off the few yards down the road to thank Alice for thinking of us. They were, of course, friends of many years' standing, and Mrs. Pitt had tried previously to rent a wooden bungalow situated in Chapel Lane and owned by Alice and Cyril Knipe. Unfortunately, the land had to be sold and the bungalow demolished in order to fund work on the stone house they were renovating for their own use next door to their family farm, so that idea, like so many more, had failed at the outset. But, at last, real hope came into sight, though only as a tiny shoot. So many problems rose up around it, threatening to choke it at birth. But, when problems beset us, to whom did we always turn for help? You've guessed – Bert Coombs, of course, and that is where I turned on this occasion.

On acquainting my friend with the new turn of events, I found him both enthusiastic and encouraging. We collected the key and examined the little cottage from all angles, Bert with his builder's expert eye, and myself from the possibilities of it housing three people all with individual requirements. One good-sized living room, containing the front door which opened in from the road and a back door, covered by a tin porch, took most of the ground floor. A narrow kitchen, with a sink under a small, south-facing window, completed that level. Narrow, twisting stairs led up from this room to a small landing with a large bedroom straight ahead. The second room upstairs had been halved to provide a bathroom and toilet, but this only left what might well be called a wide passage for a second bedroom. It all seemed awfully cramped after the open spaces of the bungalow. Headroom was adequate, except for the lower stairs where Bert managed to knock his cap sideways before learning where to duck the head. He opined the building was very well constructed, with thick, stone walls and red-tiled roof. Getting really into his stride, and waving his arms around like mill sails, he outlined plans for knocking this out here, and putting a door in there, until my head spun. With a final flourish, an extension was built at the back, and in Bert's eye the job was complete. What frightened me most was the oft repeated phrase, "You can do this, and you can do the other", when I knew I could do nothing of the sort. Buying a house terrified me, let alone almost rebuilding it to suit my needs, and after spending all and more of my money at the outset.

"Hang on a minute, Bert", I managed to gasp out, as his enthusiastic flow checked for a moment. "I know nothing about building."

Taking a long drag on his cigarette, he considered the situation, before voicing another opinion, whilst I waited with bated breath. On his reply the whole rescue operation depended, and I could not expect him to take on more building after all the work he had done and still had to do on his own cottage.

"Get it bought if you can, and then we'll get over it", was all he said, and when he used the word "we" he meant what he said.

He was the biggest part of that "we", as events would show when the time came. I could never repay him for his practical advice and support throughout this most difficult and crucial time of my life, let alone for his tradesman's skills later.

I went home to report our findings with a spring in my step. As Bert had suggested, I put the fears generated by all the alterations needed behind me, and made scant comment of them to Mrs. Pitt. She had enough worries as it was, but, like me, she trusted Bert's judgement implicitly, and if he said the cottage was a sound investment then it was. Without doubt, he was right on all counts, but there were to be a few heart-stopping moments before we finally entered our Promised Land, not least of all our severe lack of money.

Chapter 15

The Promised Land

As just intimated, money, or the lack of it, was initially our biggest stumbling block. In the days to which I refer £2,200 was a huge amount of money to ordinary, working people, of which I was one. Although I had a small nest egg, it would only make a fraction of the required sum, and so a mortgage seemed the only answer. Enquiries made with normal mortgage lenders met with polite refusals when wage rates were disclosed. It quickly became clear that not only were agricultural workers trapped by the tied house laws, but their low wages set by a wages board precluded them from obtaining a mortgage in order to escape.

With every financial door seemingly shut in my face, a lifeline was thrown by the District Council. In a flush of available money, and subsidised by the Labour government, low-interest mortgages were on offer to extreme cases which were refused by normal sources in the private sector. After a couple of nail-biting interviews, my case was approved, although only for a percentage, obviously, of the full amount. It would need a severe belt tightening to make up the deficit. When all the paper work had been completed, the sum required per month as repayment was £10.0s 7d. My heart stopped; how ever would I afford to pay all that and live? Never having borrowed money before, or since as a matter of fact, the idea sent shivers down my spine, but needs must when the devil drives, as the saying goes.

Despite all the worries, and I did worry over every little twist and turn for anything of which I had no previous experience turned me to jelly, the situation at last seemed to be working out. Admittedly every step forward went at a snail's pace, whereas the two months' stay of execution raced away in double-quick time. I applied to the N.U.A.W. for their solicitor to seek, on my behalf, another court hearing, thus allowing me more time to remove. After numerous frantic phone calls right up to the last day, thanks to Major Browne, my employer, the gentleman in question did move himself to reapply to the judiciary, although he expressed his opinion that such a move was a waste of time and money. To say I was livid was an understatement, and I told him, in no uncertain manner, that as a fully paid member since leaving school, it was my money being spent and me who was on the verge of eviction. Feeling completely drained, I sincerely thanked the Major for the use of his telephone, for which he would accept no payment. He expressed extreme embarrassment for the whole distasteful situation, although of course if was not of his making.

As we sat uneasily over the next few days, still half-fearing a sudden appearance of bailiffs, despite having been officially informed of the suspension, we were completely unprepared for two severe reversals of luck coming our way. The first was an appearance at the weekend by the owner of no. 2 Rack End, who uncomfortably told me that another potential buyer for his property had offered him £100 more than I had, and so it needed consideration. If he had punched me in the stomach I couldn't have felt more sick; in fact, it took quite a physical effort not to vomit over his shoes. I could have been the first person to use the phrase, "completely gutted". Feeling that I was being conned, but without any strength to fight back, I managed to blurt out words indicating that I would pay the extra £100, but any more increases would mean the end of negotiations as there was no more money available. I didn't add the simple fact of this £100 not being there either. As he walked out of the gate, proud, I was sure, of having squeezed an extra drop of blood out of an already dry stone, my very low opinion of those with money and education, who took every opportunity to depress life for those less fortunate in order to gain for themselves, dropped below zero. Staggering indoors like a beaten boxer to his corner, I put the latest setback to my loyal friend who, as always, produced that uplifting cup of tea and put as upbeat a slant on things as was possible. It can't get any worse, was her phlegmatic summing up, but for once fate seemed set to prove her wrong, but only for a short time.

Being dependent on earning as much as possible prior to the exchange of money for property made me very aware of my need to keep physically fit. Never before had the labourer's Achilles heel of sickness crossed my mind. My health and physique had always been taken for granted, a state to which I was entitled as a God-given right. A sudden slip and heavy fall on to my wrist was a shock. Even more shocking was the confirmation that my right wrist was broken, and when encased in plaster, would restrict my working capacity somewhat. Of all the unfortunate times to break the first bone in one's body. I certainly couldn't afford to go on the panel, so, fervently hoping no further damage would be done, I soldiered on with one arm and a bit. At least it got me back to feeding mink as that was one job I could manage left-handed. After practice I found many more were added, and I became quite adroit at working left-handed.

The second court hearing before a judge, was set to be held in Oxford, at the beginning of October. Fearing the worst, but hoping for the best, I set off for my ordeal, standing in the dock accused of law-breaking in that I unlawfully occupied a dwelling owned by Eric Wallis Spilman in the village of Standlake. Although I felt defiant as I prepared myself for the full weight of the law to descend upon me, I suppose I presented rather a pathetic figure with my arm in a sling and not the best of well-cut suits. None of this was intentional, but there is a certain difficulty in getting one's jacket over a heavy plaster. The judge heard Mr. Spilman's solicitor tell the heart-rending story of how his client needed the bungalow to move into as the Manor had to be sold to meet urgent financial commitments to others. The whole deal depended on immediate sale, and was an integral part of a chain of property sales. The learned judge would have been excused if a tear had trickled down his cheek at the sad tale recounted by my opponent's brief. To give my opposite number his due, he produced a very plausible case, which sent my heart and hopes into my boots. I visualised our furniture outside the gate, covered by a rick sheet to protect it from the weather, and we three souls homeless for six weeks. Six weeks was the estimated time which would elapse before exchange of contracts could be made between myself and the present owner of Dunmore, No. 2, Rack End. This was clearly put to the judge by the Union representative speaking on my behalf. He also stressed my disability with the broken wrist, a point I would never even have considered as helpful to my case, and I was quite unaware that it would be used. In fact I almost felt embarrassed by its use, but was soon to learn of its significance. As it was used, the judgement went as far as was possible in my favour. How could my ex-employer even contemplate turning a temporarily one-armed man, a widowed housekeeper and her young daughter out of a house when only six weeks' grace would solve the problem amicably? November 14th was the date set, exactly six weeks hence, by which time I was to give up the property to its lawful owner. Did my ears deceive me? Did I hear aright? Was this the rich man's law, so roundly condemned by me only a few weeks before, showing a heart to the hard pressed peasant? My feet hardly touched the ground as we walked from the court. There were many bridges to cross before those six weeks were out, but we had been given a lifeline by the grace of God. No other explanation could be construed, for the solicitor was as surprised as I was myself at the success of his strategy. My surprises, however, were not over for, as we walked outside, my late employer and work companion over many happy hours turned from a conversation with his solicitor to display such an out of character side of him that I was rendered speechless. Snarling at me, he openly accused me of making my injury out to be worse than it was, almost intimating I had donned the plaster as a ploy to defeat him. Having not said a word in court myself about it, I felt his accusations to be more than unjust. Thankfully for both him and me the plaster wasn't a fake for, had it been, there is no doubt it would have flown off as my fist felt an uncontrollable urge to crash into his contorted face. Thanks to the quick-thinking action of the solicitor, who pulled me very forcibly away, no serious harm was done. We two would-be combatants growled away like a pair of frustrated dogs, realising later that an unseemly, ugly brawl outside the law courts would have done our reputations very little good. In the short-term, that skirmish forced what little friendship we had left to disappear completely, and we never passed another word during the short time the Spilman family remained in Standlake. In later years I liked to think the uncharacteristic outburst was caused by financial worry, a result of losses incurred by the mink business failure.

Several years later, Gillian visited us in our new abode, and on her insistence, we visited her father, now a widower, at his home on Boars Hill, Oxford. It was a visit of reconciliation for which I'm sure both sides felt the better. There had been too much friendship in the past for bitterness, due to circumstances really beyond our control, to be carried to the grave. With both his daughters married, Dick lived alone, and gave us a laugh with his early efforts at cooking. Starting with simple stewed apple, he had neglected to peel and core them, finishing with a mind-boggling mess of pips and hard lumps. Mrs. Pitt's soft heart went out to him, and had she been within cycling distance, she would have provided him with succulent meals such as he had enjoyed in bygone days when she cooked at the Manor. We never mentioned our past disagreements, which have lain buried until now. He, I suspect, was driven on at the time by financial advisors and solicitors, whilst I had to fight tooth and nail through sheer necessity to survive. The two things that aggrieved me at the time were the fact that I had to pay his court costs, and that the bungalow stood empty for a long time after my eviction date and subsequent removal had taken place. There was a great temptation to return at dead of night in order to smash all the windows, but it never happened. I must record it was not my better self that prevailed, but sheer fatigue at the end of each long and tiring day.

Having gone on ahead much too quickly for the sake of this story, now let us return to the time when I drove back from Oxford, in a fairly cheerful mood, to tell my fellow condemned prisoners of conscience about our temporary reprieve. Tea was a meal taken in celebratory mood, and even if our battles weren't over we felt as if the worst was past, which in fact it was. Some financial juggling was called for, as there can be difficulty in stretching an empty purse beyond its limits. Major Browne presented me with the excess £100 needed to cover the gazumping that had been sprung upon me, on the pretext that it was owed to me as rent unpaid in wages over my time with him. I believe it was a gift from a gentleman to me in my time of need, and yes, it came as an absolute Godsend. Even to the last, our nerves were over-stretched, as the doctor could not get down from London until two days after the court order expiry date to move out, and we had to beg those extra days from the clerk of the court. Consumed with worry and frustration, at 3 p.m. on the second and last day of our concession, we stood on the doorstep awaiting the all clear to come in as the last of the Doctor's furniture disappeared through a hole in the hedge and into next door, which he had purchased.

As I stepped on to the bare, concrete floor of my own living room, the thought struck me that I, a member of the Bumfrey family so long chained in tied houses, had at last broken those shackles and become a property owner in my own right. Through hell and high water I had come, but at last here I was, a totally free man, a slave no more. Unfortunately I had no more than a moment to savour the thought before practical urgency took over for at 3 p.m. on a windy November afternoon there is precious little daylight left for romantic musings, however historic the event may be. Andy Andrews, a friend from Tackley, had brought Major Browne's pickup truck in order to transport our worldly goods. Jean, Mrs. Pitt's eldest daughter, was sweeping out the house. Gill, her second daughter, who was expecting her first baby, was banned by her mother from taking part for fear she lifted too much, thus causing injury to herself or baby. This was a big loss to the moving gang, for Gill's zest for work and in-built knowledge of how to work would have been invaluable, but Mother's word was law and had to be obeyed. Bert was into the fray immediately he returned from work, as was John soon afterwards. The wind blew through the open doors, and down the chimney sending ashes over Jean's newly-swept floor, and generally made much nuisance as only wind can. A loose trolley- top took off, cracking Bert on the head, and dislodging his famous cap, sending it behind the missile spinning into darkness down the road – a little light relief for us all, except Bert perhaps, who was left feeling the new bump of knowledge rising on the side of his cranium. More than half the furniture lay on the garden, covered by a large, waterproof sheet held down by stones. There was no way to get a quart into a pint pot, for the bungalow had been twice the size of our tiny cottage, and we had bought additional items to furnish it. At our leisure, we would choose what to keep as furnishings for our new abode, and what to sell in order to raise badly-needed cash. At last the chaos subsided, and weary bodies relaxed over a cup of tea. Gill came to join us as Mother's banishment of her was relaxed, the lifting done for one day, thank goodness. What a huge burden had lifted from my shoulders as the keys to the bungalow dropped through the Manor letterbox. The end of our dream-turned-nightmare, a book closed, a new dawn for Derek Bumfrey, property owner in this parish of Standlake.

Bone-weary bodies dragged themselves home against the gale, with my sincere thanks being their only payment, and I'm sure this was the only reward they would have accepted. Jackie was worn out by all the excitement and we other two seasoned professionals in life were just so relieved to be home at last that we felt like weeping. No words could describe my feelings after all the trauma of past months. We had survived as a unit under one roof, and that along with being left alone to live our lives in the way we wanted was all we asked of life.

Two beds had been hastily put up for Jackie and her mother in the large bedroom, and my single bed was placed in the narrow, passage-like second room. There was no space to walk down the side of my bed. To enter it meant walking along the bed itself, but that was of no consequence to me. I could have walked on, or even slept on, a bed of nails, I felt so tired. It was lights out all round in double quick time.

After about a week we found most of our equipment where it had been hastily thrust in the hectic move. The funny, little kitchen seemed very strange, after the large one at the bungalow, but Mrs. Pitt was soon turning out lovely meals from it, despite cramped conditions. Larger pieces of bedroom furniture were taken to pieces in order to negotiate the narrow, twisting stairs. Much swearing and laughing alternated from Bert and myself as we struggled, pinched fingers and cracked heads, whilst trying to get wardrobes and dressing tables above stairs. Items were hauled out from under the rick sheet, and others crammed back underneath. Oh, what fun we had with torches in the last dark days of that year when I tried to cope with getting things straight and pelting mink at Finstock. I owed it to Major Browne, who had been so good to me, to put in as much time as possible, and the money earned was crucial. My wrist had been out of plaster for some little time, and apart from an initial stiffness, it was none the worse for its inactivity. Mrs. Pitt was already making plans for a house-warming at Christmas, and Bert was working out ideas for the proposed extension, which must be started on no money in the spring.

My first job, after pelting had been completed, was to plan and build a substantial shed in order to get my pile of surplus furniture and miscellaneous objects under permanent cover. This project I enjoyed, as did our Corgi dog who spent hours with me down at the bottom of the garden. Being a shed builder of some wide experience, for once the work held no terrors, and I could enjoy myself. Constructing my own shed, on my own ground, was like a drug to me, and I spent every hour of daylight in my new little world, savouring its delights. Mrs. Pitt did not neglect her little chapel, but once again I was much too busy to give thanks for my eventual good fortune. Using materials salvaged from my lean-to car shelter of yesteryear, I banged away with gay abandon, whether it was a weekday or the Lord's day. I was master of my own salvation now, and I needed to build up my empire. Jackie also rebelled against accompanying her mother, except under protest, and would have much rather spent the hour passing me nails or playing with her dog, Pepie. Remember the time she had been propelled to Sunday School after falling from the apple tree?

My Morris 1000 now stood on the roadside bank, under the front window, as the cottage had only a side gate entrance. I recall having to cover the engine with an old coat to prevent damp penetrating electrical parts and thus causing bad starting. On one occasion I had just passed Witney when I realised it was still under the bonnet. A hasty check revealed a very warm, outer garment on the verge of conflagration. After that, a note was always stuck on the dashboard, "Please remove coat from engine". In later years, as the road became increasingly busy, and a footpath had been needfully constructed so restricting my frontage to a narrow, eighteen inch garden, parking was impossible on such a sharp bend, so I rented a garage, firstly from Mrs. Druce, and later from George Caswell. George lived almost opposite, with his wife, Ada, in a cottage that ran end-on to the road, with a garden through to the river. When I first came to Standlake there were several allotment gardens between long-established properties in Rack End, but slowly these had been sold as building land. All the bungalows existing now are part of this infill. Half way down this road, where large houses now stand, open pasture with grazing cattle gave a more rural look to the village. It was the advent of these more expensive properties that caused Rack End to become Oxford Road for a short time, its newly- acquired opulence demanding an upmarket name. It didn't take very long before the older residents in our part of the village rebelled against this trend, thus forcing the parish council to put up road signs stating categorically that we lived in Rack End. I wonder what the posh incomers of that period would have thought of the name, "Rats Hall", where my Grandfather Bumfrey had brought his family to reside. I don't suppose they worried about such things in darkest Norfolk.

George Caswell, already mentioned, was steward at the Methodist Chapel, and often called in to chat to "May", as he called Mrs. Pitt. George was profoundly deaf, and a real Oxfordshire character. He had driven a lorry for Tarrants of Witney, grocery wholesalers, in the early days of road transport. His delivery round was up into the Cotswolds, and he had some tales to tell of hair-raising, winter journeys. He once walked about five miles in order to get a farming friend, who owned an early-day, rubber-tyred tractor, to tow the lorry out of a ditch. He was a great-hearted man who would do a good turn for anyone. If the preacher decided to omit a verse or two from a long hymn, and George didn't hear the instructions, he would sing straight on, until a poke in the back from Mrs. Pitt stopped him in full flow. After a hurried rectification, off he would go again, for with only a single figure congregation, he had to lead the singing. Yes, it was dangerous to omit any verses when preaching at Standlake. Ted Wilkins from Bampton told me he was leading the service one day when the old tortoise stove began to smoke. Eventually the room became so full of smoke, the door was barely visible from the pulpit. George, in his capacity of steward and chief stoker, lifted the lid causing more smoke and smuts to belch out into the already polluted atmosphere. A gasping Ted suggested an adjournment, and the sparse congregation coughed and spluttered their way outside, whilst George opened the sash windows before giving the wretched stove another good riddling. With a better drawing fire, and a less smoky atmosphere, they duly returned to business, and, after blowing a thick covering of sooty residue off his notes, Ted finished his sermon. Such were the vagaries of heating appliances when the wind blew from certain directions.

To return once more to my newly-acquired property at the very bottom of Rack End, we enjoyed our Christmas celebrations, with a good meal produced from the tiny kitchen. It was impossible to pass another person in it as, with a cooker on one side and a fridge on the other, the passage left was for standing room only. The open stairs leading off allowed steam and cooking smells to rise into the bedrooms. Like the chapel, our only fireplace smoked when the wind was due west, and it was only wide enough to hold a minimum amount of coal. The front door was splashed with mud from the road and opened into the living room. The back door opened on the other side into an old, tin porch, which rattled in any wind above a brisk speed. It was not a palace, and in fact it couldn't even be classed as a contender for that "Oxford Road" level of address. But to us it was home, our home, which couldn't be taken from us on a whim, just as long as we could pay the mortgage of £10 0s.7d per month.

During that first winter, all the battered board games came out – Ludo, snakes and ladders, draughts, as well as dominoes and cards. The old dog snored by the fire, and we enjoyed peace of mind, not allowing thoughts of all the work waiting to be tackled in the coming days to mar our family fun. I am sure that if none of the planned improvements had been possible, we would have made the best of what we had, and still been happy. Good health and peace of mind make the simplest things heaven, and it's a blessing to be thankful for small mercies.

Meanwhile Bert tackled the proposed plans for an extension, with the help of an architect friend for whom the former had carried out some work. On the strength of this, the plans were drawn up at no cost to me; I had little or no available money, but obviously my mate had paid in an indirect way. They were passed, with one or two minor adjustments, and consisted of a two storey, flat-roofed extension, with a kitchen below and bedroom above. Situated at the back of the Cotswold stone-built cottage, it could be constructed of brick or concrete block rendered in a neutral colour, this being as cheap a way as possible. Still being employed at Finstock for six days a week at least, my possible work time at home was at first restricted by lack of daylight. As the days lengthened, it was advantageous to work at both ends of my day. By rising before dawn it was possible to get at least an hour in before setting off to work. I recall digging away at footings just after 5 a.m. when the existing bedroom window opened above, showing the head of Mrs. Pitt demanding to know if I was mad trying to work twenty-four hours a day. Having got the bit between my teeth, and realising just how much others were doing for me, I felt it only right to do my best at those jobs I could manage alone. I had cut the overgrown garden down to a tidy length, and could tip my surplus soil away from the house. Digging was easy as it was an ancient garden which had been dug over many years. In fact, it was too easy, for when the council inspector came, he decreed deeper and wider footings were required because of the soft ground. Eventually my excavations satisfied even him, and concrete was mixed on the roadside and tipped into my ever-hungry footings. At last we were on the way up, even if still below ground level.

Special engineering or semi-engineering bricks had to be used below the damp course. I knew nothing of this, but my bricklayer-cum-clerk of works knew it all, and organised materials. Site clearance materials destined for landfill dumps found their way to me. One man's waste built another man's extension. Broken bags of cement and Walcrete were bought cheaply from builders' merchants. The boots of both my car and Bert's were full of cement dust. Chipped blocks, muddy bricks, twisted wall-ties, all were brought back to life in our hands. Cost price windows, second-hand doors, swept up nails and screws, in fact anything destined for the scrap heap, was checked just in case it could be utilised for No. 2, Rack End. Itinerant labourers were paid with a slice of home-made cake, and an endless supply of tea. Sometimes I felt embarrassed, but I had no money to pay. The many necessary building materials we couldn't pick off the scrap heap ate all my meagre earnings.

All the time, Bert worked on, chivvying any slacker should he, the tradesman, run short of materials. When we reached scaffold height I knew my best labouring efforts would not keep up with him laying blocks. By rising early, I filled the scaffold boards with everything possible before my day's work at Finstock, leaving only the mortar to make on return. Even then he beat me to it, for no matter how quickly I gobbled my tea he was on that scaffold before my first mixing reached his "muck board". If you failed to take advantage of a slight lull as he set his corners up, you were caught short as he sped the middle wall in. It was a silent competition to see if he could use all the materials before I could climb the ladder with refills. At least we had a good ladder which prevented anyone falling through. By that time Mr. Townsend had got his wish and sawn the old one up for firewood.

I learned a great deal about building then – how to reinforce and box-up concrete lintels, what damp courses were for, the distance to set joists in order for plasterboard sheets to fit exactly as ceilings underneath, how to get the correct consistency for bricklaying mortar in order that it flows from the trowel and sticks on a block. This was a hard apprenticeship, but one that would stand me in good stead in days to come.

On 25 May of that year even the workaholic Bert managed to stop in order to celebrate the birth of his daughter, Yvonne. We were all very pleased for the two proud parents as Yvonne entered a happy and secure home. Not for her the fear of bailiffs, and not being sure where to return after a day at school. Mrs. Pitt, the proud grandmother, and Jackie, a schoolgirl aunt, were just waiting the opportunity of pushing the pram along the street.

Despite all the excitement, tools were soon taken up again to make the most of long, summer daylight. In fact, the weather was very kind to us for, apart from an occasional day's rain to dampen the dust, we had no hold up. Almost to order the weather broke on the day after the flat roof had been felted. I well remember the Saturday Bert completed the task. I had to go to work, and felt terribly bad about leaving him to work alone. I tried in vain to persuade him to leave it one more day, so that I could help, but grim and determined he battled on. As it happened, that action prevented the inside being swamped with water, for the heavens opened on the Sunday, testing the roof in no uncertain manner.

Ern Pratley came from Finstock to render the outside and plaster throughout, making a beautiful job of it. Andy Andrews, a qualified electrician, and a friend made through the Finstock mink farm, had carried out the electrics. When I look back at all the varied people who helped us to get on our feet in some way or another, the balance of previous bad luck was more than redressed by good turns. At last, under strict guidance from my mentor, I began to come into my own. A hole for a through-door between the existing and the new building had to be knocked out at the head of my bed. What dust we found between the two layers of stone in that thick wall. I learned how to fix tongued and grooved floorboards tightly by using large cramps before nailing. At last my bed could be moved, and I entered and left it by the more conventional method of the side. One night I went upstairs covered in dust and plaster, so tired that I felt to just sit on the edge of my bed was a must. At three in the morning I became conscious of the fact that I lay, fully clothed, across the bed.

Exhausted, I had just fallen backwards complete with dust-laden clothes and into oblivion.

It was an unforgettable day when I took Mrs. Pitt to Stephenson's kitchen showroom to choose her double-drainer sink unit, kitchen cupboards, and her lifelong wish – a Rayburn cooker heated by solid fuel. Her son-in-law, John Culley, had derided her wish for such, in his opinion, an outdated form of heating and cooking appliance. Brushing aside his opinions, as one might swat away an annoying insect, she remained set in her ideas even if, at that juncture, we couldn't afford the high price. For once in her life she was determined to have something new and of her own choice. The units were chosen and paid for, but the light-blue Rayburn had to be left on hold until sufficient funds were raised --we didn't realise that twelve months would elapse before her dream was finally fulfilled. Bert plumbed-in the sink unit and tiled round the top. I painted windows, walls, skirtings and cupboards. It was decided no other major alterations would be undertaken until the spring of the next year, once the new kitchen was operational. Everyone was due for a rest, and it was felt we had chewed enough builder's dust for one year. Our living room carpet, which I had obtained from beside someone's dustbin, had become an off-yellow colour, with all the ground-in stone dust, plaster and mortar, but we decided to let it soldier on for more of the same was destined for it later. One slick move I've forgotten to mention was the entry of a large, need I say second-hand, wardrobe into my bedroom. Bearing in mind the narrow stairs, we lifted it up on to the scaffold and fed it in through the open top, before building in the roof joists. It is there for ever now, unless it be dismembered for removal in sections. To date, over thirty years on, no such thought has ever entered my head.

It was whilst building up a flower garden at the back, during my "idle" winter months, that my fork struck something hard just at tine depth. Being curious, and joking to Jackie about buried treasure, I used my spade to clear the soil. By degrees, rusty metal appeared, and on further clearance a sheet of roofing tin became obvious. Reaching its disintegrating edge I hauled it up, and to my amazement uncovered a well with sparkling, clear water below. A sick feeling went through me as I realised how easily the rusting metal could have given way sending me to an untimely death by drowning. It was ironic that, having struggled to get rid of brick rubble for months, I now had a home for barrow loads, but none remained. That open well became a depository for all my solid waste, until it reached ground level, and it is now hidden under my flower garden. Thankfully I am not under there as well, or this book would have had no happy ending.

Chapter 16
Onward, Christian Soldiers

Work continued at Finstock into a second year, for me that is. Major Browne's food supply came in the form of tripe from a Thame slaughterhouse, and chicken offal from Princes Risborough further away still. This he usually collected himself, with Susan taking over as relief driver on the rare occasions he took a holiday. I think my trips out numbered only two in the time spent there, one of which was to acquaint me with the route. Again, you see, there were quite a number of time-consuming miles involved, especially for the small amount of food required for half the year when only breeding stock were kept. However little food was brought back, contact had to be maintained in readiness for summer and autumn months when kits were growing. As the season progressed it became increasingly clear that a closure would be inevitable at the year's end. As in the case of Manor Mink Farm, profits, if there had ever been any, were now negligible, and the whole enterprise was quickly sliding into the red. Pelting out completely was set to take place, and this time it would include my former pet mink who had received a number at Finstock, and had disappeared into the mass of brown females housed in the semi-light of the Dutch barn cages.

Uncertainty clouded my future once more, but not as regards housing, which was quite safe just as long as work and wages covered that £10 0s. 7d. per month mortgage repayment. I hadn't any fixed idea of what I might do after Christmas, but, as no other mink farms were left in the area, a change of course was inevitable. Before I had time seriously to consider my work alternatives, something else was to occur which would have a monumental effect on my outlook and on the basis of life in general.

Walking up the centre aisle of the long shed, at twelve o'clock on a dull, November day, I was completely alone at the farm as the two girls were just away home to dinner. Most of the animals were on the run from one end of their cages to the other, a ritual they usually undertook before feeding commenced after our break. Striding along towards my own box of sandwiches waiting in the dry food shed, I suddenly heard a voice. It was very plain, and despite its suddenness, I understood every word, for it was not repeated. The short and to the point message was as follows: "I want you to keep Standlake Chapel open". No more, no less, and as I say, not repeated. I had not been thinking about a chapel or anything in particular, except my dinner I suppose. I stopped, looked around, and there was nobody there at all. The tiny mink feet continued to drum up and down the wire cage floors without interruption, which, in normal circumstances, a human voice would have caused. They would have stopped and climbed their wire-cage sides to investigate, in the nosy manner of such inquisitive animals, when something strange occurs in their bored little lives. There had been no flashing light, or clap of thunder, and I was neither struck blind nor dumb. On the other hand, there was no doubt that I had just heard a voice outside this world as I knew it. I knew then, just as I still know now, that the voice I heard was the voice of God. The passage of time has not dulled the conviction, nor the words that I heard. The more I thought about it, as I chewed reflectively on those sandwiches, the more puzzled I became. Why speak to me who last went to chapel for Harvest Festival, enjoyed it and then got on with my work on Sundays? Hadn't the Rev. Turner called for Mrs. Pitt one Sunday afternoon and asked me, perched up on my scaffold, to come along? Hadn't I sharply asked him if he couldn't see how busy I was putting my house in order, and that I had no time to sit in chapel? What was all this about keeping it open? Churches and chapels were always open, and had been for hundreds of years. It was all very confusing, to say the least. I certainly didn't mention it to my work comrades for fear of my own embarrassment. They may well have sent for men in white coats to take me for treatment, thinking the pressures of the last few years had been too much for me, causing strange voices to enter my head. As for myself, I had no such worries as my feet were very much on the ground in a very stable home environment.

It was into this home that I took the day's strange happenings when I returned. Over tea I tentatively broached the subject about the voice and "keeping the chapel open". It was then that part of the picture cleared. Mrs. Pitt informed me that a decision had been made by the Witney Methodist Circuit, in line with a Methodist Conference directive, to close all chapels with less than twelve members, on grounds of them being uneconomic to the organisation. Standlake had one member, so was to cease to exist as a place of worship in only seven weeks' time, at the end of this, its centenary year. In all honesty I knew nothing of this, for wasn't I too busy with my own closing-down sale at work to bother my head about out of date and apparently surplus to requirement places of worship? Anyway, it seemed quite sensible to close buildings where hardly anyone wished to gather. On further discussion it seemed that Mrs. Pitt and the few regular attenders, who had never been invited to become members, held a different view. For a hundred years the small, brick-built, one-roomed chapel had been run by a local church council, first under the umbrella of Primitive Methodism and then, after 1933, the combined Methodist Church, which joined the former with the Wesleyan section. Now that "Big Brother" had taken the decision to close their chapel over their heads, it had not gone down too well. The more I heard, the more I began to warm to this task of supporting David against Goliath. At no time did religion or religious thoughts come into the battle, just my ingrained determination to support the weak against the strong whatever the situation. I was, in effect, a mercenary fighter willing to give time and energy to any unequal struggle with a blind determination to win at all costs, without thought for the effect on my job prospects, popularity or life in general.

So it was head down and at them, without calling on any divine help, about which I knew nothing, anyway. Prayer for help and guidance was not in my armoury. A few bloody noses on the faces of opponents, in the first round, usually put them on the back foot, especially when coming from an unexpected angle. But where to start was the big question. Mrs. Pitt, a doughty fighter in her own right, suggested I go into Witney to visit a gentleman by the name of Sam Mouser, an avid opponent of this chapel closure scheme. He had helped to bring life back to a small town chapel in the Newland part of Witney. This was now thriving under the leadership of local people, encouraged by Sam at the outset. The only drawback was the fact that he was a retired farmer, and without doubt held conflicting political views to my rather rosy-red self.

So it was with more than my usual trepidation that I set out on this new mission. Given a warm, if somewhat bluff welcome, and referred to as "Mr. Pumfrey", I was led off to the quiet of his study-cum-office. After outlining all the details surrounding the voice, and the feelings of Mrs. Pitt and her friends who, of course, he knew himself, being a local preacher, we settled down to pray about the situation. Well, Sam did the praying and I, being a Philistine, considered ways just short of physical violence as to how I could inflict the most damage on those advocates of the devil who held the future of Mrs. Pitt's chapel in their dirty hands. The Superintendent Minister, of whom I had no personal knowledge, definitely had horns and a forked tail, as I sat in Sam's study. After the long conversation my host had with his God, he invited me to invoke help from above, but I suggested he had done a good job and I would pass on this occasion. To me it seemed a lot of mumbo-jumbo, and I was eager for some practical advice on how to theoretically spill some ecclesiastical blood – "Who will rid me of this turbulent priest?" kind of action. My in-built (from Pretoria), early days respect meant that I always called him Mr. Mouser, and only Sam when out of his hearing, which was not terribly good. He, in return, always referred to me as Mr. Pumfrey, although in early days I tried to explain my surname began with "B". The upshot of our meeting was that my host would throw his support behind us within the Methodist ruling body, his wife would give every help on the ladies' side of fellowship, and I would do the best I could until such a time as I learned a little of the Christian faith, for it was very obvious that a fairly rough diamond had landed on their doorstep. Incidentally, I'm sure my friends of today would say that the diamond must have been both hard and rough, for those edges have not been rounded too well in the intervening years. I still do things in the way I believe to be effective, without giving thought to religious etiquette, and boy, has that brought a shower of pious indignation from a succession of "Holy Joes" down upon my head! We are told a Christian life is not intended to be dull, and my personal experiences bear that theory out.

My first bright idea was to gain some signatures against plans to close the local chapel. With Mrs. Pitt's help, I approached anyone who had the vaguest connection with the establishment over the last fifty years. In my enthusiasm to thwart the holy powers that be, I would have accepted signatures such as Christopher Robin or Donald Duck. Despatching my missive and covering letter to the Superintendent Minister in Witney, I sat back to receive a congratulatory letter to the effect that, with all these supporters, the services must continue. Imagine my surprise when the reverend gentleman wrote, with some vigour, to tell me to mind my own business and let the Methodist Church get on with theirs. The future inhabitants of Standlake would have no need of, or interest in, chapel services, and in fact he virtually put our village on a par with Sodom and Gomorrah. To intimate that local affairs had nothing to do with local people was tantamount to waving a red flag in our faces. But what could we do now, in the face of the all-powerful circuit and conference edict?

When approached, Mr. Mouser was more philosophical, and put the whole strategy down to a few powerful men who mistakenly thought they were blessed with a mission from God, when in fact they were led by a creature with horns and forked tail, which tallied exactly with my picture of the under-fire cleric in charge of the Witney circuit. In all fairness to this much maligned man, things were almost down and out in several village chapels. Bert Edmunds, a local preacher, told me recently of a time, just prior to this, when only he, the preacher, and very deaf George Caswell attended the afternoon service. When he shook hands with George after a short prayer, he felt that would be the last meeting he would lead at Standlake. You see just how low things had become, so it was no wonder closure was imminent.

Sam Mouser was certain that nothing could stop closure under officialdom, but not under God's authority. After the last planned service, we were to retain the key and allow him to get in preachers from among his friends and associates, who were legion. My task was to find an organist locally, not something I relished the sound of, for I am the worst person to request favours from others. With fear and trembling I called on suggested musicians, both young and not so young. Eventually I found four volunteers to undertake one Sunday each. One young lad admitted to having only a limited number of tunes he could play, so on his Sunday we sang the hymns he chose, but we got by somehow. I'm not saying "I Vow to Thee My Country", or "Hills of the North Rejoice", went down too well on Easter Day, but needs must when the devil drives, as the saying goes. I regularly attended chapel now, not for my spiritual leanings, but more for my bloody-minded cussedness not to be defeated by the cleric who told me to mind my own business. I must presume "the voice" was happy with my efforts, for He had placed no restrictions on my methods of carrying out His order. No doubts ever entered my mind as to the authenticity of that instruction as I laboured away, totally against my natural inclinations and past record. The villagers who knew me must have marvelled at this unbelievable "conversion" taking place in their midst.

At Finstock my final days as a mink farmer took no such dramatic turns. I left a week before Christmas, with no deep regrets this time, feeling that this interesting section in my life had run its natural course. Bert Coombs was my saviour once more when he, as foreman, set me on to work with him in building maintenance for the Luxicars Group of Oxford garages. What I knew about building could still be written on the back of a postage stamp but, with him as my mentor, I would do my best to learn quickly. Riding to work in the firm's van, I saved using my car and of course had weekends free to pursue my own house alterations and chapel commitments. The Group had their original garage showroom in Cowley Road, and a new set of premises in Iffley Road, as well as a site for work at Kidlington. Holding the franchise for Mercedes and Renault, they were an organisation on the way up, having originally been a taxi firm under Mr. Jewson, senior. His two sons, Peter and Stanley, now ran things, the latter being our boss on the building side. Spending the first week at Cowley Road assisting the completion of an office area above the showroom, I had a grand view of the road below. My first reaction was one of surprise, for almost every pedestrian was coloured. Coming from the very agricultural environment of Finstock, it was quite a cultural shock. Except for the December temperature, I might well have got to the Caribbean. With plenty of tea breaks the work was pleasant and not too exacting, although we were expected to turn in a good day's work. Stanley Jewson called, and poured over plans with Bert, whilst keeping well clear of his cigarette smoke as Stanley was, like me, a non-smoker. On the morning of Christmas Eve I was instructed to journey to Watford in order to pick up two special asbestos vents for the roof. Driving a strange van for the first time, which had an even stranger dashboard umbrella-handle gearstick, was not my idea of fun, and those stomach-wrenching nerves worked overtime. My sweating was such that the heaterless van was more than warm enough for me. How relieved I was to return safely to base in good time to break off for our two days' holiday, unpaid for me of course, having only just joined the firm.

After this short break – two days was normal practice in those days – we went out to Kidlington to begin work on an open site where the old Orchard Café had been, but where now only a toilet block and one shed remained. Petrol pumps stood on the new forecourt, and a caravan served as an office. A showroom, garage and office tower were planned, and we were to dig the footings by hand. Armed with pick and shovel my new navvying job began. The work was hard, but the company cheery.

Almost at the outset Bert suffered a reoccurrence of a back injury and was off work for around three months. Bang went my transport, for the van was commandeered by Ray Teasdale, a car mechanic, who had upset the staff at Iffley Road by trying to do two days' work in one, and was reallocated to the building section. Under his erratic guidance we battled on, occasionally digging in the right places, but at the wrong depth, or vice versa. I prayed for Bert's return before we all lost our sanity or Stanley sacked the lot of us. An ex-army lorry had been purchased from a depot at Eynsham, and this old tipper transported spoil to an in-fill site on the village edge. Ray needed glasses to drive, and after laying them on the seat whilst working, made a habit of sitting on them when leaping into the cab in his usual haste. Ray was a character in his own right, and very sociable to work with. He acted first, and then thought afterwards. On one occasion, whilst driving the van at high speed over a steep, humped-back bridge, he shot off the seat (no belts, of course) and banged his head on the metal, unlined roof, almost rendering himself unconscious. Miraculously he stopped the vehicle, but suffered a massive headache for his pains. It was so funny that tears ran down my cheeks at the way he told it. I got to drive the old lorry when the novelty wore off with Raymond, which gave me a rest from digging. We had various short-term labourers from the employment exchange, but hard work didn't suit them, so their stay was limited. Bert eventually returned, so we began to get the building the correct way up, and it is now the Motorworld Garage, which, at the time, was a subsidiary of Luxicars, dealing with Volvo. The door on my stairs is the one which adorned the old toilet of the Orchard Café, and was transported to 58, Rack End, when demolition finally finished its work there. Originally painted a lurid lilac colour, it is now a more respectable brilliant white, and does a much higher class job.

Sundays were, for a time, free, so work and chapel did not clash. Led by Mr. Mouser, our congregations grew slowly, and a friendly fellowship developed. Having retained the large, old-fashioned key, the only one to the building, we continued our unofficial occupation. Eventually the circuit officers, in their infinite wisdom, decreed the building was not for use on the Sabbath, so our Sunday afternoon meetings ceased. Sam, in his worldly wisdom, read the wording of this latest edict and, having ascertained that it said nothing about Mondays, decided to continue meetings there at 7.30 p.m. on that day. Many happy times we had too, with varied speakers from all denominations. Another bright idea he had was for us to visit houses, much as the Jehovah's Witness folks do today. I was literally dragged along on Wednesday evenings, and almost hid around the corner in fear and trembling as he knocked on doors. My heart wasn't in that operation, and the "voice" gave me no support whatever. It wasn't very successful either, but Sam was all faith and marched on. I detested it so much that, on one or two occasions, I feigned illness to get out of it, for one week at least. Why, I thought in despair, had I got myself into this mess? He also wanted me to give out the announcements at chapel, but I assured him my nerves would not allow this. Even with all these crosses to carry and worry about, there was never any doubt but to carry on. Like Jonah, I seemed to have no escape, even if I wished for it. Sam, who loved his cup of tea, purchased some larger cups – seconds from Worleys in Witney – for welcome refreshment after our meetings. Mrs. Pitt manned the teapot and served her home-made cakes as well. After the aforementioned coke-burning stove collapsed, Sam found a vitreous enamel replacement from the then defunct East Leach chapel. Myself and Bert fitted it up with a chimney pipe out through the roof. We had a real warming fug with that one, and very little in the way of back draught fumes. Naturally it was a scramble after work to light the fire, have tea, and get back to chapel in time to open up, but the fellowship was well worth a touch of indigestion.

Moving back to the building side of my life, I must, at this point, mention John Day, a young man who worked with us at Kidlington for a time. On his own admission, I'm sure, John would agree that he was what one might call a "one speed horse". It would have been a surprise to anyone who knew him if he had been panicked into a sweat over work. Ray, who was always in a gallop, used to be constantly shouting and goading him to move more quickly. One particular afternoon, Ray had been even more noisy with his criticism, until John had the chance to get his own back. Hearing his tormentor shouting about something or another, John strolled over to investigate, and came upon Ray with his fingers trapped under the edge of a heavy object which he had been trying to lift, foolishly, by himself. Sizing up the situation, John enquired the reason for Ray's shouting. Interspersed with quite a number of swear words, Ray indicated the obvious to his tormentor now that rôles were reversed.

"How did you manage to get stuck like that, Ray?" questioned John.

Even hotter language, which obviously cannot be recorded here, came from the man with bruised fingers. Hearing the rumpus, I joined forces with the grinning John to lift the offending object, thus allowing Ray to regain the use of his hands, which he thrust under each armpit whilst he stamped around in an effort to dull the pain. John refuted all Ray's rather heated accusations that he purposely delayed lifting the heavy object, declaring he could do nothing to help until I came on the scene. Just how long he would have left his tormentor trapped, had I not come to the rescue, I dread to think. As luck would have it, no real damage was done, apart from a couple of black fingernails and some loss of dignity on the part of Raymond. John, on the other hand, carried a slight suspicion of a malicious grin around for the rest of that day. I met John Day a week or so back, doing his interpretation of a supermarket trolley dash in slow motion. I enquired as to whether he had met Ray in recent years. "Probably burned himself out", was the reply. I could see no visible sign of this happening to my late work-mate, John, although he was almost at the checkout when I left with my purchases, so he may be speeding up just a fraction in his later years.

One lasting memory of John, in those past days, is the fact that he always drank relatively expensive pure orange juice, whilst we morons guzzled orange squash. "That stuff will give you cancer", he declared, and of course we laughed in the same way as we did over wearing protective masks whilst cutting asbestos. He was, in fact, deadly serious, since his mother believed, and was many years later proved correct, that additives and artificial sweeteners could cause the disease. Although I for one took not the slightest notice, I remembered his words when the matter came to light only a few years back. The same applied in the case of asbestos – and we had sawn asbestolux board, by hand and without wearing masks, to make soffits to insert under overhanging eaves. Unknowingly, I had moved from the dangers of farmer's lung to others just as lethal in the building trade. It wasn't just bruised fingers we had to look out for.

At the height of the Kidlington job, we had quite a large gang of workmen, of various trades, and some, like me, of none. A tea boy made sure we were well supplied with builders' favourite brew. For this beverage we each paid a weekly levy from which the lad purchased tea, milk and sugar. It so happened that a scourge of stomach upsets swept through the gang, and, after a night spent seated on the toilet, Raymond decreed it must come from partially-washed tea mugs. It was obvious to the naked eye that severe staining had taken place over the length of time handles had remained on individual mugs, no change being contemplated whilst a handle remained in place. Gathering our faithful tea containers, he proceeded to smash them in the waste skip, to our horror. When he looked in the teapot, he howled in disbelief. It was almost full of mouldering tea bags. Our money-conscious tea boy had added one bag each day to the pot, leaving weeks of previously used bags inside to be re-soaked. I must say our gorges rose at the thoughts of what we had slurped down in previous days. Presumably the money saved on ingredients had helped to buy fags or cakes for the lad who didn't stay around long enough for us to find out, as Ray threatened to break the pot over his head. After that our bodies should have been resistant to anything nature could throw at us. Tea never tasted the same after a drinks dispenser was installed by the management – it had no "body" to it. See what I mean?

Another attempt to finish me off came when painting the upper walls of the high garage workshop. The fumes from cars being tested, with engines running below, gathered above, where no vents allowed them to escape. Although special attachments were provided for exhaust pipes, mechanics rarely bothered to put them on. I found my breath difficult to take, and could have collapsed from carbon monoxide poisoning. When I complained to the workshop foreman, he sucked on his pipe and intimated I was making a fuss over nothing. Some nothing, had I fallen from that high scaffold on to a concrete floor! If anyone says that health and safety officers are not needed, I have just about survived to tell a different tale.

When the boss refused to pay us a promised bonus because the job, through no fault of ours, was not completed on time, I felt it was time to organise a sit-down strike, and that was the action we few remaining workers took. When he came out and saw us thus seated, in the middle of the afternoon, he demanded of Bert what was going on. "When I told them you had reneged on the bonus deal, they refused to work, saying bugger him, and sat down." After a whole day blustering, he did pay up to a degree, but my victory was only short-lived, as I was to find out, making me love my bosses even less than my writing has already indicated. You cannot take on money and win, but being a glutton for punishment, I have never given up trying.

Not having a telephone in the sixties meant that any contact with me had to be made through Bert or Gill at Copanda. Thus it was the latter who brought the sad news of the sudden death of my father, due to a massive heart attack. I was floored by the news for, although he had been unwell for some time, no heart trouble had exposed itself. In all probability the rheumatic fever of earlier years had weakened that organ. When my little, black Morris arrived at Pretoria, it was a very sad family reunion. Cremation was arranged, after all the necessary forms had been released, according to my mother's wishes. The only contact I remember having with the village was to visit Leslie Turvey to have a piece put in the local paper. Westacre was dead to me, I wanted to be no part of it, and I was glad my father would not be buried in the churchyard. Why I was so bitter, I cannot explain, but it was so at that time. Sadly, I left once more to return to my own life, with never a thought of returning to Norfolk, and knowing full well that my mother and I could never live together, for we were of the wrong temperament and too alike it seemed. We were both fiery of temper, always right in our points of view, determined to the extreme in battle, and we could never back down – these were stout virtues in their ways there is no doubt, but we rarely saw eye to eye, and a distance of around 150 miles worked wonders in keeping the peace. What the eye doesn't see, the heart doesn't worry about.

Returning to work on Monday morning I found Bert rather quiet on the way to Kidlington, but thought it in deference to my recent bereavement. Eventually the truth came out to the effect that Stanley Jewson had given him the unenviable task of terminating my employment as from the end of that week. On the pretext of cash flow problems within the Group, he had exacted revenge for my leading that sit-down strike. This was how I saw it, at any rate, although there had often been rumours of cash flow crises during previous months, especially at the time of our strike. Even in those days the threat of job uncertainty was a useful tool in the employer's armoury.

So it was back to the good old Oxford Mail Jobs Vacant column once more. The Oxford & District Co-op weren't the only firm to stake a permanent spot in that part of our local paper. Stephensons of Oxford, the local family builders' merchants, ran them a close second, and sure enough there was a request for a paint-van driver. This looked interesting, so I made a detour with our works van, in order to enquire further. Being a frequent customer with Luxicars order book, I knew quite a bit about the firm and their premises. Taking Sam, a paint-counter assistant to one side, I quizzed him about the post.

"No good to you", he said, "they only pay peanuts for that job. Go along to see Mr. Stevens, the personnel manager, and tell him I sent you to see if any better paid posts are vacant".

This I did, knocking nervously on the door bearing his name. A very pleasant man genteelly greeted me, and listened to my request. Sizing me up, he eventually offered a post in Lamarsh Road yard, where they hoped to expand their house-brick business. Although under the main yard foreman, I would eventually be in charge of that side of things if I proved suitable. The wage rates were on a par with those I was getting at present, so, apart from extra motoring costs, the change would not be too bad. A possible future wage rise (where had I heard that before?) was in the pipeline, so we shook hands and a start was to be made on Monday. Thanking Sam on the way out, I returned to Kidlington with wings on my heels. Bert was relieved when I told him, as he had felt so bad over my notice being given on the day I returned from my father's funeral. I knew it wasn't his fault, and had told him so, but that didn't help him much; after all, we were mates of long standing.

On the Wednesday, Stanley Jewson came over to me and said that if I hadn't a job to go to immediately, there could be work for another week or two. How I enjoyed telling him I already had a job lined up. Hindsight – what a great help it is – tells me that possibly Stanley Jewson occasionally had a prick of conscience, and this was one of those times. In actual fact I got on fairly well with the man, and was glad we never had words about my leaving. For once my tongue restricted itself to the minimum of words, which was a good thing for, although neither of us knew it, I was to be tempted back to work for the Jewsons in a short eighteen months' time. Can work, will travel, became my watchword, and as previously mentioned, I never stayed where I was not happy.

My work on the cottage continued almost day and night in the summer. On one summer morning, I was merrily mixing concrete by hand down the garden, in order to re-floor two old cupboard spaces in the living room. Mrs. Goodall next door suddenly woke to my scraping and, in panic, dug her husband, Mike, in the ribs exclaiming, "Get up, we're late". Mike, who was by habit an early riser, flew downstairs only to find his watch had not stopped, as the kitchen clock also showed 5.30 a.m. Pat, his wife, was not amused to have her beauty sleep disturbed by my early morning shift. Is it any wonder that, although we are still friends, they now live at the opposite end of our village, and who can blame them?

Chapter 17

Life goes on – but never the Same

Gardens and sheds have always played an important part in rural lives. As well as being the venues for quite a lot of hard work, they were also, most importantly, a place where men could escape if domestic pressures became intolerable. Such times usually came about in the spring, when gentle hints on interior decorating became stark reality. How could a man mess about with distemper brushes when the garden needed digging and planting? That was a line I have heard my father take when in a desperate situation regarding the job he hated most. Obviously, in earlier days, produce from the garden was vital to feed the family but, by the time I owned a garden, this age had passed. The garden at Dunmore was long and narrow, running down to a row of tall trees on the southern boundary, with a thorn hedge on one side and a panel fence on the other. As I was not really a garden lover, and had no need to fear house redecoration, this lack of a good vegetable plot did not worry me. Apart from runner beans, every other type of vegetable refused to mature under the shade of overhanging trees which, being on the southern side, prevented direct sunlight getting through.

My interest lay in and around the sheds. Having built a second as a lean-to alongside the existing one, I felt the need to upgrade from dusty, dirt floors, and so set about mixing concrete to form a cement base for each. New, felt-roofed rabbit hutches were constructed, allowing me to continue with my rabbit meat trade, which had been started at our other ill-fated abode in High Street.

During my working days at Finstock I had called in to Keymarket, an early day supermarket in Witney, where trimmings from greens were dumped in a disposal skip. This waste, along with a dry mixture bought from Ducklington Mill, made good rabbit food. Since moving to work towards Oxford, the first source of green food had finished, to be replaced by roadside herbage in summer and hay in winter. I often thought back to George Hall and his rabbits at Pretoria. Mr. Hall, as we knew him, could often be seen striding past with a long sack of clover or hogweed on his shoulder. Not much had changed in thirty years, although no beehives stood in my garden as they had in his. My rabbit keeping continued for a few years more, until the thought of myxomatosis, which was widespread in the wild rabbit population, turned the housewife from the meat that had sustained poorer families for years, especially during the Second World War.

The most important operation to take place in and around my sheds was the storage and sawing of firewood. Ever since those Sunday morning sawing sessions at Pretoria, so graphically described in my first book, I have been a sawyer. On the end of a crosscut saw, with my father, I had been from an early age indoctrinated with the firewood bug. My poor, little arm ached, but the weekly pile of sawn logs had to reach a specified height before relief came. Well, I have sawn on ever since, and to date my arm has never fallen off, although it has often threatened to do so. Having, through the years, upgraded myself into using Swedish-designed bow saws, I do not yearn for a much faster, mechanical chain saw. They are easier to use may be, but a certain key factor was missing when I tried one, amidst flying sawdust and nerve-shattering noise. To me there is nothing more therapeutic than a saw easily slipping through a log of wood, with spilled sawdust speckling a growing pile of cut sections below. Having made up a good wood- stack from fallen timber collected in and around Rack End, I could settle myself at the task, whenever time or need for fuel allowed. With Pepie, our Corgi, as observer, many happy hours were spent bending over my sawing horse, made up in the workshop of Bartlett Bros., after the desecration of my previous model. Mrs. Pitt would carry two mugs of tea from the kitchen, where a large window allowed her a clear view of work outside. Usually a slice of home-made cake came as an accompaniment, and we would sit in the shade to enjoy the peace and a rest. Needless to say, Pepie would sidle up, with a view to a cake crumb or two, for had he not done his duty as observer all morning? After losing two lovely cats to road fatalities at the bungalow, we didn't attempt to keep them, and the dog could be confined behind the gate.

In earlier days pigs had been kept just over the bottom fence, at a time when Bill Harrison used the land as a smallholding, but the air was sweeter now. Times were changing, and natural farm smells weren't quite so popular within village confines as in the past. Mrs. Savory owned the property now, and ran a small shop there. This had superseded a tiny "front room" shop of many years' standing, run by Mrs. Eagles, at the property now known as Hampdon Cottage. Jackie recalls the time when Granny Pitt, who lived opposite the Green, brought her down, as a little girl, to do the weekly shopping, which was carried home in a very small, home-made shopping bag – some difference to the huge, overflowing supermarket trolleys of today. Is the extra space taken up by packaging, I wonder, or do we buy to waste?

Whilst on the subject of sheds, and, as you will have gathered, a very important subject to me, there is one more tale I must tell. After the death of my father, mother came to stay for a short holiday. Mrs. Pitt's granddaughter, Yvonne, was by this time very mobile, and full of energy. Gill called one afternoon with her daughter, and was invited to leave her in the care of the two older women while she went up into the village. This was agreed, and after a while, the three walked down the garden to look at the rabbits. Peering into one hutch, my mother saw, to her horror, a dead rat lying inside. Not wanting Yvonne to see it, she and Mrs. Pitt opened the shed door and went inside to find something to cover it. Suddenly the large door shut with a bang as Yvonne put her robust little body behind it. The vibration shook a wooden button, designed to hold it shut, into place. The pair were nicely trapped, and their charge was free to roam.

"Open this door at once, Yvonne", commanded Mrs. Pitt, "or I will give you a good smack".

This was not a threat to be taken seriously when a wooden partition separated the two parties. Another serious drawback to carrying out the command was the small fact that Yvonne's hand, even at full stretch, was about three feet below the offending button.

"I get a 'tick, Nan", said the ever-resourceful Yvonne as she proceeded to poke away with a cane.

"Call Mrs. Goodall, Yvonne", was the next instruction, so without further ado, the little girl ran up and down the path shouting, "Goodall, Goodall", to no avail, whilst Pepie joined in the fun by running behind, barking his head off for good measure.

The two prisoners, suddenly remembering their promise to look after Yvonne, began to fear she might go out on to the road in her efforts to find help.

"I shall have to put my shoulder to it", decided the well-built Mrs. P.

"Derek will be pleased if we break his door", rejoined my mother.

But help was at hand in the form of Gill returning from her errand. On hearing all the commotion as she approached, she naturally hurried into the garden. Yvonne, who was still running up and down shouting, "Goodall, Goodall", blindly collided with her mother, and was instantly taken to task over all the noise. Pepie, who considered his work now done, wasn't too sure about the tone of voice being used, and withdrew to an observation post under the rabbits' hutch. Hearing agitated voices coming from a closed shed, and now being led by Yvonne, Gill released the offending button, looked questioningly at the two red-faced ladies inside the shed, and thus saved my precious door from being split asunder by a quite hefty shoulder charge. My mother hastily absolved Yvonne from all blame, for wasn't it plainly stupid for two adults both to go inside the shed at the same time, leaving their charge unsupervised outside? With no harm done, apart from a few ruffled feathers, the amusing incident has gone down as a good laugh in the annals of family history. There must be a door-slamming gene in the Pitt family because Jackie's son, Mark, tried the same trick on me, but I just managed to put my foot there before the door closed. Yvonne often recalls the afternoon she shut Nanny and Mrs. B. in the shed. Were their faces red?

On another occasion, winter this time, Mrs. Pitt made a huge pot of soup, or "shackles" as she called it. It simmered away on her beloved Rayburn, which had been installed after the first year of the new kitchen being in operation, for several hours, giving off mouth- watering smells in the process. Florry Harris, an ex-Linnet (exiled from King's Lynn), who lived in Rack End, called and remarked on the appetising odours, but Mrs. Pitt refused to be tempted into giving her a taste. "It's not ready yet, Florry", she opined, so the luckless lady returned home, her drooling unrequited. After feeding her own table, the cook set off up the road with her container on what we called the soup run. Gill, her daughter, had been suffering from flu, as had Granny Pitt who was now well into her eighties. They were both supplied with strengthening "shackles", and perhaps Florry too, if supplies held out. An Irishman working on the sewer also caught the mouth-watering scent, but was definitely unlucky on that occasion. My mouth still waters at the thought of those succulent meals that came from Mrs. Pitt's skilful hands – steak and kidney pies with pastry made to melt in the mouth, beef puddings, bacon clangers, apple dumplings, there was no end to her simple but wholesome dishes. It's a good thing we worked so hard, otherwise our waistlines would have been excessive. She never weighed any ingredients, but worked by rule of thumb. When Jackie studied cookery at school she was tempted to inform the teacher that her mother didn't mess about with scales or measuring jugs, and the cooking turned out fine. A disgruntled instructress assured the critic that things would be done her way in her class. Jackie remained unimpressed, and although her school culinary efforts weren't too bad, they fell well short of the standard produced in our home kitchen.

The two girls from next door, Joanna and Alison Goodall, came round to try their hand at cooking, for Mrs. Pitt had great patience with children, just as long as they refrained from shutting her in the shed or sitting on her fire guard. Aprons were found for them, as Mrs. Pitt never worked without first donning her apron or overall. Flour tended to fly around to a fair degree, but hopefully they learned something whilst enjoying themselves. Their mother often said that she could not put up with their mess, but Mrs. Pitt enjoyed passing on a few, basic tips. Even when grown up and married, they still returned to visit their early friend and mentor, bringing, in turn, their own children, but not for cooking lessons as, by that time, severe arthritis had limited Mrs. Pitt's work in the kitchen where, for so many years, she had ruled supreme.

I have just one more memory which I'm sure Alison won't mind me sharing with you. Jean had volunteered to take some of the youngsters to a Christmas church service. On the way, Alison quizzed Jean as to how much collection money she had. Thinking perhaps the young lady was a bit short on funds, Jean kept her sum down to ten new pence.

"Oh", said Alison, "Dad gave me fifty pence; do you think they will give me change?". Jean, who always saw the funny side of things, laughed about Alison's change whenever church collections were mentioned. Jean left a big gap in the family life when she became a cancer victim and passed away, only in her forties.

It was in the aftermath of our being turned out of the bungalow that I began to work in lay positions for the National Union of Agricultural and Allied Workers. Charlie Brown, our District Organiser, encouraged me to become involved on the back of my experiences over the tied cottage system. Charlie was a great motivator, and used to take me to Witney for district meetings. Big Jim Godfrey, Tom Rance and myself from the village, piled into his little, blue Morris, and off we would go to put the agricultural scene to rights, as best we knew. Bill Harris from Carterton took the chair, and his wife recorded the minutes in her post as secretary. The union represented their members on matters relating to wages, which were then set by the Agricultural Wages Board consisting of our members, and members of the N.F.U., along with an odd number of independents. Wages, being relatively low when compared with industrial counterparts, always came top of the agenda, with the tied cottage chestnut a close second. Quite a few of our members lived, by this time, in council houses, and tended to command higher wage rates, but of course they had a rent to pay. By living independently, not in tied houses, they could bargain for better rates, and the farmer knew he could quite well lose a good man to factory work unless he stumped up a few more coppers. In many instances the men did leave the land for better paid work in factories, night shift workers especially being always in demand at Cowley car works. Very few really relished working inside after many years in the open air, but wives, who were liberal spenders whilst keeping up with the Jones family next door, forced their hand. Indirectly, this drift helped those left on the land in that a few shillings above basic rate were paid to key men, but not overly so even then.

It was as a Witney representative at County Conference that I first met Ron Warwick, who was organiser for Northants and North Oxon. Ron lived in Raunds, on the far side of Northampton, so had a long trek to Oxford. A family man, with sons, and a wonderful wife, Mary, Ron had worked his way up from agricultural worker to his present post, and so knew all the problems of workers in his field. We became, and still are, firm friends, although our lives have long since left the scene of practical agriculture, as have 99% of the then workforce, with farm workers being only a minute part of the Transport and General Workers Union today. Huge machines have no need for Trade Union representation, neither will the robots that will soon drive them. As it is, most large-scale cultivations are handled by contractors who work day and night, seven days a week. All those precious safeguards for workers we sweated blood to obtain have been swept away with one swipe of the iron lady's handbag. I am left wondering what such agricultural union stalwarts, as Joseph Arch and Edwin Gooch, would have thought of the gutless display of men in the 1980s, who allowed a woman to sweep them aside like dust before a broom. I do not deny that some unions had become too powerful for their own good, but for many they worked tirelessly, although their work never hit the headlines. Good works never make good news stories.

The N.U.A.A.W. had a tent at the annual Thame Agricultural Show, and the day seemed to attract a deluge of rain, without fail. Mrs. Pitt and I went to assist Charlie and Ron, along with their respective wives. Refreshment was served to any union members who called in, and as the rain pelted down, the shelter and cuppa were much appreciated. Ron's youngest son, Geoffrey, was with us, and whilst carefully stepping through the quagmire surface, he slipped, landing face down in the mud. What a sight he looked as he squelched into the tent. On catching sight of the muddy apparition, Ron made the understatement of the day by saying, "You've made a mess of yourself, boy". Poor Mary had the unenviable task of wiping down her bedraggled son, without any rag, or change of clothes available. Any mention of Thame Show brings back memories of mud and more mud.

Although no longer working in agriculture, I was chosen to represent the union on various committees, which I quite enjoyed. Having found my voice to a degree, and using my background knowledge of farmers' thinking picked up from the young bloods at Grammar School, I found it all very interesting. One of these committees involved agricultural apprentices, and the need for periodic visits to them and the farmers with whom they were placed. I often accompanied Mr. John Wilmer from Friars Court, Clanfield, who was a fellow member, but from the farmers' side. John was also a Methodist local preacher, and as such we had often met up at our unofficial chapel meetings. Riding through the Oxfordshire countryside was very pleasant, especially on a summer's evening, and in John's posh car. Being a deep-thinking, public-spirited man made him good company, and we put the world to rights as we rode along.

Eventually I was elected Chairman of the Union County Committee, and remained so for several years. I attended two biennial union conferences, one in Aberystwyth, and the second up in Filey where we had spent our Butlins holidays in days of yore. My chairmanship came to an end when Oxon and Berks were combined in reorganisation. As a consequence, Ron Warwick lost his post in a rather bitter controversy, eventually working in an administrative position at the Northamptonshire County Council. I believe this was much less stressful for both him and his wife, but not so close to his heart as was helping his fellow workers in agriculture.

All this unpaid union work took place whilst I was shuffling backwards and forwards between Luxicars and Stephensons, where no unions existed. I still displayed my union car sticker depicting horses ploughing, already a figment of the past and a period where the union itself was due to go in a few short years' time. As the rural worker was still very much the underdog, I felt it my duty to use my education and background to help where I could to improve his lot. My own lot seemed to be of no importance, although, as a virtual yard labourer, there was ample room for improvement both in wages and conditions. As I write, I realise just how mad I must have been. There was I, picking up carpets off other people's dustbins, refurbishing toilet doors, sitting on second-hand furniture, and struggling to keep a car on the road, whilst rushing around in an attempt to better the lot of others. What did I do for myself? Nothing! We had no union which, in turn, meant no protective clothing, even when handling bricks and slates, no catering facilities, and a queue for toilets with no wash basins. It was sweated labour, for a mere pittance per week. It appears I could not see the wood for the trees. On the rare occasions I mentioned trade unions, hushed whispers informed me of the fact that Mr. Norridge, company chairman, was so anti-union, that any man even mentioning them would be instantly sacked. Later developments gave light to the fact that though my car carried a union sticker, it was thought that neither it nor I spelled danger to the firm. It just shows what information is passed on to the board room, for I had never met Mr. Norridge in my yard or near my car. In an age of America's "reds under the beds" outbreak, perhaps it's not surprising if they feared another Red Robbo in their midst.

Strangely, no union moves came from me directly, but from a new yard employee, John Fox. After only a few days there, he approached me, along with one of the more Bolshie drivers, to talk union possibilities at Stephensons. As a fully paid up member, I was prepared to back him if he could persuade enough men to support such a move. Warning him to keep his head well down below the parapet in case the management shot it off, I left it to him. I'm sure those huddled groups around the place didn't go unnoticed by the official spies, but nothing surfaced. A meeting was called for all those interested in joining the T. & G.W.U., and was held at John Fox's house in Windmill Road, Headington. Contact was made with Transport House, Cowley Road, the local union office, and arrangements were made for officials to meet management. In spite of being one of the instigators for union recognition, I did not join, but retained my N.U.A.A.W. card, as my work for them continued. It was not a closed shop in any way, although all the drivers and yardmen joined up, but the nearer staff worked to the main office building, the more prepared they were to take any perks gained without actually throwing their hats into the ring. As for myself, I stayed only a short time after that, for there were many things taking place at Stephensons which I didn't like, and when Bert offered me more money to rejoin him at Kidlington, I shook the dust of Lamarsh Road off my feet and left. Things there had come to a head when I suggested that, as I had the running of the yard to organise, a reflected monetary reward should be given. A very sarcastic personnel manager, successor to Mr. Stevens, informed me that my pay scale was along my new union lines, so I could like it or lump it. As Bert's offer came just at the right moment, I told him, in no uncertain manner, where to put his job, which, if it were possible, would have been quite painful. No amount of persuasion during that week could make me change my mind, so off to work for Stanley Jewson I went once more.

It was nice to be back working with my mate again, and we soon settled into our old routine. The lads around the garages welcomed me, and the Kidlington centre had worked into full swing. We had an old workshop at the rear, and some lockup garages for our stores. Sid Holmes worked as car cleaner, having the task of bringing part-exchange vehicles back to showroom condition. This was a formidable task as many came in from farmers who are notorious for their mud, straw, and dogs' hairs left in the car boot and interior, as well. Being an anti-car cleaner myself, I marvelled at the before and after shots of Sid's work. "Soapy", a long time servant of the Jewson firm, came to help sometimes, but never reached a standard set by Sid Holmes. Soapy would do anything for the price of a pint and a pinch of snuff. He seemed to know every pub in the county, and many more outside it. He came over one afternoon with a new car, for which a very influential customer had been waiting several days. The salesman pressed upon Soapy the urgency, instructing him to prepare and polish the vehicle, as it was being collected that same afternoon. After a quick wash down, for the car – not our man – he armed himself with a good pad of mutton cloth, and prepared to polish. Now industrial polish comes in gallon cans, with screw tops. Inside is a second metal seal, which Sid knocked out with a screwdriver. On this occasion, the screwdriver had pierced the seal, leaving a jagged edge pointing inwards, but the seal had not been removed. Tipping the can up on to his rag, Soapy failed to notice the metal coming loose and thus following the polish. Taking a wide sweep over the bonnet whilst applying good pressure resulted in the jagged metal edges scouring the paint through to its base. Hearing the scratching noise, and staring in horror at its result, Soapy called Sid. There was nothing short of a paint respray to repair the damage, and that would take days. With quaking knees, our hero sped into the showroom to report this piece of really bad luck.

"You are joking", gasped the whey-faced salesman, whose day was already almost past redemption.

Tears were in the eyes of them both as they viewed the damage. What tale was concocted for the customer, I dread to think, although I have overheard some pretty tall stories when working around.

"You will have to forfeit some pints to pay for that lot, Soapy", were Sid's comforting words.

Whether is was snuff or tears over his lost pints that produced Soapy's handkerchief was difficult to tell, but I did feel sorry for the poor old soak. It could have happened to anyone.

It was during my second spell with the Luxicars Garage Group that the Salvation Army Corps at Abingdon agreed to send some of their members to lead a meeting at the chapel, as part of our Monday evenings programme. Geoff Chadwick and his wife called to check on the size of our building in order to ascertain whether or not their band could perform for us. Obviously musicians need a certain amount of room to wield their instruments, and although a tight squeeze was anticipated, the evening was set to go ahead. Now Jackie, Mrs. Pitt's youngest daughter, declined to join us on these Monday evenings, preferring to do what most teenagers do after work. Her mother issued the normal invitation on this occasion and, to our surprise, Jackie said she thought she might come. This, in fact, she did, and along with all of us, she enjoyed this lively form of worship. It wasn't until we returned home that she expressed a special interest in the Salvation Army, and what they stood for. When, after a couple of days, this apparent interest hadn't waned, I offered to contact them again, on her behalf. This I did, and we were invited to a series of special meetings being held in the town. After being introduced to Captain Hiscock, his wife and one or two members, Jackie agreed to join their Sunday evening service in order to test the water. Being unable to drive herself, I volunteered to deliver her at the citadel, without committing myself to join in. The transportation complete, I preferred to sit and wait in the car park whilst she joined the fellowship. This system continued for a couple of weeks or so, with my taxi passenger returning all bright eyed and bushy tailed, full of the spirit, having really enjoyed the fellowship. This got me wondering why I was sitting outside when I could join in. The next week I ventured into the very old citadel building, and thoroughly enjoyed singing hymns to band accompaniment. So began, in earnest, Sunday evening visits to the Salvation Army. Were these the much maligned group of Christians, the likes of which my schoolgirl mother and her cronies had danced behind as they marched through Briston streets, cat-calling, "Salvation Army, all gone barmy"? Admittedly the ladies looked rather strange in those bonnets, but at least no one had two heads.

At the end of a few months' settling-in period, Jackie finally decided to become an official member of the Abingdon Corps. I too had leanings towards this new, to us that is, form of Christian worship, and expressed my feelings to Captain Hiscock. It was duly arranged for Jackie and me to meet him at his house – the quarters, as it was known in Army parlance – for instruction in basic beliefs and rules of the organisation. After our first lesson the good captain enquired as to whether we had time for a cup of tea. When we said we would love one, he rustled up a brew in next to no time. Perhaps, in his nervous haste, he omitted to put any tea in the pot, or maybe supplies were running out, because the resultant cup fell a long way short of our chapel cuppa. The proverbial newspaper could have been read through it. When pressed for a second cup, we almost blew him over with the force of our need to be on our way. The trouble was that when, on our second visit, we stressed our tight schedule, he made a pot even faster, so that it was definitely more of the standard Mrs. Pitt called water bewitched and tea begrudged. We may not have remembered the poor man's teaching, but his tea will never be forgotten.

So it was decreed that we two, along with Jackie McIver, an Abingdon girl, would be enrolled at the last Sunday service in the old citadel, before its demolition. We received and signed our Articles of War, swore allegiance to God and the Army, and then they knocked the house down. There must be something significant there, I'm sure. On receiving the news of my joining, my forthright mother was heard to say, "I should think he will soon make up his mind what he wants to be". I am still pondering that, as I'm not one to be hurried into decisions.

Even this latest move did nothing to curtail my work for our local chapel, and in fact it had the opposite effect, for doors to new ideas were opened, and access gained to more and varied speakers for the Monday evenings. I even had courage enough to tackle the announcements, as a help to Sam, but still allowed him to continue with his long prayers, much to Mrs. Pitt's chagrin; she was of the opinion that he went on much too long. He also had an annoying habit of standing, with the door open, letting out our carefully nurtured heat. For this Mrs. Pitt often gave him a very audible reprimand, whereas, with the first fault she only thought the more. Our unofficial occupation of the chapel building meant no maintenance was carried out, except that which we did ourselves. The roof and walls were very sound, although the windows needed attention and painting. Sam paid for this, along with insurance premiums, and a token sum to the Witney circuit in order to retain good favour (although it was doubtful whether any existed), from our meagre funds. This may have been an assumed doubt over the existence of good favour, since, whenever the thorny question arose about enforcing the closure and selling the building, Sam would rise to give his, by then, famous oration, "If you really believe it is God's will for this little Bethel to close, then vote to do just that". The vote was never taken, let alone carried, so there was some goodwill for us there. I suppose this became more and more self-evident as lay preachers came to lead and find out more about these stubborn people who fought to keep their identity.

It was the rotting floor which gave us most concern, as the joists supporting the boards slowly sank. By taking up part of the floor, I managed to crawl underneath and, by using lengths of reject-timber and second-hand bricks, the areas affected were supported. The damp course between the ground and the bricks prevented rising moisture from attacking my new work, and so it was safe to continue using the chapel for a little longer. Ominous creaks and groans gave warning of trouble to come, but, in good faith, we soldiered on. Various patterned old carpets covered the floor, thus preventing a foot going through failing boards. These carpets were covered with slug trails, which had to be rubbed out before each meeting, and mousetraps were kept busy in the corners and around the pedal organ, a gift from the closed New Yatt chapel. With Mrs. Mouser organising a weekly Women's Fellowship meeting, we began our slow rise to the civilised level we find ourselves in today, refurbished and official, but not before much blood and sweat had been shed for our cause. I'll not say we didn't enjoy some of the skirmishes, for cut and thrust is all part of living, but they were harder to understand when both sides ought to have had the same aims in promoting the Gospel, when the going is pretty tough anyway. We never quantified the rights and wrongs of the situation, but just kept on doing the work required of us to give the local people, especially the elderly, an alternative place of worship.

At work I continued quite happily with Bert, on garage building maintenance, collecting materials from various merchants and odd-jobbing at Stanley's house on Boar's Hill, knowledge of which had to be kept from brother Peter for fear he would demand a like period of "free" labour at his home. Almost every time I visited Stephensons for materials people would say, "When are you coming back here to work, we need you". One of the most persistent was George Day, transport manager and age-old trouble-shooter, loved by none and hated by all just out of habit. Jesting, I always gave the same reply to him, "When you offer me £1 per hour – £40 for a forty hour week". This was like asking for the moon at that time, which was why I plucked the figure out of the air. George would bluster on about talking sense, and then march off. I was very happy where I was, but felt pleased that someone had at last recognised the fact that honesty and hard work had something to recommend it. This type of exchange went on for some months and was, by me, treated as a joke between friends for, although strange bedfellows, I got on O.K. with "miserable old George".

Meanwhile, I trundled along under Bert and "Stan the Man", as we called him. We did some painting at the house, and Bert painted the back of a toilet door. On his own admission, he never cared for painting, and spent as little time as possible at it. A few days later it appeared that Stanley had used the toilet, with time to study the back of his door. Being of a very fussy disposition, he noticed an odd brush hair or two left in the paint. Having ascertained who actually painted the door, he enquired of his foreman whether there were any bristles left on the paintbrush when he'd finished. "Sarky old bugger", said Bert – after Stanley had gone. I was awarded the task of rubbing the offending paint down, and providing a satin-like, bristle-free surface for Stan to admire when seated on his throne.

On another occasion he requested us to call at the house on our way home, to help him move a grand piano. This we did, without undo exertion, and as we prepared to leave, our boss handed Bert a £5 note. Knowing that Stanley was universally renowned for his careful handling of money I, without thinking, blurted out, "I'm blowed, Stanley, are you feeling ill?". A pregnant pause developed, and eventually he forced a sickly grin as Wendy, his wife, burst out laughing, and the touch on the raw passed off without rancour. Mrs. Jewson always treated me well when I worked up there, and her husband didn't deserve these malicious rumours scurrilously circulated about his tightness of pocket, although, on second thoughts, how did he amass his empire?

From these examples you will gather I was happy in my work, although those rumours of cash flow problems and take-overs still came to the surface occasionally. The next time George Day approached me, he was in earnest, having been directed by Mr. Norridge to contact me with the object of persuading me to return and take sole command of Lamarsh Road brick yard as a foreman in my own right. A meeting could be, and was, arranged for me to discuss terms with the big white chief himself. Determined to stick to my off- the-cuff wage scale, I entered the inner sanctum, with George's plea for me not to get Bolshie (as if I would) ringing in my ears. So it was that, for the first time, I came face to face with E.P.N., as he was spoken of in awe throughout the company, Edward P. Norridge, Chairman of Stephensons of Oxford since 1950, having joined in 1916 as office boy. What a chance for me to jump up a few rungs on a promotional ladder, for hadn't I been chosen to lead where others had tried and failed? For once it was a task I relished and knew how to succeed at, but would my self-destruct button be pressed? Poor George sat on pins, as two diametrically opposed, strong wills met, with only a desk between them.

Chapter 18

From Arbitrator to Author

I found in Mr. Norridge a man with whom I could talk face to face, with no difficulty at all. We discussed the problems of running the branch yard without proper security, in that goods were taken out on to the road with only the customer's honesty to be relied upon in order that these items be booked out to their accounts. He fully understood the building fraternity, after a lifetime in the industry, and agreed with me that a certain percentage would "forget" to return to the main yard office for this purpose. We dealt with all aspects of the job and its responsibilities, and he agreed my requested rates of pay were not excessive. After this interview I could not but be dismayed that such a practical man would have allowed himself to be surrounded by a load of clownish "yes" men in managerial positions. With thoughts like these, you can see how popular I was with management throughout my career, for I rarely kept my opinions to myself. Even so, an official contract was drawn up and signed.

After only a few days in the job I knew I would earn every penny of my wages, both in hard work and effort, to get middle management to implement any of the necessary changes in the way things were done. Only the hard-nosed George Day had guts enough to stand up and be counted when unpopular moves needed to be made. For a time I was at odds with men and management, but determination eventually won the day. By proving that good organisation saved work in the long run, and with co-operation from the fork-lift driver, Gerry Stapylton, the ship was slowly turned around, but not before much sweat had been shed. Changes in staff caused bad feeling, and at times it was only my faith, through the Salvation Army, that kept me going. This faith was well known as, on Sunday evenings, I assisted in the open-air meetings on Carfax in Oxford's city centre. What you stand for on Sunday in public, you have to stick by during the week. If you refuse to weaken your fight for honesty and fairness, people eventually respect you, even if grudgingly at first. Once this was done, life began to be much easier for both myself and the men under me, as there is a great temptation to all, in the flash of a pound note, when wage rates are low. It would not be quite so favourable for the tempter, if he knew I would check his load before it left the yard.

My best move by far was to persuade young Sid Holmes to leave Luxicars and join my staff at Stephensons. This was difficult at first, as he was a few months under eighteen at the time, and did not qualify for an adult wage. Eventually we got around it, and he joined as the junior of my gang. All in all, my squad was what you might call an oddball outfit, but, as a working team, we were second to none. Sid turned out to be my star signing, even if it took me all my time to keep him out of police custody for his rather high-spirited antics at Oxford United's away games. His father summed him up by saying, "Sid will be a good chap if he ever grows up". I must say, he was good enough for me, and I take some pleasing. Eventually he became my charge hand, forklift driver and right hand man. His father, Sid Holmes senior, also moved from Luxicars to Stephensons as foreman over the main yard. Prior to this the personnel manager persuaded me to oversee both yards, but when a promised pay rise failed to materialise on the old pretext of me being paid above union rates, I once more told him what to do with his extra responsibility. I think that man was a slow learner. In actual fact, we always remained on good terms, and he just looked at me in disbelief after I made some seemingly outrageous statement, but I'm sure he didn't understand manual workers.

Our disagreements became even more heated when I was persuaded to become shop steward. I'm sure it was the first time drivers and yardmen ever elected a foreman to be their union steward. It was nice to feel that they had faith in my even-handed way of dealing with work problems. I enjoyed the cut-and-thrust arguments with management, and they rarely had an easy time. It is fairly obvious why I never climbed promotion's ladder, nor did I want to. Any fair case I fought, but lame duck claims got short shift from me. Lazy men could not hide behind me either in my foreman's capacity or under my union cap. On the other hand, when I got my teeth into unfair treatment of any member, especially youngsters, I never let go until justice was seen to be done. At meetings with management I now laid my brief case on the table, with the open side towards me. My bible was always just visible and, by seeing that, I remembered to curb my temper which, as you will have already gathered, was pretty fiery. By losing your temper you lose an argument – a good saying to remember, and I needed to do the remembering on numerous occasions.

We only had one strike, as I remember, and that was instigated by some hotheads whilst I was otherwise engaged in having the mumps, caught from Mark when he was a small boy. He also managed to give his mother, Jackie, a dose as well. That strike did very little good, especially when one fool, acting on their picket line, spat at a customer trying to enter the front building. From that time on, the firm, and consequently the union, began to decline. Life there no longer held the happy family feeling we had enjoyed.

Mondays had always been reserved for football rivalries. Saturday winners displayed scarves, and losers kept a low profile. One driver, Bob Betts, was a prime example to mention. If his team, Chelsea, had an especially tough fixture he would get his loading tickets from the office late on Friday afternoon and load in our yard in order to escape our taunts on the Monday should the worst happen. Once, when an outside contractor pulled into our yard, with Norwich City colours proudly displayed, Sid was heard to remark loudly, for my benefit, "Here's their other supporter; I knew there must be one more, besides Derek". My allegiance to Norwich City was very well known, especially when they lost, which was quite often, and all and sundry remarked on it.

Slowly trade diminished as a building slump took effect. The firm had just passed their centenary as a family concern, although a Mr. Stephenson, if there ever had been one, was lost in the mists of time. Talk of take-over was rife, and redundancies seemed imminent. Downsizing became an "in" word, and the two yards were to be merged, with me moving over to the main yard. The writing was on the wall, and I could read it. Time for me to move on, but not without somehow being made redundant and drawing the statutory money attached to this at that time. My brain had to be put into gear, for once to my own advantage. The new managing director explained that, as my job was continuing, I wouldn't be able to claim redundancy. He was so sorry, but rules were rules, as I should know well. But when I produced my contract, which stated specifically where that employment would take place, I was proved to be redundant, for there was no work there for me to do. I did, tongue in cheek, suggest I could sit in our hut office all day and be paid for it, but my offer was turned down. I left at Christmas, with a great send off from men and management. The latter could have been relieved to see me go, and more than likely they were, but whenever I returned to buy materials there both sides welcomed me warmly and I was always pleased to renew acquaintance with them.

It seemed very strange not going off to work after the Christmas and New Year break. Actually it was a blessing in disguise, for my friend, Mrs. Pitt, had become very unsteady on her feet due to progressive arthritis, and it was a worry to leave her all day with no help. Mark was only three, and enjoyed coming to Standlake to visit his Nan. The phone would ring and a little voice on the other end, pleading for a lift from Oxleas, Witney, would say, "My dad has gone to work and can't bring us over. Do you think the little, red car can come to fetch us, please?". The little Renault 4 could always oblige, and we spent many happy hours in my shed at the bottom of the garden during those winter days. We even had to return after dark with torches in order that his dad could see the jobs we had been doing. Michael declined his son's offer for him to sit on our dusty seats, much to Mark's disappointment. Office-style suits don't go too well with dusty sheds. Mark was being indoctrinated into country ways at an early age, and enjoying it, but no more so than his mentor to whom cobwebby sheds were a way of life.

Whilst on the subject of sheds, firewood-sawing, and other rural pursuits, may I just hark back to the days when my mother stayed during her last illness. I had acquired some large logs, which were difficult to split small enough to fit our open fire. Not to be outdone by this slight problem, Mum and Mrs. Pitt armed themselves with a poker apiece, and sat one on either side of the fire, holding the blocks in place until they burned down small enough to lay in the grate by themselves. I dread to think what they would have done if one had rolled on to the mat. But, one with arthritis, and the other an advanced cancer sufferer, they were game for anything, determined not to waste good, natural fuel. My mother enjoyed her last days, despite the pain. Mrs. Pitt played her mouth-organ, having a constant request for, "Now the Day is Over, Night is Falling Fast". The day was almost over for my mother, and she passed peacefully away in the John Radcliffe hospital a few weeks later. Two simple but wonderful parents were gone, but they had left with me the sense to value those things in life that last – honesty, faithfulness and a good name. Money cannot buy any of these since they are beyond price. My parents had them, and I pray I shall never lose them myself.

My interest in politics, both local and national, was born out of a will to help those less fortunate in society through no fault of their own. Everyone is entitled to the basic necessities of life, especially in a country like our own. Being born into a household with the Daily Herald the only newspaper allowed over the threshold (we couldn't afford two anyway) and the Landworker, a monthly trade union newsletter, it was small wonder I was a Labour man. Many of their members, and indeed leaders, had only a limited education then, most of which was obtained by their own efforts after a long and hard day's work. These were men I could acquaint with, and follow in their efforts to bring better living conditions to the masses. At one time I flirted with Communism, but found their wonderful theories failed dismally in practice, as has been proved in the fullness of time.

I've never been over-enamoured with politicians, especially modern ones, finding most of them to be self-centred windbags who can never be wrong. Not all socialist M.Ps changed their views after exchanging the cloth cap for a bowler hat, but I fear many did – or were forced to by circumstances. They learned all too quickly that money rules this country and not an honest conscience. This applies even more so today, when an unscrupulous speculator on the other side of the world can send our finances into a rapid, downward spiral, ending in money-saving cuts to vital services. Mind you, I am always amazed that we can find unspecified amounts of money to fight other people's wars, at the drop of that bowler hat. Still, this isn't a book to highlight the virtues of any one political party. I would just like to record one or two lighter incidents at election time.

It was always a good policy for election candidates to stand on the biggest pile of stones available when visiting tough villages. At least opponents couldn't throw those stones at you! I've never known feelings to run that high in Standlake. Good humour tended to be to the fore between Mick Ayres, Conservative, (who, in my father's parlance, was as blue as a whetstone), and myself and Dessy Knipe who held opposite views. I always wore a bright red jersey when going to cast my vote. On one occasion, a Tory supporter left his car running on full throttle just outside my window, whilst he ran round delivering leaflets. Incensed at his audacity, I hurled a stale egg at his windscreen, which produced a bull-like roar from across the road. During this election, when Maggie Thatcher was securely seated on her self-ordained throne, I had made known my views of both her and her policies at work. I met Mick at the polling station and he termed me as the mad egg thrower, and promptly plastered a Conservative sticker on my car. I left it on, and drove to work, knowing full well the stir it would cause when the shop steward rolled up with a blue, Tory sticker on his car. "If you can't beat 'em, then join 'em", I told my disbelieving onlookers. I then explained how it had come about.

My own dabble into politics didn't go beyond the parish council, which hardly counted, I suppose. It was in the early days of my life in Standlake, certainly when I still, if only occasionally, went to the Bell and local issues were bandied about. The proposed and much-needed sewerage plan seemed to have been put on the back burner once more. Every time Standlake appeared to be approaching the top of the priority list, another village jumped over them. Naturally, the tap room experts blamed the parish council for failing to push our case, whether it was their fault or not. In a fit of madness I agreed to join Dessy Knipe and force an election for perhaps the first time. It did seem as though, by carefully co-opting a new member as a straight swop for one retiring, it was possible to keep a closed shop. Bob Burt also made it known he intended to stand, making ten candidates for seven places. Jackie helped dash my morale by declaring that only six people knew me, so I could only hope for six votes – which was very encouraging, I must say. By canvassing as joint candidates with a "get the sewerage system" policy, with Dessy, who carried a large vote from the council estate, I was elected, although in seventh position. My total votes well exceeded the minuscule amount forecast by my former errand girl, who perhaps didn't want me to become overconfident. The election of we uneducated oafs, their words not mine, didn't go down too well with our self- appointed, former leaders, but we were the ones attending the meetings at the school. With help from Jack Rolph, the incumbent clerk, we soon learned the ropes, enough that is to be an irritant faction in questions which would have received rubber stamp answers in past days. When we ran a petition in the village over the sewerage question, without the chairman's knowledge, we were promptly told we couldn't do it. But we replied that we had already done it, and really there was no answer to that. The main sewerage system came quite soon after – hopefully, with some help from us, I would like to think. Two years later my father died, and I stepped down from the council, having no heart for the unequal struggle against the old guard. I did serve for one year at a much later date, when no one wanted to fill the vacancies, but domestic responsibilities were too heavy for me to continue. I have often been a stern critic of the parish council, but in having to deal with acute village apathy for many years, they secretly have my sympathy, if it is any consolation.

After I left Stephensons, I could not apply for dole until twelve weeks had elapsed. I signed on towards the end of March, with not much hope of a job at my age. I did apply for work with the heavy horse at Cogges Farm Museum, Witney, which I felt well able to do after my early working days with Uncle Will at Soigné. Nothing came of it, and I was sorry for my heart was set on being with horses again. When Mark and I visited the museum, I saw a girl, wearing green wellies, handling Boxer, so I presumed she knew much more about horses than I did. One thing which was certain though was the small fact that she had not been in the business long enough to have a ton of horse, with iron shoes, tread on her foot accidentally. Green wellies don't give the same protection as a stout, leather boot, with metal toe-cap. Perhaps Boxer wore carpet slippers. Neither did I recall many farm labourers, in the past, wearing wellington boots, let alone green ones. I believe the staff wear more authentic clothes now – I hope they do, for their clothing stood out like a sore thumb at that time, and spoiled a day of memories for me meeting tight jeans and tee shirts around every corner.

Mark spent most Saturdays with his Nan and me, for he much preferred our "olden days house", as he termed it, to an afternoon spent in a modern supermarket. Fresh cod, chips cut straight from our potatoes, and spaghetti was his favourite lunchtime meal, after which he always volunteered to wash up. This was a novelty denied him in the world of dishwashers. Admittedly, the suds were softer to his hands than those non-existent ones were in days when washing soda was used to soften water in real, olden day houses. "Chaps" and cracks were the order of the day then, especially in frosty weather. Hands that did dishes were not as soft as your face, as I remember. After this, my near sixty year old legs were subjected to games of football, cricket or tennis, depending upon the time of year. Brian Gunn, in the Norwich goal, made full length saves in our make-believe games between my team and his Manchester United. A full, running commentary would ensue, as long as breath lasted. Then, very red-faced, we would return to be told what silly fools we both were by Mrs. Pitt, freshly wakened from her sleep, a ritual always adhered to after dinner. Cricket usually went better when Mark's dad arrived after tea, making an extra fielder. My mind went back to occasional Sunday evenings in the Squire's Field at Pretoria, when Uncles Will and John, plus our father, made extra fielders for we boys. The hay stubble gave a very rough pitch, but who cared, as long as everyone had a hit.

Helping Mrs. Pitt deal with her increasing disability had proved a problem when trying to earn a living at the same time, but months on the dole were not for me, if I could avoid it, and eventually I prepared to strike out on my own with gardening and any odd job which might come to hand. A scheme for self-employment became available for those on the dole, which paid £40 per week for one year, to augment one's earnings, thus allowing a one-man business to get started. The first day of my business empire building was a cold, wet one in October, and I earned the princely sum of £4.25, putting a couple of safety chains on doors. Trade never looked back after that lowly start, and decorating took up most of my time once the first winter was over. During those cold, early months I worked at Brighthampton for Peter Bury, who wanted, amongst other things, to change the white-painted windows of his converted barn and garage block to wood stain. This involved a lot of work, but it saw me through the worst weather. Being employed in the village allowed me the freedom to pop back home occasionally and be at the end of a nearby telephone, should any emergency arise. Grass cutting, outdoor painting, room decorating, fencing, wood sawing – you name it, I took it on. Mostly for pensioners and at affordable rates, my work was both interesting and fulfilling, my books remaining over full no matter the time of year. It was so enjoyable being my own boss that I began to regret not having begun earlier in life. Bert and myself had seriously discussed going into business as builders some years before. Well, he would have been the builder, planner and quotation expert, and I would have been labourer and general factotum – not a very balanced partnership, but we worked so well together that it could have been a success. We decided not to take the risk, for building is a fluctuating trade. Perhaps Bert had a portent of his early death, at the age of 54.

As I approached my sixtieth birthday, it became increasingly obvious that I could no longer work full time and care for my friend at home. Her arthritis was becoming markedly worse, the pain being almost unbearable, especially when she lay down at night. Often we would make up the fire, and remain in chairs until the early hours of the morning, before trying to get her a short time in bed, thus reducing swollen legs. It was a vicious circle of pain and broken nights for us both – physical pain for her, and mental stress for me who felt so helpless at being unable to ease that pain. Arthritis is so debilitating, as movement becomes more restricted, but by sheer determination and with chiropractic help, Mrs. Pitt fought its fearsome progress over many years. Her hands were kept mobile with knitting and crochet, and she made coloured vests for Save the Children, knee rugs, blankets and pram covers for all and sundry. Most importantly, her mind remained as keen as ever, allowing her to take an active interest in T.V. quizzes, and run the chapel from her chair. Our cottage, although warm and cosy, was not conducive to wheelchair access, being very small. The close proximity of furniture did allow her support from one piece to the next, but this was rather fraught with the danger of falling when no help was at hand. As you can imagine, all these pressures were beginning to take their toll on us both, and the time had come to take decisive action. Either Mrs. Pitt would have to be taken into a home, which was unthinkable for she was so contented and happy with her simple life in a house where she had lived for a quarter of a century, or I would have to stay at home and look after her. There was no real decision to make, for true friends do not forsake one another in times of need, and so the second option came into being. The Social Services were very helpful, after a notoriously slow start and we became alternately frustrated and despondent, with a few bright spells in between. But, by remembering that Rome wasn't built in a day, we soldiered on, as one must under adverse circumstances, adjusting our lives as we went, enjoying the few days when pain eased, and then snatching sleep where possible at bad times.

My cooking improved under instruction from the sitting room, and I came to enjoy making meals, which a number one cook would enjoy. Problems, however, arose when gall bladder trouble developed, and my charge could only eat certain non-fatty meals. Three hospital stays for her changed our scene during one winter, but she took it all in her stride, and after skilful work by Mr. Britton at the John Radcliffe hospital, no further trouble occurred. Beef puddings and bacon clangers were furtively brought back on to the menu, without ill effect, although a dietitian might not have been impressed. I must mention here that Mrs. P. gave scant credence to advice given by the latter, having long since forgotten the sylph-like figure of youth. Not for her a body resembling a broom handle or as straight as a yard of pump water!

It was during our after dinner rest periods (we still had dinner at mid-day) that my mind went back to the wonderful boyhood days at Westacre. Mrs. Pitt always tried to have a nap at that time, and often I did as well, especially after a broken night, which had become more the norm rather than the exception. I would drop off whilst mentally walking the fields and footpaths around Pretoria, which had been so peaceful even in wartime. The idea of making a record of those times began to take root and germinate. Writing a book for the world to read was not with me at this initial stage, for I had no idea so many people would be interested. As I sat down at the kitchen table, with an A4 pad and Biro pen, my aim was just to record my memories of a way of life now gone for ever. By mentally placing myself back into the situation, writing became easy. Not only was I able to work easily, but recalling the stress-free, early life seemed to relax me in my present situation. Whilst listening for the alarm from upstairs summoning me to help, I could go birds' nesting with Cyril Jones and David Bunker, or catch rabbits in the harvest field with Grandad Eke, an event of summer days long ago. Step by step I grew up, went to school and shared wartime days with evacuees. We moved house, harvested, threshed, laughed, grieved, all in the environs of a small village almost unheard of in the big, wide world. Yet we had lived a complete life, so full that it was almost impossible to fit everything in. Never being bored or led into malicious damage, it was an ideal life, to my way of thinking, and I am not alone in this as subsequent letters I have received bear out. It was strange perhaps to evacuees, but healthy there is no doubt, even under rationing restrictions.

Every quiet moment, when my friend sought relief from pain in exhausted sleep, was utilised in writing. A chapter pattern developed, both in length and content, although no firm thoughts of publishing were as yet in mind. Subconsciously, my pattern followed the form I liked books to take, with chapters just the correct length for a one per night read before falling naturally to sleep. That was how it used to be for me, at least.

So it was that twenty, A4, hand-written pages constituted a chapter, finishing one subject, and the next chapter started on a fresh theme. Very little unnecessary padding was needed to reach that point or, conversely, to severely prune a situation to shorten a chapter. The easy flow, often remarked upon, came naturally, and as long as I enjoyed reading that which I had written, it was left alone with only very minor adjustments made by myself.

As the pile of pages grew, I began to wonder quite what the outcome might be. As I said, like Topsy, it just growed and growed. My first move was to read it on to a tape, which seemed to make it more professional, at least. Our friend, Mrs. Noël Collins, listened to the first tape and then tentatively suggested that she should ask her married daughter, living near Ipswich, if it was possible for it to be put on to computer. Celia and her husband, Alan, volunteered to take the job on, even though they themselves were busy, professional people, with two children, and also working for the scout group in their village. As I've learned more of my venture, I do not know how they managed to complete the task, but they did. Alan produced the finished article in ring binder book form, complete with photographs. To me it was a miracle, far beyond anything my wildest dreams had ever conjured up. My ambition had been achieved and revelled in, and I would have settled for that pinnacle, being a chap of very modest aims in life.

Having passed these copies around friends and family, I awaited their verdict on my efforts. They all came back with the same cry that I must get it published. Well now, was my creation going to cause me worry and uncalled for expense at a very inappropriate time? Having no income, apart from a very small care allowance, and no financial prospects beyond retirement pension, the outlook for investment was not encouraging. Expert amateurs cheerfully informed me not to worry as publishers would want to take it up and would finance it. On the basis of nothing ventured, nothing gained, I consulted a long list of publishers at the Witney library, selecting a few likely ones connected with countryside books. Again, following advice, I sent a couple of selected chapters, with a short resumé of the book content, to them, hoping obviously for a quick reply to tell me of their eagerness to take up the book. Not so, I'm afraid, as each one came back with advice to try publishers of autobiographies. This I tried next, but still without success, for they had so many people clamouring for their life stories to be published that there was a "no room at the inn" syndrome in operation. Losing hope quite rapidly, I tried a few more in desperation, and one replied with an offer to print and market it, as it showed promise, just as long as I was prepared to back my book with a sum of money just in excess of £7,000. If I could have done so, I doubt if I would have been persuaded to throw that kind of money behind a dream. As it was, there was no question to be answered, and the lid had to be slammed down very firmly on the whole idea. Periodically, questions would be asked as to publishing progress, and the same answer had to be given, "Out of the question, I'm afraid". It was more for the good people who had encouraged me that I felt aggrieved, rather than for myself at the non- progress.

Tucking a slight disappointment behind me, I began the enjoyable task of recording my days on the farm at Soigné, the draft eventually becoming, "All Mangolds and Muck Cart". It was at this juncture Jean and Ian Little became involved in a practical way. Jean was of course Jean Andrews, when I knew her at Soigné where she grew up, before making more of her higher education than I did. Jean had furnished me with some photographs, and during a telephone conversation suggested I should continue with my writing, despite temporary setbacks. Eagerly telling of my most recent efforts, I was more than thrilled to hear her volunteer her services to transfer my scrawl (my description of my handwriting, not hers, for she is far too polite to say things like that) on to a computer disk. As she had just ceased a part-time job, it would keep her occupied, perhaps more than she imagined at the time. If this turned out to be the case, she never let on but, with the help of her husband, Ian, contrived to do a wonderful job for me. Having been born and brought up at Soigné, Jean had no trouble with local place name spellings or with surnames either. Most of my memories would be familiar to her, although she is much younger than me – well, a few years, anyway! A friend indeed she turned out to be, for as well as all the practical help she gave me, both she and Ian were so encouraging in urging me to get the work published. Every avenue suggested and tried failed to bring even a hint of success, and it began to look as if all our efforts, which ranged from Standlake to Ipswich via Bedford, were destined to be filed in an upstairs drawer forever.

Chapter 19

Success at Last

Mrs. Pitt enjoyed an occasional read, but unfortunately, for me that is, only read love stories of the most slushy nature. Coupled with this, her failing eyesight for small print meant a concentration on the large print section of the mobile library was the order of the day. As I had to choose her books, the onus was on me to produce something new each fortnight. Mrs. Wilcox had the same problem as she tried to choose for another lady with the same tastes and eyesight. We did our best to exchange volumes, which were not to contain violence, had to be non-historical, not too heavy and not too long.

During these exchanges, I got to know the driver of the library van very well. It emerged that he, Colin Taylor, was a keen Oxford United supporter, whilst I boasted of being a Norwich City man. Knowing of Colin's love for countryside books, I lent him mine to read, and having done so, he returned it with compliments, expressing his view that it ought to be published. Efforts to publish were also discussed, but again with no firm ideas, apart from those already tried. Unfortunately, as a result of a freak accident sustained as a spectator at a football match, his shoulder was badly injured and this prevented him from driving the van, and we lost contact for a time. Somehow, unkind rumours circulated to the effect that, whilst in the unaccustomed act of applauding an Oxford United goal, a scoring feat as rare as hen's teeth, his shoulder gave out under the stress. This tale was in fact invented by myself when, in reality, he slipped on a patch of ice whilst innocently fielding a loose football at a local match. Having been a referee, he loved to watch a game at any grade. Joking aside, it was very bad luck, with ongoing consequences too painful to contemplate. I know Colin will forgive me for this sick joke, as he always enjoyed our football exchanges, we being two long-suffering supporters of teams with very indifferent records. Well, to cut this long story short, I received a phone call one evening, from Colin, asking whether I knew of a publisher in Witney, a certain Robert Boyd, whom he had worked with a number of years back. His name had been mentioned in the local paper, in connection with the publication of an Oxfordshire book. Armed with a phone number, I contacted the man in question, explained briefly my situation, and enquired whether he was interested. Interested and keen he certainly was, arriving at my house in double quick time to look over my efforts so far.

We struck up a rapport immediately, both being very interested in recent history, which, in effect, only dated back half a lifetime, but was in danger of being lost before it left living memory. Promising an estimate for the work within a week or so, he departed, leaving me on cloud nine, for at last there was a chink of light at the end of my black tunnel which, for so long, had blocked me off from being a published author. I felt like Archimedes of old, shouting "Eureka", except I wasn't in a bath of water or naked either.

As the days passed and the time for Bob to return with the quotation came, self-doubt and fear of disappointment deflated my new-found joy, bringing those stomach-griping, nervous pains back into my life once more. Settling a maximum figure in my mind, I prepared to face one of those ultimate disappointments in life that members of my family seemed destined to receive from our very dates of birth. How very different things were to turn out to my morbid and downbeat estimations. Bob arrived, his usual smiling self, and accepted the offer of a cuppa, before passing over the vital papers. My white and drawn face must have betrayed my fears as a shaking hand opened the missive. Despite my worst fears, the bottom line came to a fraction below my reserve, and I felt able to launch the project there and then. I'll not say my knotted stomach relaxed, for everything discussed held new, hidden terrors for me. Most, if not all of the technical terms used, were foreign to me, but I tried to look intelligent, even if I wasn't, as things were being made as simple as possible. Bob said that I should not worry as I had done the hard part in writing the book, but I was far from reassured. Was all this worry really worth it? Was I throwing away hard-earned money which we would need in coming pensioner days? Why wasn't I satisfied with a simple life, such as my father had pursued? Poor, little Westacre hadn't been big enough for me, and now recording its happy memories was doing my nervous system no favours. On the other hand, there was no turning back, and the die had been cast.

Mrs. Pitt viewed all these exchanges from her chair by the fire, giving support where she could by saying how nice it would be when finished. Helping to choose cover colours and photographs, she was in her element, for she had a good eye and wisdom to go with it. Colin Bough came down to take the cover photograph, and it was Mrs. Pitt's suggestion that I sit by the shed and wear my cap and jacket. The resultant photo was the one used to adorn the cover of "A Boy's Eye View of Norfolk Village Life", making me look the countryman I really am. Jean and Ian were over the moon with the news, the former doing computer adjustments after Ian's proof-reading, and my last minute, visual checks. With these final touches to the text, and photographs mounted and labelled, everything was ready for off. Each time the publisher's voice came on the telephone, I died yet another death, fearing the worst over any small query. Bob used to hesitate on purpose to set me up at the outset of his calls. I dare not think what I would do with the minimum 500 copies my agreed estimate told me I would receive, ready-boxed at my front door. How did one dispose of 500 books written about life in a county 150 miles away, whilst caring for a disabled friend twenty-four hours a day? The question begged an answer, but nobody could give me one, least of all myself.

Just recalling my nightmares of brown, cardboard boxes, piled from floor to ceiling, gives me the shivers, so I will turn aside from the problem for a moment to record a few domestic details. It was shortly after Mrs. Pitt's periods of hospitalisation that the social services officials agreed the need for a through-floor lift to be installed, in order to get their applicant between floors. Just how I had managed to get her up the twisting stairs was a miracle re-enacted every night, except when she elected to stay in her chair, the effort needed to get upstairs proving too great. Nick and Ann Clack, who owned a bungalow opposite, kindly volunteered to lend us their property for the four estimated days needed for installation. Working in London, they normally stayed at their flat during the week, so things were set to work out well. Being people of good Christian principles, they remained in the city, enduring the August heat wave for the whole four weeks it eventually took for the work to be completed. In fairness to the workmen, I felt it was a minor miracle for installation to be possible at all, in such a tiny cottage, without one straight wall in the place. We, in turn, enjoyed a holiday away from home, able to sit by a large, picture window, with wonderful views across to the river. Toby, our neighbour's cat, who had recently moved in to live with us, heroically braved the dust and noise in order to lay in a chair and observe all the upheaval.

What a wonderful relief it would be to just press a button morning and night in order to get my gallant companion from bed to chair and back again. Our little friend, Mark (he was little then, believe it or not) came over to try the lift out for his Nan, before trusting her to such modern inventions. In fact he tried it several times before passing it safe to use. Even then, its lady passenger viewed it with some suspicion, fearing a breakdown in mid-journey would leave her suspended overnight. Built-in safety devices prevented any such situations arising, although we did have occasional teething troubles, but nothing serious. The whole set up was so neat that very few visitors noticed its presence until Mrs. Pitt proudly pointed out her new helpmate, which enabled her to continue living at home, to everyone's satisfaction. She was a home person, and would have pined away in any other environment. Always cheerful, even when her face was drawn and grey with pain, she made the most of life and never complained of her lot. Her only cross word with me came when I failed to take her advice on the virtues of an after-dinner nap, and I then fell asleep in the middle of our evening game of cards, an event she looked forward to and rather liked to win, I might add.

When Mark came, as he did most Saturdays, just in time for cod and chips at 12.30 p.m., we needed to play "Kings" for coppers. Out would come the two plastic bags of pennies, along with Nan's red purse. There was no need to mark our respective bags as mine, without doubt, was the smallest since our guest was a habitual winner. Ludo and dominoes also took their turn, although they could develop into mock violence as killing- off and blocking-up weren't always taken in good spirit by the elder stateswoman taking part, and we two innocents were branded as cheats when things went against her. We also had a competition, wherein the person with the most fish bones on the side of their plate had to wash up. Nan couldn't lose, as she was unable to get up to pay the forfeit. I always gave Mark a tail fillet which was boneless, so I lost out every time. Luckily my young mate liked the novelty of helping as this gave him the opportunity of playing in suds. He was, and still is, a great help in any situation, and jolly good company the while. His Nan and I felt very much like poor, old Puff, the Magic Dragon, when music school and increasing school work kept him from regular weekly visits. Our games of football, cricket and tennis were things of the past, although, as my legs grew older, a halt would have had to be called anyway. Growing up can be hard sometimes for youngsters, but their growing up is hard for us old ones as well, you know. Mrs. Pitt's two grandchildren had given us hours of pleasure with their company, and we were grateful for that.

When the day of book delivery finally arrived I was on tenterhooks to see the finished article. Thankfully the pile of boxes didn't reach the dizzy heights of those in my nightmares. To hold a published book, which has been written by oneself, is a wonderful feeling "A Boy's Eye View of Norfolk Village Life, as seen by Derek Bumfrey", was a dream ultimately come true. I pinched myself to make sure I was awake. The publication was everything and more than my wildest thoughts had envisaged. Bob Boyd left, with his final cheque, and I was now the proud owner of 500 books, with one copy held for posterity in the Bodleian Library in Oxford, and one each at the national libraries in London, Edinburgh and Dublin, I believe. Ah well, I had made Bumfrey family history.

After tentatively selling one copy to my neighbour, who had been keeping an interested brief on my literary progress, I only had 499 left to sell. Not many to go now, I told myself, as Mark and I humped the boxes upstairs. By stacking them in a space behind his Nan's recently realigned bed, we could use them as a rest for her bedside lamp.

"What happens when you sell lots and the pile of boxes sinks", questioned Mark.

"We will have to think again", I replied, whilst silently contemplating there wasn't much fear of that happening yet awhile. Oh ye of little faith! If only I could have foreseen how, step by step, sales would develop, and age-old acquaintances return to my fold, my mind would have been easier.

A few years previously, Captain Birkbeck had written and published a book entitled "The Birkbecks of Norfolk", a copy of which I had purchased by post from the Westacre Estate office. The Captain himself wrote a short letter to me for inclusion with the book, and I felt that action to be a small step in repairing our slight altercation, which developed between us just prior to my leaving Westacre, and after thirty-five years probably only remembered by myself. So I decided that, as it was the Birkbeck Estate that my story had been lived upon, a copy should be despatched to him. I also posted a book to Leslie Richardson at Soigné, my work-mate and provider of photographs. A phone call from Leslie quickly followed, asking for price details and points of purchase. The Captain followed up with the same request in order that he could arrange for details to be placed in the window of the tiny post office. Gobsmacked by this sudden influx of interest from my public, I flew about getting postal rates, details of packaging materials, and other relative facts for mass marketing. Galvanised by the receipt in the next post of an order for six to be despatched to Captain Birkbeck, and four to Leslie for various interested parties, I felt the need to get my brain into gear in double quick time. Included in the Captain's letter was an invitation to visit him and, if possible, take lunch. All this was almost too much, and a rapid chain of events was overtaking me. I felt my legs couldn't keep up, let alone my brain. Admittedly, after suffering a severe attack of glandular fever during the summer, I had little strength at my command for everyday tasks, let alone directing sales in a market 150 miles away. In the event, Jackie's husband came to my rescue by offering to drive me up to Norfolk for the day, whilst his wife took care of her mother. Thus it was arranged for the following Saturday, only to find Captain Birkbeck unable to be there on that day. This meant that lunch was out, but notwithstanding, we prepared to set out, carrying a packed meal and boxes of books in the boot. Mark had charge of the maps and football quiz books, so necessary on a long car journey. He was highly delighted to be visiting, for the first time, this county he had heard so much about. Being a modern man, who never wore a coat unless really forced to do so, he had heeded warnings from all sides that it could very well be much colder on the eastern side of England, and how right we turned out to be. Later that day his well-thatched head was so cold he wished for one of his Nan's woollen hats as extra protection.

We made steady progress towards our target, having arranged to meet Leslie Richardson before he set out on his weekly trip to Swaffham.

Obviously, not wishing him to miss his date with destiny, we tried to rendezvous on time. It was a very strange feeling to return to my roots after such a long time. The roads seemed to be much narrower as we swept up Tumbler Hill and through the woods, slowing down for pheasants which seemed to view the road as their own. Slowly, Michael turned towards Soigné, pulling up at No. 6, Pretoria, to allow Mark to take a photo of the old homestead. Then on we went to the farm where Leslie lived in retirement, his garden being the very one Leslie Lloyd and I had dug for Charlie Wilson, the story of which is told graphically in "All Mangolds and Muck-Cart". I wondered whether its present tenant had inherited the wonkey-handled wheelbarrow designed by Barney Hooks to rupture its user. Just to prove that, in Norfolk, things were built to last, Leslie was still using his grandfather's wheelbarrow, which must have seen a long life, as Leslie was 79 by then himself. His cheerful greeting of, "Come on in, I thowt yewed got lorst", confirmed to me this was the same mate I had shared so many hours of work with over forty years ago. The same cheerful grin accompanied a firm handshake, and we were back to leg-pulling companionship, which gave us so many laughs in earlier days. I had to act as interpreter for Mark as Leslie told us of his wood store in the "shud", and how he "hulled" rubbish into the "pithole". We shared memories and swapped news over a cup of tea, and promised to call back later in order to meet Barry Osborn, the farm manager who had been on the same course as myself at Kesteven. Remarking that we ought not to delay Laddie from meeting a girl-friend in Swaffham, we prepared to depart. Naturally, he denied my insinuations, saying that talking to authors can be dangerous – as if I, the soul of discretion, would have written anything about it.

We left my friend with boxes of books for distribution, as Olive Ashby, the then Estate secretary, had agreed – with Captain Birkbeck's permission – to sell them from the office in Westacre. Proceeding the short distance to the Hulver, we decided to eat our picnic lunch in the car. It was whilst stretching his legs here that the strong westerly wind froze Mark's scalp, causing a need for the woollen hat residing in far away Standlake. My ever-present cap gave me protection, and I comforted Mark by telling him that it would have been twice as cold had the wind blown from the east. He took several pictures of deserted stock yards, and of long-unopened stable doors where Gipsy and my Uncle Will had plied their trade. Not a soul stirred, neither did one animal call. The soft lowing and rustle of feet in fresh, barley straw was long gone, as was the squeak of piglets fighting for the best milk tap along a fat sow's side. On that Saturday afternoon it was a dead farm, the few large tractors as silent as those animals of the past. Everything was as cold and sterile as the wind biting our ears.

The village itself showed no sign of life. The old school, now divided into two houses, brought back memories of rough and tumble playtimes. I just had to point out the site of the wheat stack where rat catching at threshing time had resulted in a late return from dinner, and a caning for we boys. Brother Brian's tiny stone still stood in front of the churchyard holly trees, as it had done since 1945, following his death at the age of three the previous year. I pointed out the large headstone, with three small ones on either side, standing opposite, just inside the old churchyard, where seven other children lay at rest. These were the victims of a diphtheria outbreak in 1881, all seven of one family dying within thirty days between 14 November and 14 December. My mind just could not take in the trauma for those poor parents, bearing in my memory the heartbreak suffered in our family when our small brother passed away. Walking back into the new churchyard we sought the stone standing over Grandad Alfred Bumfrey and his sons, Will and John. All around were memorials to men and women who were active friends, workmates and well-known village residents when I plied my trade on Soigné Farm forty years previously. It was a strange feeling, almost as if I had slid back a trapdoor in order to look down into a world I was no longer part of. My feelings were torn in two directions, firstly to find out more of present day Westacre, and secondly to leave the village wrapped in the frozen state my memory recalled, as if nothing had changed or would ever change – Horrie Everard tending his prize chrysanths and not lying here cold in the ground, Leslie Lloyd, my work-mate, getting new hoe blades put on by his father – both were now here for ever silent. Was it the wind making my eyes water, as I pretended, or was I regretting all those lost days lived away from the village? Well, we all know there is only one life to be lived, and mine had taken me to pastures new, making many friends in the process.

Continuing our tour we looked across the cricket field towards the Abbey ruins. My mind went back to that special evening when Soigné Farm sent a team to play one from the Abbey. I took a brilliant catch one-handed above my head, to dismiss Brian Reynolds, one of their leading batsmen. In truth, my hand went up instinctively, and the ball miraculously stuck, a point which Brian remarked on as he passed me on the way out. Leslie Lloyd was struck on the nose whilst fielding a ball in the rough outfield, and took no further part in proceedings. Geoff Thaxton scored a half century for us, though I'm not sure if we won in the end. With only three men between two farms today, such a game can never be fought out in the future. How good that we were there spilling blood and taking accolades for the honour of our farm. No cheering crowd stood on the bank that chilly November afternoon, not one moving soul had we encountered on our wanderings. Westacre was a "Marie Celeste" of the modern, rural village, where life, as we past inhabitants knew it, seemed to have passed away. Mind you, if even a shadow of past days still lingered, several people would have observed us and wondered who those three strangers were, and why were they taking photographs. I had a feeling we were under surveillance, and our presence would be discussed at length during the coming week.

Leaving the village behind, we travelled over to Litcham in order to see Aunt Ivy. This was a surprise visit as there had been no time to warn her of our sudden trip to Westacre. After failing to recognise me initially, we were welcomed in and spent a comfortable hour there, before returning to our promised meeting with Barry Osborn at Soigné. As we had a short time in hand, we returned along the Litcham to King's Lynn road, turning off at the Patch corner and pulling up at the Milestone gateway. This was the route taken by Grandfather, at the head of the Bumfrey family, when they moved from Baconsthorpe to Rats Hall seventy years before. As my previous books have shown, I've always had a special affinity with Rats Hall, and was very pleased when Michael decided the track up over the slight rise was car passable. Leaving our vehicle at the top, we walked down into the slight valley, in the shelter of which the tiny hamlet of three cottages, two bungalows and farm buildings had stood. Now all that remained of the settlement was one wall of the huge barn. Of houses there was no sign, trees had encroached where bungalows once sheltered on the wood edge, broken walls surrounded nettle-filled bullock yards and the barn had been reduced to rubble. Beside the one remaining barn wall stood a large, yellow demolition machine awaiting Monday morning, when the last rites of Rats Hall would be administered. How very strange that I was drawn over 150 miles, after almost forty years, to an almost unknown backwood of Norfolk to be present at the passing of my old friend, where many happy hours had been spent on Sundays sixty years before. Being a sentimentalist, I conjured up the ghosts from the past – Grandad with his striped shirt and black trousers carrying water for Monday's wash, Jeffrey Warner with white beard, and Grandfather Welham's horse looking over the stable door. Selecting a brick from the rubble heap, I carried the soul of Rats Hall back to Oxfordshire where it resides on my coal bunker, a reminder of my Sunday teas so lovingly given for the "heir to the Bumfrey millions".

Returning to Standlake, through the murk of a November evening, allowed me ample time to reflect on the events of my day. To me it had been quite a momentous event, so suddenly activated by the publication of my book. Without it the journey wouldn't have even been contemplated, let alone made. Having dreamed, relived and then written about Westacre as it was fifty and even sixty years ago, I was steeped in the past. To be suddenly thrust into its present, with virtually no warning, was likely to have burst my bubble of happy memories once and for all. Thankfully, this had not happened as, on the surface, the village looked almost the same and my reception at Soigné had been both warm and welcoming. The village slept on, as it had for winter afternoons immemorial. Work had ceased, it appeared, at twelve o'clock as it had in the days when we young bloods leapt aboard Jack Eagle's coach bound for football at Carrow Road, Norwich. Pheasants roamed the quiet roads in time-honoured fashion, safe for a time before shooting began later in the month on this game-oriented Estate. Leslie Richardson had visited Swaffham market, a tradition upheld from the days when he cycled there, before the car made his journey faster and much easier. Had there been no changes in my forty year absence? Certainly the machines, standing in the much higher cart shed, were larger. The farmyard itself looked very uncared-for, shorn of the metal windmill, which had been its central feature pumping water for humans and their stock. Of course it at last came to me – the "Marie Celeste" atmosphere of the farm, Pretoria Cottages and Westacre village itself. Not one person had we seen outside. Doubtless many had seen us, but we had met no one. Apart from Leslie and Barry Osborn in the former's living room, not one solitary human being. The farmyard, in turn, gave no animal sounds, the soft snuffle or scrape of iron shoe on cobbles was missing from the stables, and there was no rattle of Charlie Andrews' milking pails or swish of milk spurting on to their metal sides. Where was the army of cats, so beloved by my Uncle Will, who always waited so patiently for their saucers of milk? The place was sterile from sound, and as I was to discover later, almost without labour as well. Only a shell remained, the lifeblood of Soigné, as with farms in general, had slowly drained away as machines replaced man, and contractor replaced direct labour. On the plus side, the warmth of Leslie's welcome, and the easy way our comradeship had been resumed, made me eager to return to see if anything of the world I knew remained hidden below the surface.

I think it only fair to the men running the farms on the Estate to make clearer my earlier reference to the general neglected appearance of the yards. With virtually no direct labour, and three farms rolled into one unit, no manager or foreman on earth could hope to achieve the standard set in the days when surplus labour was available during in- between seasons. Not that we labourers enjoyed being around the steadings under Charlie Wilson's eye, either mud hoeing, scraping, sweeping with stiff brooms or nettle cutting – soul-destroying jobs, but their value showed up when completed, giving the place a lived-in look. Having at one time no idea what the name Soigné meant, I have been informed by those more learned than myself that it translates as "well cared for". I believe, also, there is a connection to a battle of the same name which took place during the Napoleonic wars. My informant told me that the huge Soigné Wood was planted in the same unusual shape as the British Army formed up in before the battle. These facts you must take at face value, as I have no written proof. I know the gamekeepers say that its shape makes it very difficult to drive for shooting purposes, so perhaps Napoleon had the same difficulty in defeating we Brits in his day.

I have mentioned the strange coincidence which brought me to Rats Hall in the final days of its demise. It appeared I wasn't the only person to have thoughts of Rats Hall when far away from the area as the following poem arrived in the post a few days later.

Rats Hall by Jeffrey Rye

This is a poem about Rats Hall,
The Place we knew as home,
Out there amid the woods and fields,
But now my house is gone.

While Grandad fed the horses
Mother made the bread,
This was left on the hearth to rise
While we were all in bed.

The morn' is dry, a fox runs by,
The huntsmen gallop round,
But the fox runs on and, by now, is hid
On Massingham Heath, in the ground.

The shoot is on, the birds fly high,
The beaters walk in line,
But some are missed and will fly again
To be shot another time.

A loved one's going to pass away –
We find the parting hard,
As the coffin is gently borne away
To Gayton Thorpe churchyard.

The time goes by, a war is on
And off we have to go.
It was never thought a boy from here
Would go to Anzio.

The good, old barn still stands there
Rather sadly and forlorn,
While I treasure a brick to remind me
Of the place where I was born.

Jeffrey Rye had been born in the cottage next to Grandad Bumfrey; his grandfather was Jeffrey Warner who I just remember as a very elderly gentleman with a white beard and wearing a brown jacket. Jeff's father, John Rye, was, he tells me, a lay preacher and had been requested, by my grandfather, to say a last prayer over my Uncle Stanley, who died at home aged only fourteen. It could have been his coffin referred to in the verse, but more likely it is that of John Rye, who died only weeks before Jeff's call up papers arrived, leaving his mother to live alone in that isolated hamlet. I am sure her neighbours did all they could for her, especially as they had lived side by side since the Bumfreys' arrival in 1927. It was a sad time for the two families, for they both had sons in the forces, Uncle Sos being a member of the Tank Corps. Granny Bumfrey also died in 1940, so there were several coffins being borne over the hill to the little, Saxon-towered church at Gayton Thorpe. No visible stones mark any of their resting places, but they are not forgotten. Obviously the above poem was penned in days before the barn became unsafe and before my subsequent visit. How significant that we should both take a brick as a reminder of our days there.

Another poem arrived a few weeks later, from two people who had lived and loved there, Daisy Easter and Billy Smith.

Rats Hall by Daisy Smith

Hear the wind in the tall trees
Moving the boughs to and fro;
I walk the path through the woodland
Where you and I used to go.

The houses no longer are standing
For nettles cover the ground –
Just the old barn is still with us
From where the white owl flew around.

Hares were seen in the fields, boxing,
Rabbits were always at play,
Pheasants ran across my path
As if to get out of my way.

Once there were people who lived here
Right near the Half Moon wood.
All I see now is rubble
Where three little cottages stood.

It does not seem long since they have been gone
From the place where we fell in love.
Our hopes and our fears have changed with the years,
But I would not change those days, if I could.

The post brought many more letters of memories stirred up by reading my first book, and we waited each morning, almost with bated breath, to discover who next would return to the fold. It was almost akin to the T.V. programme, "This is your life", only in my own home.

Chapter 20

The Final Round-up

The post continued to roll in, as folks from the Westacre of almost sixty years ago came back into vision. The joy expressed by all made the sweat and worry suffered by myself in getting to publication well worthwhile. When sales reached one hundred copies, I was thrilled beyond belief. Encouragement from all sides pushed me on to finish "All Mangolds and Muck-Cart", for wasn't everyone asking for a sequel? Photographs flowed in from Westacre and East Walton, covering school groups and local events from the fifties and sixties. My hand was being forced, but all I needed was a return on my initial investment, in order to finance the second. Having qualified for my basic pension in January, I was in no fit state to flash money around. Jean and Ian Little prepared the computer disk, which enabled me to check and correct my work from their printout. Precious photos were mounted and named in readiness for the great day, should it ever arrive. "It's coming", was the message I gave out at every query asked me on the subject of Book Two.

The joy of meeting up by letter with so many friends of the past was tempered by the marked decline in the mobility of my friend and ally, Irene Pitt, for whom I had cared over several years. I found she slept in her chair for much longer periods, and the drive, which had been her hallmark, had begun to lose its edge. Her brain, however, was as keen as one half her age and she could still outwit me at cards – which was usually being played at the time I began to doze, much to her annoyance; she forgot that she herself had enjoyed several snoozes during the day. While she slept, of course I had beavered away at writing letters, despatching books and setting up my second book. Her sudden death, so peaceful in itself, was a tremendous shock for me, as well as for her devoted family and many friends. Having been cook/housekeeper, nurse and companion to her for twenty-four hours a day, life, as I knew it, had suddenly vanished completely. To say I was devastated would be putting it mildly, and the thought of the void, which everyone assured me would be left in my life, terrified me. That void never materialised, thanks to all the friends locally and those newly-returned to me by post. My dear friend passed on to her rest in May, which, luckily, coincided with lighter days, if not real summer weather. Surprisingly, after all my broken nights, I slept wonderfully well from 10 p.m. until 5.30 a.m., waking with the dawn chorus. Long walks around the village footpaths helped me come to terms with my grief for I am a great believer in things of nature bringing balm to a troubled mind. My days were full as I cleaned, washed and painted my house from top to bottom, inside and out. Cooking one good meal every day, I took care of stomach as well as mind – with all my exertions I needed to feed the inner man.

Thanks to the good offices of Mike Goodall, who, through his work, had contact with the farming fraternity, I was put in touch with Ian Victor-Smith, the proud owner of four Suffolk Punch heavy horses. With my, by now, famous nervousness and trepidation, I phoned him to seek permission to take photographs of myself with a harnessed horse to use on the front of my book soon to be published. He turned out to be very enthusiastic and invited me down on a Saturday afternoon, when he would have a horse in harness. So it was that Mike drove me, complete with cap and jacket – as used on the cover of Book 1 – and Colin Bough, my photographer friend, down to Darkwood Farm, Nettlebed. Our reception couldn't have been more welcoming as we were invited into the house by Ian and his wife, and offered refreshment. It turned out that a children's birthday party was planned, to include a wagon ride around the back roads prior to a picnic on the lawn. Two horses were to be used, Duchess and Punch I believe, and we were invited to take pictures before and after, but even more importantly, we were asked along for the ride. Who were the more excited, we three men or the children, I don't know, but, ducking my head to miss overhanging branches along narrow lanes brought back the most poignant memories of Honeypot Lane, where I rode behind Beauty on the way to High House.

As so often in my life, this chance meeting, scheduled just to be a one-off photo session, turned out to be an ongoing engagement. Ian invited me back, when convenient to myself, so as to enjoy working with the horses. To date several happy days have been spent harness cleaning, in readiness for shows, and exercising the four animals pulling the wagon along beautiful lanes around Nettlebed. As well as Ian, my other companion has been another Derek – Derek Hunt, a retired postman from Slough, who has had much more experience than I with the shows. We can spend hours putting the world to rights whilst getting a good shine on four sets of harness. The only show I managed was Stoke Row steam rally, where we hoped to give wagon rides. Instead, the skies opened soaking everyone to the skin. What price our shining brass harness and martingales! Oh, to be in England in flaming June! I'm getting to know my four-legged friends quite well now – Duchess, the only mare, and her manger-companion, Jake, who is about twenty years old. They are what I considered Suffolk Punch size. Punch is bigger, and apt to take a sly nip at one's posterior if given the opportunity. Boxer, the youngest and the largest, is a grand lad who loves to put his head above reach at harnessing time. It's no wonder boys of years ago had to climb into the manger to get a collar on. Just the smell of their stable and the rattle of iron-shod hooves on cobble blocks, bring back memories of happy mornings and evenings in Uncle Will's stable. Gossiping whilst sitting on the corn bin at the end of a "horsey" day lives on, even if Beauty, Gipsy and my uncle are no more. A trip to Darkwood Farm, the home of Country Ways, is the highlight of my days – just another example of the joys I am encountering through my efforts with a biro and an A4 pad.

After the photographs became available, the decision to seek out the publisher was made. Hopefully, publication would give me the book by August, thus enabling me to take copies for sale to Norfolk and to enjoy a holiday there at the same time. As August approached I couldn't make up my mind if I really wanted to go back, after so many years. The need to market my books finally forced me to make a move. It's surprising how the pile of boxes in the hall gets one into action. As good as his word, Bob Boyd had delivered on time for me to set off. Whilst seeking information on local B & B accommodation, June and Colin Deasley invited me to stay at their home, Keeper's Cottage, in East Walton. Colin had been our neighbour and mate at Pretoria when his father, Ernie, held the keeper's post there. East Walton village is part of the Birkbeck Estate, being roughly one and a half miles nearer King's Lynn than Westacre, my old home and basis for the two books published.

Leaving a good food supply for Toby, the lodger cat, with my neighbour, whose small son, James, was an eager, volunteer feeder, I prepared to start early on Sunday morning. It was with mixed feelings that I set off as I keenly missed my late friend and companion, for it was, in effect, her death that had released me to be able to go on this journey. The fresh, August morning helped to lift my spirits, and I soon began to realise this was, in a way, an historic journey, a story in itself, if it turned out as I hoped it would. A misty start soon gave way to the promised, brilliant sunshine, and by the time I reached a picnic area on the edge of Thetford Forest, it was uncomfortably hot in the car. Eating my prepared sandwiches in the welcome shade, I felt able to begin to enjoy this trip of a lifetime. The final chapter of my proposed third book was being written and, in modern parlance, this was the squaring of the circle. But would it be like the return of the Prodigal Son? What would the welcome be like, always allowing there was a welcome at all? After all, I had only met Leslie Richardson and Barry Osborn on the last, whistle-stop trip. Pushing these negative thoughts to one side, I drove on towards Brandon, determined to enjoy this return to my beloved county, which I had boasted about for forty years. My blood lines were purely East Anglian, drawn from North Norfolk to be precise.

On reaching Brandon I felt the urge to visit Feltwell, where my R.A.F. National Service had been spent. I was quite surprised at the distance involved, when remembering my cycle journeys home for a part day whilst off duty. Although I didn't really expect it, a base remains there, housing 48th Fighter Wing, R.A.F. Feltwell. Memories of guardroom duties flooded back, as did scuffles between American airmen and their military police at the gate, when W.R.A.F. personnel were prevented from returning on time to camp. Although all was peaceful, I noticed a guard watching me closely, so I left, not wishing to be close questioned in that old guard room I knew so well. It wasn't the way to start my long-awaited return to native soil. Two pubs remained – The Chequers and The Bell – but, of the most frequented Cock Public House, there was no sign, unless I missed the street along which we stumbled back to camp after yet another demob party. Proceeding on to Swaffham, with the sun burning down, I was very glad to be motorised and not pedal pushing on my green, Sunbeam bike, as in days past. Leaving behind Swaffham, my seat of learning, I travelled towards Narford, but took the fork into a narrow, single-track road, along which I had cycled to school. The first thing I noticed was the absence of carrot crops. In my youthful days, acres of the root vegetable had been grown on the light, sandy-soiled fields bordering this bye-road. In fact, I had briefly contemplated working with a carrot gang whilst on the dole, and seeking gainful employment. On reaching the brow of the steep hill leading to Westacre, I stopped to enjoy the view of the village nestling in the valley just above the River Nar, which meandered through water-meadows. Something had changed besides the clearance of a rough, triangular piece of ground to my right. It was the electricity pylons carrying power along the valley that I hadn't noticed forty years before. If they were there then, my eyes wouldn't have seen them, as attention would have been focused on the long sweep of pedal-free road before me, a rest before an equally long climb up out of the village, culminating in the notorious Tumbler Hill.

If I had any worries about the reception I would receive on the Birkbeck Estate, they were immediately dispelled by Colin and June. It seemed as if our friendship picked up where I had left it four decades earlier. In those days, of course, Colin was not married, and I had only met June, his wife, once before, and then only briefly. I can never thank them enough for making my stay so memorable. A barbecue had been planned, and their family invited prior to my visit being arranged. June had set the cool, front room at my disposal should I care to take a rest after the journey, and I felt this was so very thoughtful on her part. She gave me a key to the door, thus allowing me to come and go as I pleased, to do my own thing as it were. I expressed a wish to walk very early in the mornings, and with my own key this caused no problem.

After enjoying an open-air lunch on the lawn, and being introduced to Sandra and Keith, my hosts' grown-up children, and their respective families, I asked if they minded me taking a stroll to the nearby church. Again, they impressed upon me that my holiday was my own, and I should go where I wanted and whenever I wanted. Earlier, I had stood with Colin, looking over the stubble field at the back, reliving its previous life as East Walton's cricket field, where sacrificial blood of Westacre heroes stained the grass as the home team's deadly, fast bowlers wreaked havoc amongst our batsmen on many occasions. Mrs. Leah Petch, my scoring opposite number, was remembered as formidable opposition in the pavilion area. We often had our own, private match, irrespective of what went on in the middle. What characters rose up in the heat haze shimmering across that old battlefield. We wondered how many poor umpires had been lynched there, if the home team failed to triumph, which wasn't very often, for they were a force to be reckoned with. This we found on one occasion, when Westacre were dismissed for eight runs, and Fred Petch hit a six off the first ball the home team received. I hope the victors bought us a drink at the Greyhound before we pedalled our way back home, with tails between our legs, and trying to convince ourselves that it was only a game.

On entering the churchyard, the first grave I noticed was that of Fred Petch, or "Young Fred" as we knew him. Taken far too early in life, with a defective heart, I knew by the fresh flowers that he was not forgotten. Nearby was a memorial to Barry Jackson, a friend of my brother Michael, killed in a motorcycle accident. Wandering further on I found "Whiffo" Jackson's headstone – I remembered him as one of the first combine drivers at the end of World War 2 – and also Walter High, the temperamental blacksmith. I had ridden horses from Soigné to his East Walton smithy for shoeing. The smithy is now a private house, and an ancient wheelwright's oven outside is the only sign of its previous lifestyle. Inside the peaceful Church I met a lady who, it seemed, recognised me – Oh what it is to be famous – although I did not know her. It was Mrs. Lewis from the nearby farm, a gracious lady and tireless worker for church and village. We chatted for some time as I tried to recall local characters of the past, known to us both. I was eventually directed to a cottage further down towards Watery Lane, where Jean Petch, wife of the late Fred, now lived. Tentatively knocking on her door, as there was a car parked outside, I awaited this first real reception as I hovered in the guise of a blast from the past. As in the case of Colin and June, I need not have worried for, after the first introduction, we were away with our reminiscences, taking "fourses" to the harvest field. Her father was "Whiffo" Jackson. Memories of her husband, "Young" Fred, with red-spotted neckerchief, combining in clouds of dust, came easily to mind. An hour soon passed before her family, the car owners, came back from their dog-exercising walk. After being introduced, especially to Jean's faithful dog, I took my leave to stroll back and rejoin the party. My length of absence indicated to my hosts that I had met up with someone, and they expressed their pleasure in the fact that I was settling in.

After a good night's sleep, I woke early for my proposed walk, and crept downstairs as quietly as possible. My key lay on the side, with a half tube of peppermints to sustain me as I walked. June left a similar packet there every morning, and this simple, thoughtful act really touched me. Such simple actions make all the difference in life, and I set off up the track towards Soigné with a very upbeat spirit. Many times, since my book-writing began, had I walked this way in thought. Now I was actually here in person, seemingly the only thing alive in the world, apart from birds and animals whose footprints crossed and re-crossed my path. There were pheasants, partridges, rabbits, hares, and even a stoat, which took a careful look at me before disappearing into undergrowth. The latter, as well as the squawking jay, were rarely seen in my day on this game-conscious Estate, but I was to learn that a more "live and let live" tolerance exists today. The very thought made me imagine those gamekeepers, mentioned in previous books, turning in their graves. Standing beside the resting place of Charlie Welham later in that day, it would have been no surprise to see the turf disturbed as the process took place. On the surface, and at first glance, very little seemed to have changed on the Estate, but further investigation showed otherwise. Along the verges familiar flowers still grew, as in the days when I rode Beauty and Violet down to Mr. High. Blue bugloss, corn cockle, knapweed, poppies, Scottish thistle, and yellow charlock kept their appointed places on the field edge, but not one could be seen amongst the green-leaved sugar-beet, or in uncut barley. Crop-spraying, indicated by tell-tale tramlines, had done its job. There were no weed-infested plots, side by side with clean ones, to indicate where a hand-hoer had put in the "slubbery" (our expression for poor workmanship). Headlands had not seen the pitch-halfpenny games at dinner time, the swish of beet hooks slicing tops from roots would not be heard through the autumn mists, and there was no back-ache now as machines did the work, but gone also were the life and comradeship of field gang work I had left behind in November 1958.

Despite no influx of men into the fields at 7 a.m., all life and leg-pulling hadn't left the Soigné fields.

As I turned to retrace my steps along the Hulver, a vehicle drew up alongside me, and the voice of Brian Reynolds called out, "What are you doing out here at this time in the morning?".

Seeing who it was, along with his manager, Barry Osborn, I replied, "Captain Birkbeck asked me to check up on the timekeeping of his men, so I will be reporting back".

After a few words, they continued on their way, but seemingly reported my arrival on the Estate to those in possession of two-way radios. When I met Colin on his rounds, he told me of the reported sighting, and the message received.

"Yes", I said, "if anyone enquires who the strange man is walking the Estate, tell them it's a lottery winner hoping to buy it as a going concern".

One had to keep up tradition by circulating tall tales. It was revealed later that Barry had returned to Soigné in order to tell Leslie Richardson that I had called at his house at about seven o'clock, but could find no one up. Leslie, who was a notoriously early riser, refuted this slur upon his early morning routine, and checked with me later that day, in order to be able to accuse Barry of lying. In all this, I found, to my delight, that at least the sense of humour, enjoyed so much in my Soigné days, was still around, and as active as ever. In that field it felt as if I had never been away.

As soon as it was known that I was in the area, June had to act as my secretary, taking appointments. I already had a list of people to visit through the letters received from previous book sales. Colin proved to be an excellent salesman with that latest edition, and kept me busy signing copies for him to deliver on his rounds. He also arranged for me to meet Captain Birkbeck, at his request, the appointed time being 2.15 p.m. on that first Monday afternoon. Being instructed to enter the side door of the Hall, and then follow my nose upstairs, I set off. Forking away from the road at Pretoria, I went up the private drive and into the park. How far from my thoughts would have been this visit, as I cycled down from my interview and dismissal in Captain Birkbeck's study forty years earlier. Then I was determined to shake the dust and mud of Westacre off my feet, never to return. Well, here I was, returning and looking forward to our meeting this time around. After passing through the side entrance, and glancing at the huge mantrap displayed on the wall, this present-day peasant mounted the stairs, whilst imagining the frowns of ancestors gazing down upon me from their gilt-framed portraits. I'm sure the Captain and I enjoyed our half-hour chat, which ranged from my books, to changes in farming methods, and hopes for the future. We enjoyed a cup of tea together as I declined his offer of anything stronger. His severe disability, suffered as a result of a motor accident, now restricts his outside activities, but he gets around when possible. We parted with a strong handshake, and with me sincerely hoping his plans for the continuation of the Estate in its entirety will come to fruition. How strange it was that the Estate, which I had wished would be broken up under my Karl Marx leanings of fifty years before, now seemed to be very precious as part of a way of life I had enjoyed, but had failed to realise it at the time. Let's face it, how could I have written three books without the Westacre Estate? With these chastening thoughts, I retraced my steps out into the sunshine, and set my car towards Leslie Richardson's house at Soigné.

Harvest was in full swing, making the most of a fine spell of weather, which was destined to bless me for the full ten days I stayed in Norfolk. Those days were unforgettable, as I was welcomed wherever I went. My correspondent and photo provider, Iris Gooderson, and her husband, Buff, turned my proposed half-hour visit into three times that. Tall tales about the size of tomatoes in Buff's greenhouse were given me, for passing on to Jeffrey Thaxton should I see him. This I duly did when I met Jeffrey a few days later, and as soon as I mentioned a Walton man who had to cut his tomatoes in order to get them through his greenhouse door, I got the response, "I know, I know, it's one of Buff Gooderson's tales – him and his giant tomatoes".

Reg and Ethel Meachin, at Westacre schoolhouse, showed me how Miss Wiskerd's infants' room had been divided between their house and the renovated school – now another house – to make a toilet and bathroom. Such sacrilege should have brought our much-feared schoolmarm back to haunt the perpetrators. That "short" visitation, along with an unscheduled visit to Lou Abel at High House, meant it took me from 9.30 a.m. until 3 p.m. to travel the twelve or so miles to visit Aunt Ivy at Litcham. Lou was such a mine of local information, and I could have talked with him for a week. He urged me to return later, but lack of time prevented this, much to the disappointment of both of us. It was the same with Leslie Turvey, who had been local correspondent for the newspapers for more years than he cared to remember. He recalled the days when working on Estate maintenance painting at Pretoria, on a wet day in the 1950s, they sheltered at Grandad Bumfrey's. Being Friday, Reg Meachin called to pay them, and whilst there, was accosted by my grandfather who, in his broad Norfolk accent, enquired, "Mr. Meachin, are yar min sneck hendle putters on?". Reg, who was not of our county and not acquainted with a north Norfolk accent, stared in bewilderment at this strange request. After much amusement, his men gave the more understandable explanation that Mr. Bumfrey had broken the handle on the latch mechanism designed for door fastening. To this day, Lou, Leslie and Reg himself had remembered the incident when a new language came to the ears of an Estate official. Reg wasn't the only person from outside the county to fail in understanding

Grandad's broad accent, and in fact, some inside couldn't understand it either.

On Sunday I joined the congregation at Westacre church, where I had been first drawn to worship under Canon Caley. Jean Plummer still played the organ, although without the assistance of manual pumping of air through her instrument. I joined my erstwhile workmate, Leslie Richardson, in a back pew, keeping well near the door for fear the roof timbers might collapse with two such characters under them at the same time. June and Peggy Thaxton, as their names were before marriage, suggested I might come more often to help with the singing, but I declined on the grounds that a round trip of almost 300 miles made it uneconomic. Their final try, explaining it would be only once a month, failed to move me, I'm afraid. The thought was nice, though.

Onwards I went across the county to West Beckham and Baconsthorpe, where Grandad Bumfrey had been born, and from where he had brought his family to settle at Rats Hall, and then back to Briston, my mother's home, where I joined the afternoon Salvation Army meeting. I myself had been born on a Sunday just opposite the Hall in Plumbs Cottages, so doubtless their band had played me into the world. Plumbs Cottages and the band are no more, such is the march of progress. Even so, I enjoyed the fellowship and met the daughter of the late Vic Dewing, who was for so long the Corps Sgt. Major at Briston. She told me he had often cycled to neighbouring villages, with the big drum strapped on his back, for open-air drumhead services. There's dedication for you.

The time passed so very quickly with each day and evening filled by people visiting me, or me visiting them in their various homes. They told me tales of youngsters biking from King's Lynn to Rats Hall with groceries, in order to keep the business in the family. Roger Reynolds told of his father, Jimmy, leading young Laddie to the schoolmistress by his ear, after alleged bullying. I met Mrs. Beryl Watts, now past 90, at High House; she remembered my parents arriving immediately after their 1931 March wedding, and seeing my mother picking her way through the muddy field gateway, and her heart going out to the young bride. Despite all the adverse conditions, the marriage survived, as they did in those days, giving we children the wonderful, stable start in life, which has stood us in such good stead throughout.

There are so many more people and instances worthy of mention in my life, but one must stop somewhere. What better time to call a halt than when looking back over that pasture where two honest and faithful young people set out on a marriage, to which I owe my existence and the happy life I've enjoyed. May the despoiling tentacles of so-called progress never touch that little piece of Norfolk at the back of Home Farm, Westacre. Just as with Rats Hall, my heart will forever be there among the sweetest of memories. Only a tangle of briars and brambles cover the garden, which was once so proudly tended by the young husband, and there is no sign now of those brick floors scrubbed by the ex- parlour maid straight from service in Harley Street, London. A half wild, half rotten apple tree, where my pram rested in the shade while guarded by the ever-faithful Rip, still gives a clue to human habitation, but, like Rats Hall, it's only in my mind and now in my books that the "cottages across the meadow" will live on.

The Epilogue

This is the epilogue of all three books, the trilogy outlining my life up to the age of 66.

The circle has been completed in as much as I have been reunited with the county and village of my birth. This is not strictly true, for I was born at Briston, but returned to my parents' home at High House, Westacre in the first weeks of my life. When I left that village in 1959 I had no wish to return at any time, but the pull of roots is much stronger than we bargain for. Who would have imagined all the strange coincidences that led me back. The Estate, which in my own mind, I had so many times nationalised, along with all its contemporaries, in my great plan for a modern Britain, had called me back. I had written about it, realised what it had meant to our lives, and examined its chains and often-unsung advantages to those under its umbrella and above its safety net. My father, who was nobody's fool, saw more than I did since he had experienced other employers, and my grandfather more than he, of course. They were hard workers who fully appreciated there were many agricultural workers in worse conditions of employment and housing. Things could have been better, and hindsight shows us all what could have taken place "if only". I could never have believed that I would sit upstairs in the Hall with Captain Birkbeck, gazing out over the sunlit park, discussing the future of the Estate within the present unstable agricultural climate. Can it survive as a unit when all around is change and in many cases decay? If it succumbs to external pressures, what system will replace it? Steeped in so much history, I sincerely hope it survives. Have I grown soft and sentimental in old age? Perhaps I have, or can I see further than the end of my nose with the help of new spectacles?

I can well remember wishing to see all old properties bulldozed down, and modern houses built to replace them. I have, for the last thirty odd years, lived in a two hundred year old, stone cottage, and would not exchange it for anything new. Refurbish and bring up to date, yes, but put away the bulldozer – yet another change of policy on my part. I know we can never turn the clock back, and it would be very wrong to do so. There were no "good old days" for the working man, but there were a great number of good and worthwhile things in life which my generation allowed to be swept away, in our charge for progress. Unfortunately, this so-called progress has not improved the quality of life for many, and a pause to take stock of where we went wrong would do no harm at all.

As a young man I never ceased to mimic and take off Charlie Wilson, my foreman, who sang and hummed hymn tunes as he strode along. As a chapel lay preacher he never held with Sunday work, except in the need to care for animals. Silly old fool, I thought, as I lapped up the overtime in the barn at harvest time. Now that I regularly attend chapel myself, I see seven-day trading as a chain around employees' necks. Not only has the Lord's Day gone, but the necessary day of rest, so sorely needed for family unity and recreation, has been forfeited. Now, who were the silly fools? By viewing my life from a distance, I realise that, at no juncture, do we know it all. There is something new to learn every day, and we should never be too haughty or proud to change our views and opinions as the pattern of life unfolds.

I don't envisage anything exciting enough, about which to write a book, happening to me in the short or long years left to come. Realistically, I have been very fortunate in getting this far, after such a sickly childhood, my health almost worrying my poor mother into an early grave. But one never knows. As they say in football parlance, the game isn't over until the ball stops rolling. Meanwhile, I can continue to make renewed contact with folks mentioned in these books - people who have had an effect on my life. George Hall and his wife are the latest of our old neighbours to come back into view. As the energetic man living at No. 5, Pretoria Cottages, his go-ahead ideas were too much for Soigné environment, and he went forth to build a new life in 1947. The same thing happened to me in 1959. George is now 88 years old and keeping busy in his garden and greenhouse. I hope to meet him later this year, but in the meantime he made the effort to write an extensive letter to me after reading my first two books. George took over the post of "Lord", or gang leader, from my grandfather when he first arrived from Narford. How strange that I too held this post in succession to those two men I held in such high regard as hard workers and leaders of men. Genuine workers have always held my admiration, and still do so today. My maxim is that a good labourer is always worthy of his hire.